1 MON
FREE
READING

at

www.ForgottenBooks.com

By purchasing this book you are eligible for one month membership to ForgottenBooks.com, giving you unlimited access to our entire collection of over 700,000 titles via our web site and mobile apps.

To claim your free month visit:

www.forgottenbooks.com/free123403

ISBN 978-1-330-93513-2
PIBN 10123403

Summarized Bible

Complete

Summary of the

Old Testament

By KEITH L. BROOKS

Author of

"Simple Studies in Bible Marking"

Published by

BIBLE INSTITUTE OF LOS ANGELES

536-558 South Hope Street

Los Angeles, Cal.

PREFACE

Chiefly for the purpose of stimulating Christians to take up the chapter method of Bible study, this work is compiled. It is designed to act as an aid to the ordinary reader in gathering into a nut-shell, as it were, the definite spiritual lessons for the daily life contained in every chapter of the Bible. Many of the statements contained in the conclusions will be found to be familiar, and the writer does not claim originality throughout the work. The work was compiled largely from notes made in the margins of the author's Bible, kept, for the most part without regard to their sources.

The course through the Bible, chapter by chapter, may well be used as a system of daily devotional reading, and we commend it for that purpose as it gives the Word of God its proper place. The "striking facts" will center the reader's attention upon Jesus Christ, while the "strong verses" may often be taken as promises for the day or as memory verses.

The work is also adapted to be used as a text book for teaching chapter summary work. Members of a class may be required to work out for themselves the points suggested on each chapter. The comparing of their "leading lessons" will make most interesting class work. The teacher may then read the statements given in the Summarized Bible as a guide to the student. In this connection, we would recommend for the use of students, the chapter summary note book designed by Rev. John H. Hunter and published by Biola Book Room, Sixth and Hope Streets, Los Angeles California. This is comprised of blank pages ruled into divisions for "prominent persons"; "best verse"; "leading lesson" and "principal subject."

The Summarized Bible will also be found of value as a reference work. For the preacher who is in search of Scripture illustrations for his sermons, the "conclusions" will often suggest helpful applications. Many suggestive outlines will be found throughout which may be used as skeletons for sermons. The "striking facts" furnish foundation material for a study of Jesus Christ, as He appears in all the Scriptures.

If this work may be used of God to bring some to apply themselves wholly to the Scriptures and the Scriptures wholly to themselves, we shall feel abundantly repaid for the effort.

KEITH L. BROOKS.

415539

WHAT TO DO WITH THE BIBLE

BY REV. W. H. PIKE

T HE Bible is wonderful because it gives us a knowledge of God, of men, of the Universe, and of Redemption. No other book can be compared to it in this respect, but it not only informs us about these important truths, but it also tells us what we are to do with it. We have within the Bible itself instruction as to our attitude toward it We are exhorted to:

1. "Read it." Neh. 8:8. And may I suggest that it be read slowly, carefully, prayerfully, in large portions, repeatedly, reverently and with a willing spirit to follow its precepts.

2. "Believe it." Rom. 10:8. Because it is the Word of faith. It has been given to increase our faith in God and His working in the Universe.

3. "Receive it." Jas. 1:21. Here it is the engrafted word that is to be received as the soil received the seed, or the tree receives the graft. Taking the Word of God in our heart life, allowing it to grow and bear its own fruit in motives and actions.

4. "Taste it." Heb. 6:5. For it is the good Word of God. Some seem to be afraid of the Bible for fear it will require them to do something they do not wish to do. Be not afraid; it is good and right in all its requirements.

5. "Eat it." Jer. 15:16. This process suggests that we not merely taste but actually live by it, as Jesus said, "Ye shall not live by bread alone, but by every word that proceedeth out of the mouth of God." Matt. 4:4.

6. "Hold it fast." Tit. 1:19. It is a faithful word. All its promises are true; all its history is true; and its statements are truth. Therefore we are to rest our faith upon it.

7. "Hold it forth." Phil. 2:16. Because it is the Word of Life. All who come under its benificent rays feel its life giving power.

8. "Preach it." 2 Tim. 4:2. Here it is called simply the Word. It suggests that we are not to preach any one part of it or any one phase of it, but preach it in its entirety and fulness.

9. "Search it." John 5:29 R. V. This suggests work and patience. The Greek word carries the idea of "ransack" as the housewife goes through the home at housecleaning time; or "to track" as the hunter laboriously follows the game through the brush, so we are to search for truth and run down the lines of God's revelations to man.

10. "Study it." 2 Tim. 2:15. Here is a word that means close application to the Word of God, as the builder minutely studies the plans of the architect before erecting the structure.

11. "Meditate on it." Ps. 1:2. This word has much the same meaning as "eat" for it means literally "to chew the cud." Turning the Word of God over and over in the mind till the sweetness of its truths feed our souls.

12. "Compare it." 2 Cor. 2:13. This is not so much what we do with the Scriptures as what the Holy Spirit does with them in our hearts. This is a divine commentary always at hand. Or as John puts it in his first epistle 2:27 R. V. "The annointing which ye received of Him abideth in you, and ye need not that any man teach you, but as His annointing teacheth you concerning all things, and is true, and is no lie, and even so as it taught you, ye abide in Him."

13. "Rightly divide it." 2 Tim. 2:15. This is not an arbitrary division of subjects but the following of a line of truth from the first place mentioned to the last place mentioned; noticing it in all its relation to other truths and as the word literally means "the cutting of a straight line" of truth in the Bible.

14. "Delight in it." Ps. 119:92. Seven times in this Psalm the Psalmist speaks of delighting in God's word. This should always be the heart ambition and attitude.

"Study it carefully; think of it prayerfully;
Deep in thy heart let its precepts dwell.
Slight not its history; ponder its mystery,
None can e'er prize it too fondly or well.
Accept the glad tidings, the warning, the chidings,
Found in this volume of heavenly lore,
With faith that's unfailing, and love all prevailing,
Trust in its promise of life evermore."

GENESIS

Key Thought: Beginnings	Number of Chapters: 50	Key Verse: 1:1	Christ seen as: Seed of Abraham
Writer of the Book: Moses	**Date:** About 1500 B. C.		**Conclusion of the Book:** The failure of man under every condition is met by the salvation of God.

SUMMARY

CHAPTER ONE

Contents: Original creation and the renovating of earth for habitation of man. Creation of animal and human life.

Characters: God, v. 1. Spirit, v. 2. Christ, v. 26 (See Col. 1:15-17; John 1:3) first man and woman.

Conclusion: An all-wise, all-powerful, loving God formed all things perfect in the beginning. He made man, the crown of His creation, perfect and capable of fellowship with Himself and able to enjoy and govern Eden.

Key Word: Beginnings, v. 1.

Strong Verses: 1, 27.

Striking Facts: v. 1. Be sure to compare John 1:1, 2, 3, 14. Not only was Jesus Christ present in creation, but creation was bound up with Him as its secret. Col. 1:15-17. See Heb. 1:3.
Gen. 1 is not a history of the original creation, but of a reconstruction following a cataclysmic judgment which had befallen the original creation. v. 1 Original creation. v. 2 Its destruction. v. 3 and on, Reconstruction.

CHAPTER TWO

Contents: God's Sabbath rest. The creative act of Gen. 1:27 explained. The Edenic covenant.

Characters: God, Adam, Eve.

Conclusion: Man is a threefold being, body, soul and spirit. The real man is soul and spirit, conferred directly from God. The body, the outward casing, is dust and to dust it returns.

Key Word: Man, v. 7.

Strong Verses: 3, 7, 18, 24.

Striking Facts: Eve, a type of the Church, the Bride of Christ, was not formed of dust, but came from an opened side. The Church is a heavenly Body, born from the opened side of the Second Adam, God's Son.

CHAPTER THREE

Contents: Temptation of Eve and entrance of sin into the race. God's covenant with fallen man and the expulsion from Eden.

Characters: God, Satan, Adam, Eve.

Conclusion: Doubt lies at the root of all sin. Altering the Word, v. 1; adding to the Word, v. 3 or taking from the Word, v. 5, are dangerous acts.

Key Word: Serpent, v. 1.

Strong Verses: 9, 15, 19, 22, 23.

Striking Facts: Conscience, the realization of what man is, must be met by salvation, the revelation of what God is in Grace, before peace can be restored to man. Through woman sin entered and by her seed alone was salvation promised. Isa. 7:14; 9:6, 7.

CHAPTER FOUR

Contents: First sons of Adam, Cain and Abel. Murder of Abel. First civilization. Birth of Seth.

Characters: Adam, Eve, Cain, Abel, Seth.

Conclusion: Attainment can never take the place of Atonement. Without the recognition of Christ as our substitute and sacrifice there can be no approach to God.

Key Word: Offering, v. 4.
Strong Verses: 4, 26.
Striking Facts: There has been more persecution on religious grounds than on any other.
The fruit of Cain's false worship was to avoid the presence of God and to lose himself in the world and its pursuits.

CHAPTER FIVE

Contents: Generations from Adam to Noah.
Characters: Adam, Seth, Enos, Cainan, Mahalaleel, Jared, Enoch, Methuseleh, Lamech, Noah.
Conclusion: By man came death. In Adam all die. In Christ shall all who believe be made alive.
Key Word: Generations, v. 1.
Strong Verses: 24.
Striking Facts: Enoch, the seventh from Adam was translated and made the trophy of God's power over death.

CHAPTER SIX

Contents: Flood announced. Compromise of sons of God with daughters of men.
Characters: Noah, Shem, Ham, Japheth.
Conclusion: The true believer can float in peace on the very waters by which the wicked world is judged.
Key Word: Flood, v. 17.
Strong Verses: 8, 9, 18, 22.
Striking Facts: The plan whereby Noah was saved was no invention of his own but one revealed by God, v. 13. Faith is governed by the pure Word of God. Heb. 11:7. The ark is a type of Christ as the refuge of His people from the judgment.

CHAPTER SEVEN

Contents: The flood comes. Noah and family preserved.
Characters: Noah, his sons, and their wives.
Conclusion: The blood of Christ keeps out the waters of judgment and makes the believers position "in Christ" a safe one. v. 16.
Key Word: Ark, v. 7.
Strong Verses: 16.
Striking Facts: The hand that made Noah secure within, shut the others out. There was a window in the top of the ark whereby they could look up in communion with God, knowing that no judgment remained for them. Heb. 12:1-2.

CHAPTER EIGHT

Contents: Waters receding, exit from the ark. Noah's altar.
Characters: Noah and family.
Conclusion: When judgment days are past, the believer will find himself safely landed in a better world.
Key Word: Rest, v. 4.
Strong Verses: 1, 20.
Striking Facts: Superstition would have worshipped the ark as the means of salvation, but Noah looked to the God back of the means.

CHAPTER NINE

Contents: Noamic covenant. Noah's shame and Ham's sin.
Characters: Noah and family.
Conclusion: The believer is as secure as God's promises are true. No promise of God can fail.
Key Word: Covenant, v. 9.
Strong Verses: 9, 13.
Striking Facts: The bow seen upon the storm clouds of judgment speaks of the cross where judgment never to be repeated has been visited upon the believer's sins.

CHAPTER TEN

Contents: Establishing of the nations.

Characters: Noah, Shem, Ham, Japheth, Nimrod, Canaan.

Conclusion: God made all nations of one blood and determined the bounds of their habitations.

Key Word: Nations, v. 31.

Strong Verses: 32.

Striking Facts: From the seven sons of Japheth, the Gentile nations are descended.

CHAPTER ELEVEN

Contents: Failure under Noamic covenant. Tower of Babel. Scattering of the people. Ancestry of Abram.

Characters: Shem, Terah, Abram, Lot, Sarai.

Conclusion: Man ever builds under the heavens, seeking a name and a portion in the earth. The believer builds on an imperishable foundation laid in heaven by God. Man's devices all fail.

Key Word: Confusion (Babel) v. 9.

Strong Verses: 5, 9.

Striking Facts: To exalt man without God in Christ is to elevate him to a dizzy height from which he is sure to fall into hopelessness.

CHAPTER TWELVE

Contents: Call of Abram. His worship and testing. The error in Egypt.

Characters: Abram, Sarai, Lot, Pharaoh.

Conclusion: The path into which God calls the believer may often be trying to the flesh, but this does not necessarily indicate that he is out of God's will.

Key Word: Sojourners, v. 10.

Strong Verses: 3, 8.

Striking Facts: God's biddings are His enablings. Better suffer in Canaan in God's path than live in luxury in Egypt in the devil's path.
The altar marks Abraham as a worshipper. The tent marks him as a pilgrim. These are distinguishing marks of the followers of Christ.

CHAPTER THIRTEEN

Contents: Abram's return to the land and the altar. Separation from Lot. Lots backsliding and choice of the land.

Characters: Abram, Lot.

Conclusion: Material blessings are often accompanied by moral blight. Let nature range where it will, it can never take faith's treasure.

Key Word: Separation, v. 9.

Strong Verses: 4, 17, 18.

Striking Facts: Lot pictures a professing Christian trying to make the best of both worlds, v. 12.
He who puts God and Christ first will never be bereft of that which is best for him.

CHAPTER FOURTEEN

Contents: Abram delivers Lot. Abram's refusal to compromise with the King of Sodom.

Characters: King of Sodom, Lot, Abram, Melchizedek.

Conclusion: Genuine faith never wraps itself in fleece while a brother shivers in the cold. The farther a believer lives from the world, the greater power he will have over it.

Key Word: Deliverance, v. 20.

Strong Verses: 22, 23.

Striking Facts: The most effectual way to serve the world is to be separated from it.
The first mention in the Bible of the kings, finds them fighting. The last of Revelation leaves them hard at it still.

CHAPTER FIFTEEN

Contents: Abrahamic covenant confirmed and spiritual seed promised.

Characters: Abram, God.

Conclusion: The promises to faith are more certain than the conclusions of logic (v. 25). Faith is the key that unlocks the cabinet of promises.
Key Word: Seed, v. 5.
Strong Verses: 1, 6.
Striking Facts: v. 17. A smoking furnace suggests that the inheritance would be reached by passing through furnaces of trial. The bright lamp tells of God's relief which shines brighter as the road gets darker.

CHAPTER SIXTEEN

Contents: Birth of Ishmael.
Characters: Sarah, Abram, Hagar, Angel, Ishmael.
Conclusion: The moment the believer takes his eyes away from God's promises he is ready for mean devices of unbelief which bring him untold suffering.
Key Word: Despised, v. 4.
Strong Verses: 13.
Striking Facts: God promises—faith believes—hope anticipates—patience waits. Heb. 6: 12. The heart prefers anything to the attitude of waiting.

CHAPTER SEVENTEEN

Contents: The revelation of God. Abram's name changed. Covenant confirmed. Circumcision established. Promise of Isaac.
Characters: God, Abram, Isaac, Sarah, Ishmael.
Conclusion: When man is in the dust God can talk to him in grace. In spite of the believer's mistakes, God is faithful.
Key Word: Covenant, v. 2.
Strong Verses: 1, 2, 19.
Striking Facts: Abram means "father of altitude." Abraham means "father of breadth." The perpendicular of justice is transversed by the horizontal beam of embracing love. In the two names we see a picture of the cross.

CHAPTER EIGHTEEN

Contents: Abraham, the friend of God. Promise of the seed renewed. The plea of Sodom.
Characters: God, Sarah, Abraham.
Conclusion: The closer the believer walks with God, the more he will know of God's mind about everything. The secrets of the Lord are with those who fear Him.
Key Word: Communion, v. 33.
Strong Verses: 17, 18.
Striking Facts: The way to know the divine purpose about the world is not to be mixed up with its schemes and speculations but walking in communion with Christ.

CHAPTER NINETEEN

Contents: Destruction of Sodom and Gomorrah. Lot's backsliding and escape.
Characters: Angels, Lot and family, Abraham, Moab, Benammi.
Conclusion: No Christian can find his pleasure and profit in the world and at the same time bear effectual testimony against the world.
Key Word: Destruction, v. 13.
Strong Verses: 27, 29.
Striking Facts: In gaining great worldly influence, Lot had lost all influence and spiritual power, even over his own family, v. 14. Choose between the Word and the world. No heart can mature two crops.

CHAPTER TWENTY

Contents: Abraham's lapse at Gerar. Lying to Abimelech about his wife.
Characters: Abraham, Sarah, Abimelech.
Conclusion: Sin has many tools but a lie is a handle that fits them all. If the truth is stretched, expect it eventually to fly back and sting you.
Key Word: Sin, v. 9.
Strong Verses: 6, 17.
Striking Facts: One is often struck with the amazing difference between what God's people in Christ are in His view and what they are in the world's view. God sees His own through Christ, although in themselves, they are often feeble and inconsistent.

CHAPTER TWENTY-ONE

Contents: Birth of Isaac. Bondwoman and her son cast out. Abraham at Beersheba.
Characters: Sarah, Abraham, Isaac, Hagar, Ishmael, Abimelech.
Conclusion: Behind every promise of God is the purpose and power of God, therefore faith should know that God's bonds are as good as ready money "at the set time."
Key Word: Isaac, v. 3.
Strong Verses: 1.
Striking Facts: It often involves a struggle to cast the bondwoman and her son out. Gal. 5:1; Col. 3:9. Human religion would keep them in the house.

CHAPTER TWENTY-TWO

Contents: Offering of Isaac. Abrahamic covenant again confirmed.
Characters: God, Abraham, Isaac, angel.
Conclusion: The man of faith must keep his eye on God, looking not at circumstances, nor pondering the results of what God asks of him. The trial of faith is precious.
Key Word: Worship, v. 5.
Strong Verses: 15, 16, 17, 18.
Striking Facts: Isaac is a type of Christ "obedient unto death." Abraham illustrates the Father who "spared not His own Son." The resurrection is illustrated in the deliverance of Isaac.

CHAPTER TWENTY-THREE

Contents: Death of Sarah. Burial in cave of Machpelah.
Characters: Sarah, Abraham, sons of Heth, Ephron.
Conclusion: Although the man of faith knows that in the resurrection glory he shall be heir to the land, until that time he will be no debtor to those in temporary possession. (vv. 15, 16.)
Key Word: Burial, v. 4.
Strong Verses: 19.
Striking Facts: One of the most zealously guarded places in the world is a rectangular building in Palestine, beneath which the cave of Machpelah is supposed to be, and in which are the remains of Abraham, Isaac and Jacob. God has never let it come into the hands of those who were disposed to disturb it.

CHAPTER TWENTY-FOUR

Contents: Bride of Isaac secured by Abraham's servant.
Characters: Abraham, servant, Bethuel, Laban, Sarah, Isaac.
Conclusion: God leads in every detail of our lives. The marriage which is not according to His will as shown by His Word and the leading of His Servant, The Holy Spirit, will not be blessed of Him.
Key Word: Wife, v. 4.
Strong Verses: 27, 40.
Striking Facts: Abraham stands for the Father (Matt. 22:2). The servant stands for the Holy Spirit (John 16:13, 14; 1 Cor. 12:7-11). Rebekah stands for the Bride of Christ (Eph. 5:25-32). Isaac stands for the Bridegroom who is coming to receive His Bride (1 Thess. 4:14-16).

CHAPTER TWENTY-FIVE

Contents: Abraham weds Keturah. Isaac becomes Abraham's heir. Death of Abraham. Generations of Ishmael and Isaac. Birth of Esau and Jacob and the sale of the birthright.
Characters: Abraham, Keturah, Zimram, Jokshan, Medan, Midian, Ishbak, Shuah, Isaac, Ishmael, Esau, Jacob, Rebekah.
Conclusion: The natural man values only what he can see and puts no value on the things of God. Many despise their birthright as sons of God because it is a spiritual thing, of value only as there is faith to apprehend it.
Key Word: Birthright, v. 31.
Strong Verses: 23.
Striking Facts: Esau is a type of the man of the earth, Heb. 12:16, 17. In

many respects a nobler man than Jacob, yet the fact that he was destitute of faith caused him to despise his birthright. God's choice of His children does not depend on their character, but their faith.

CHAPTER TWENTY-SIX

Contents: Covenant confirmed to Isaac. Isaac's lapse at Gerar, Isaac as a well digger.
Characters: Isaac, Rebekah, Abimelech, Ahuzzath, Phichol, Esau, Judith.
Conclusion: It is peculiarly comforting to see that God has ever been dealing with men of like passions as we are and patiently bearing with the same failures. When the believer falls, God is still with him.
Key Word: Blessed, v. 12.
Strong Verses: 2, 24, 25, 28.
Striking Facts: There is a great difference between God's blessing through Christ and His presence. One cannot always judge of a believer's spiritual condition by their circumstances, but God has a purpose in all His dealings.
Before the chapter closes, we see Isaac coming into God's presence as well as His blessing, v. 24.

CHAPTER TWENTY-SEVEN

Contents: Fraudulent methods of Jacob in getting Isaac's blessing. Remorse of Esau.
Characters: Isaac, Esau, Jacob, Rebekah.
Conclusion: Human nature in prone to scheme to bring about what God would do without any scheming. He does not need our cunning or deceit to accomplish His purpose. Seek spiritual blessings in the right way or get with them years of sorrow afterward.
Key Word: Supplanter, v. 36.
Strong Verses: 28, 29, 33.
Striking Facts: One only needs to read the history of Jacob to learn that it does not pay to take things into one's own hands. The more pressing the temptation to take things out of His hands, the richer will be the blessing of remaining in His hands and awaiting His time.

CHAPTER TWENTY-EIGHT

Contents: Jacob at Bethel and the Abrahamic covenant confirmed to him in a dream.
Characters: Isaac, Jacob, Laban, Esau, Ishmael, Mahalath, angels.
Conclusion: The believer should realize that he is ever in God's presence. However no heart can feel at home in His presence until emptied of self and broken.
Key Word: Bethel (house of God), v. 19.
Strong Verses: 12, 15, 22.
Striking Facts: Bethel, to the Christian, stands for a realization, although often imperfect, of the presence of God through Christ, and the spiritual contents of faith.

CHAPTER TWENTY-NINE

Contents: Jacob and Laban, two bargain makers, meet.
Characters: Jacob, Laban, Rachael, Leah, Reuben, Levi, Judah.
Conclusion: The believer who has erred may not be forsaken of God, but he is permitted to reap the shame and sorrow of his self-chosen way. Matt. 7:2.
Key Word: Beguiled, v. 25.
Strong Verses: 20.
Striking Facts: Jacob at Haran, pictures the nation descended from him at the present time. He was away from the place of blessing, without an altar, but yet under the covenant care of Jehovah and eventually to be brought back.

CHAPTER THIRTY

Contents: Jacob's posterity in Padan-aram. Another bargain between Jacob and Laban.

Characters: Rachael, Jacob, Laban, Leah, Joseph.
Conclusion: The toiling and scheming of men is the result of ignorance of God's Grace, and inability to put implicit confidence in God's promises.
Key Word: Blessed, v. 27.
Strong Verses: 27.
Striking Facts: The success of Jacob's policy was not sufficient to justify it, had it been unjust toward the shrewd Laban, but evidently it was not unjust, for see 31:12.

CHAPTER THIRTY-ONE

Contents: Jacob's resolution to return. Laban's hot pursuit; their quarrel and final agreement.
Characters: Laban, Jacob, Rachael, Leah.
Conclusion: The safety of believers under trying circumstances is much due to the hold God has on the consciences of bad men. In the path of obedience, we may count on God's care.
Key Word: Flight, v. 21.
Strong Verses: 49.
Striking Facts: The settlement of a quarrel is a jewel so precious, one can scarcely buy it too dearly. While the believer may resent injuries, he is not to avenge them but remember that God is the avenger.

CHAPTER THIRTY-TWO

Contents: Jacob becomes Israel. Preparation for meeting Esau. Wrestling against the angel.
Characters: Jacob, Esau, angel.
Conclusion: Either we lean on God or on our own plans. The arrangements of unbelief and impatience prevent God acting for us and He must bring us to the end of our own strength.
Key Word: Afraid, v. 7.
Strong Verses: 24, 30.
Striking Facts: To be alone with Christ is the only way to arrive at a knowledge of ourselves and our ways. Jacob was a wrestled-with man, and until the seat of his own strength was touched, he did not reach the place of blessing.

CHAPTER THIRTY-THREE

Contents: Jacob meets Esau. Settles in Canaan.
Characters: Jacob, Esau, Leah, Rachael, Joseph.
Conclusion: How groundless are all the Christian's fears and how useless all his self-devised plans. "When a man's ways please the Lord, He maketh even his enemies to be at peace with him."
Key Word: Meeting, v. 4.
Strong Verses: 11.
Striking Facts: "Acquaint now thyself with Him and be at peace." Failure in this, causes one, on every fresh occasion, to doubt and hesitate notwithstanding the evidence of God's faithfulness through Christ.

CHAPTER THIRTY-FOUR

Contents: Harvest of evil years comes on Jacob and family. Dinah defiled and the bloody revenge.
Characters: Dinah, Jacob, Hamor, sons of Jacob, Simeon, Levi.
Conclusion: Untaught maidens who go out to "gad" with the daughters of the land fall into a snare and involve their relatives in great trouble.
Key Word: Defiled, v. 2.
Strong Verses: 19.
Striking Facts: God had directed Jacob to Bethel. He settled at Shechem. Partial obedience to Christ is responsible for much trouble which befalls Christian families.

CHAPTER THIRTY-FIVE

Contents: Jacob's return to Bethel and renewed communion. Death of Rachael. Birth of Benjamin. Death of Isaac.

Characters: Jacob, Deborah, Rebekah, Rachael, Benjamin, Reuben, Bilhah, Isaac, Esau.
Conclusion: There is no perfect communion with God until all idols are put away and we come into His presence as He directs.
Key Word: Altar, v. 1.
Strong Verses: 3, 7.
Striking Facts: "Arise and go to Bethel." God is ever calling the soul back to Himself. Christ says, "Remember from whence thou art fallen and repent and do thy first works."

CHAPTER THIRTY-SIX

Contents: Generations of Esau and their settlements.
Characters: Esau, Jacob.
Conclusion: Though one have not a spiritual right by promise, they may still have, in the mercy of God, temporary rights to rich estates in this world. "But what is a man profited if he gain the whole world and lose his own soul?"
Key Word: Generations, v. 1.
Strong Verses: 6, 7.
Striking Facts: Edom, a name by which the foolish bargain was perpetuated, means "red pottage." If men sell their birthright in Christ for a mess of pottage, they must thank themselves when afterwards, it is remembered against them to their reproach.

CHAPTER THIRTY-SEVEN

Contents: Generations of Joseph. Joseph hated and rejected by his brothers. Cast into pit. Carried away by Gentiles.
Characters: Jacob, Joseph, Reuben, Judah, Potiphar.
Conclusion: Envy is a canker to the soul and hates those excellencies it cannot reach. "Hatred stirreth up strife" and left to itself, only stops at murder.
Key Word: Envied, v. 11.
Strong Verses: 4.
Striking Facts: Joseph, a marvelous type of Christ. Rejected because of his testimony to his brethren, sent by the Father on a mission of love, cast into a pit, sold to Gentiles, the Gentiles blessed through him.

CHAPTER THIRTY-EIGHT

Contents: Shame of Judah and his sons.
Characters: Judah, Hirah, Er, Onen, Tamar.
Conclusion: The sins which dishonor and defile the body are evidences of vile affection and are very displeasing to God, often visited with quick punishment.
Key Word: Shamed, v. 23.
Strong Verses: 10, 26.
Striking Facts: It is evident that our Lord sprang out of Judah. Heb. 7:14. Divine grace is seen rising above man's sin to bring about His purpose. The Spirit is conducting us by this chapter, along the line through which, on the flesh side, our Lord came. Man would never have devised such a genealogy.

CHAPTER THIRTY-NINE

Contents: Joseph tested in Egypt in the house of Potiphar.
Characters: Joseph, Potiphar, Potiphar's wife, prison keeper.
Conclusion: Loyalty to God may bring a believer into serious testings but the almighty grace of God will enable him to overcome the enemy's assaults. Though stripped of possessions, we need not be stripped of virtue.
Key Word: Goodly, v. 6.
Strong Verses: 2, 3, 21.
Striking Facts: The one taken from the pit, into which he came through rejection, is coming to the place of ruler, the channel of blessing to the Gentiles, sustainer of life to the brethren. '(Christ).'

CHAPTER FORTY

Contents: Joseph in prison in Egypt. Interprets dreams.
Characters: Butler, baker, captain of guard, Joseph, Potiphar.
Conclusion: Whatever our lot in God's providence, we may ever be a blessing to companions in tribulation by showing a concern in their troubles and doing our best, by God's help, to lift their burdens.
Key Word: Interpretation, v. 8.
Strong Verses: 8.
Striking Facts: Bad dreams cannot be given a good interpretation. If a minister' of Christ deals faithfully with God's message and it proves unpleasant, it is not his fault.

CHAPTER FORTY-ONE

Contents: Pharaoh's dream. Joseph's exaltation in Egypt and his Gentile bride.
Characters: Pharaoh, Joseph, butler, Asenath, Manasseh, Ephriam.
Conclusion: The faithful believer will be abundantly recompensed for the disgrace he has patiently suffered and his righteousness will shine forth so all will know that God is with him.
Key Word: Exalted (set over), v. 41.
Strong Verses: 38, 39.
Striking Facts: As Joseph solved Pharaoh's vexing problems, so Jesus relieves the heart of its burdens. Rejected, exalted, Jesus is now taking a Gentile Bride to be with Him when the "Time of Jacob's trouble" comes upon the earth.

CHAPTER FORTY-TWO

Contents: Joseph preserves his brethren from the famine.
Characters: Jacob, Joseph, brothers.
Conclusion: Times of testing await those who are guilty and often prove the effectual means of awakening conscience and bringing sin to remembrance.
Key Word: Proved (tested), v. 15.
Strong Verses: 8, 23, 24.
Striking Facts: While Jesus is unrecognized by His brethren, the Jews, they are passing through deep troubles, but a tribulation awaits them which will bring them to the feet of Him Whom they crucified.

CHAPTER FORTY-THREE

Contents: Second visit of Joseph's brethren to Egypt in their necessity.
Characters: Jacob, Benjamin, Joseph, Simeon, Judah, steward.
Conclusion: The way to find mercy with men is to seek it of God Who has all hearts in His hand and who works in strange ways for His children, when they know it not.
Key Word: Mercy, v. 14.
Strong Verses: 14, 23, 29.
Striking Facts: Before Him, who in their blindness they do not know, the Jews will plead for their Benjamin who has been lost to them, and in the agony of the hour, the opened heavens will reveal the Christ they crucified, as their Deliverer. The sufferer and the conqueror are one.

CHAPTER FORTY-FOUR

Contents: Joseph's brethren further tested. Arrest on charge of taking a cup.
Characters: Joseph, Judah, Benjamin, steward.
Conclusion: Even in afflictions wherein the believer thinks himself wronged by men, he must own that God has a righteous purpose and possibly it is to make him confess his sin and develope his better nature.
Key Word: Sorrow, v. 31.
Strong Verses: 16, 33.
Striking Facts: As Joseph laid a plan to bring about full confession from his brethren that they might come into fellowship with him, so Christ

will deal with the Jews, culminating in a great day of confession and mourning.

CHAPTER FORTY-FIVE

Contents: Joseph reveals himself to his brethren whom he blesses and sends back to Egypt.

Characters: Joseph, brothers, Pharaoh, Jacob.

Conclusion: "He worketh all things together for good to them that love God and are called according to His purpose." He can work wonders for His own, when He has surrendered men through whom to work.

Key Word: Revealed (made known), v. 1.

Strong Verses: 5, 7, 8.

Striking Facts: A sacred scene is coming for Israel (Ezek. 22:19) when Christ shall be revealed. As they stand self-condemned before Him, He will pour balm into their hearts (Zech. 13:1; 12:9) and will show all to have been decreed for their blessing (Rom. 11:11-12).

CHAPTER FORTY-SIX

Contents: Jacob's journey to Egypt and meeting with Joseph.

Characters: Jacob, Joseph, brothers, their families, Pharaoh.

Conclusion: A glorious meeting day is coming after the trials and mistakes of earth. Jesus prepares a place for the believer and comes again to receive him unto Himself, that where He is, there they may be also.

Key Word: Meeting, v. 29.

Strong Verses: 1, 3, 4.

Striking Facts: The absolute will of God for Israel was in Canaan, not Egypt (26:1-5). His permissive will allows them to settle in Goshen and as far as possible He blesses them there. The Jews sidestepped God's absolute will by rejecting the Messiah, but a day of mingled joy and mourning awaits those living at His second advent.

CHAPTER FORTY-SEVEN

Contents: Jacob and descendants exalted in Goshen.

Characters: Pharaoh, Joseph, brothers, Jacob.

Conclusion: Notwithstanding former unkindnesses received, the believer who is prospered in this world, must not overlook nor despise his poor relatives in their need. The measure of a truly great man is the way he treats men who in themselves have been small.

Key Word: Nourished, v. 12.

Strong Verses: 12, 29, 30.

Striking Facts: Christ will, at His second advent, present His brethren, the Jews, in the court of heaven, restoring them to the place of blessing in the earth. As Jacob here blesses, King Pharaoh, so Israel's portion in the Millenium will be that of blessing the kings of the earth.

CHAPTER FORTY-EIGHT

Contents: Jacob on his death bed blesses Joseph's sons.

Characters: Jacob, Joseph, Ephriam, Manasseh, Reuben, Simeon, Rachael.

Conclusion: God in His grace, does not always observe the order of nature in bestowing His blessings, nor prefer those whom we think fittest to be preferred, but as it pleases Him, He chooses the weak to confound the mighty, thus His grace becomes more illustrious.

Key Word: Blessed, v. 15.

Strong Verses: 21.

Striking Facts: v. 17. When the tribes were mustered in the wilderness, Ephriam was more numerous than Manasseh (Num. 1:32-35; 2:18-20) and is named first (Psa. 80:2).

CHAPTER FORTY-NINE

Contents: Jacob's dying blessing, prophetic of the tribes of Israel.

Characters: Jacob, twelve sons.

Conclusion: It is a great blessing to attend upon Godly parents in their ꞁ last hours that we might learn how to die as well as live, and profit by their reproofs, counsels, and comforts. Though they cannot prophecy, they can tell us from God's Word what will befall us in the last day if we do not do the will of the Father.

Key Word: Prophecy (shall befall), v. 1.

Strong Verses: 10.

Striking Facts: The cunning, shifting and often faithless Jacob, the supplanter, bargain maker, comes forth in the calm elevation of faith to bestow blessings and impart dignities. This will be Israel's part in the last great dispensation of earth, after Christ has returned.

CHAPTER FIFTY

Contents: Jacob's burial. Joseph's death.

Characters: Jacob, Joseph, brothers.

Conclusion: As it is an honor to die lamented, so it is a duty to honor the dead who have been useful in the Lord. Sincere and humble lament over Godly men is proper, for their death is a great loss to any place.

Key Word: Mourning, v. 10.

Strong Verses: 17, 19, 20, 21.

Striking Facts: Finding man in a beautiful Eden, Genesis 1, we leave him in chapter 50 in a coffin in Egypt.

EXODUS

Key Thought:	Number of Chapters	Key Verse:	Christ seen as:
Covenants	40	12:23	Lamb of God.

Writer of the Book:	Date:	Conclusion of the Book:
		Redemption is by the
Moses	About 1500 B. C.	blood and that alone.

SUMMARY

CHAPTER ONE

Contents: Israel in Egypt and their bondage.

Characters: Joseph, Pharaoh, Shiprah, Puah.

Conclusion: God's providences may at times seem to thwart His promises that His peoples' faith may be tried and His power the more magnified. In their persecutions, He will sustain all who trust Him.

Key Word: Bondage, v. 14.

Strong Verses: 17, 20, 21.

Striking Facts: It has been the policy of the persecutors of Israel throughout the centuries to represent them as a dangerous people, hurtful to provinces and untrustworthy, as a pretense for barbarous treatment. God's counsels stand and they still increase.

CHAPTER TWO

Contents: Deliverer prepared for Israel. Moses' birth, boyhood and marriage.

Characters: Levi's daughter, Pharaoh's daughter, mother of Moses, sister, Moses, Pharaoh, seven daughters of priests, shepherds, Reuel, Zipporah, Gershom.

Conclusion: When men are plotting the ruin of God's people, God is planning His peoples' salvation. One apparently marked for obscurity and poverty may be destined to rise before the world to show God's power. Even enemies may be used to carry out God's purposes.

Key Word: Moses, v. 10.

Strong Verses: 24, 25.

Striking Facts: Moses is a striking type of Christ. Rejected by Israel, he turns to the Gentiles. In his rejection, he takes a Gentile bride, then later appears as Israel's deliverer and is accepted.

CHAPTER THREE

Contents: Moses called as deliverer. The burning bush.

Characters: Jethro, Moses, angel.

Conclusion: Those qualified for great service may expect for a time to be confined to obscurity for special preparation and the vision of God's purpose. If God gives opportunity and heart to serve Him, it is an ernest of His power to accomplish the work.

Key Word: Deliverance, vv. 8, 10.

Strong Verses: 7, 12, 14.

Striking Facts: The burning bush pictures Israel in the furnace, yet never consumed. God's relations with Israel are eternal. v. 15.

CHAPTER FOUR

Contents: Moses' objections. Unbelief of the people and Moses' lack of eloquence. Return to Egypt. Message delivered to elders.

Characters: God, Moses, Aaron, Jethro, Zipporah, elders.

Conclusion: Unbelief refuses to believe God because it does not find in self a reason for believing. With God, the merest stammerer may prove an efficient minister, neither need he be uneasy as to the reception of the message.

Key Word: Spokesman, v. 16.

Strong Verses: 11, 12, 31.

Striking Facts: The rod, symbol of power in Christ's hand, was not wrenched away from Moses, but cast down by Moses. It remained a serpent only while out of his hand   The rod, temporarily out of Christ's hand, will soon be taken up again and Satan's power will be over.

CHAPTER FIVE

Contents:—Moses' first contest with Pharaoh.

Characters: Moses, Aaron, Pharaoh, taskmasters.

Conclusion: God, in coming toward His people in mercy may sometimes employ strange methods so that people will think themselves ill-treated. God suffers it to be so that we may learn to cease from man and cease depending on second causes.

Key Word: Burdens, v. 4.

Strong Verses: 3.

Striking Facts: Those called to public service for Christ may expect to be tried, not only by the proud threats of enemies, but the unjust, unkind censures of friends who judge by outward appearances.

CHAPTER SIX

Contents: Jehovah's answer to Moses' first prayer. Covenant renewed. Families of Israel. Moses' commission renewed.

Characters: God, Moses, Pharaoh.

Conclusion: Man's extremity is God's opportunity of helping and saving. God's covenants are as firm as the power and truth of God can make them and we may venture upon all His promises.

Key Word: Covenant, v. 4.

Strong Verses: 3, 6, 7, 8.

Striking Facts: v. 12. Disconsolate spirits often cause us to put from us the comforts we are entitled to in Christ and we stand in our own light. If we indulge in fretfulness, we lose the comfort of His word and must thank ourselves if we go comfortless.

CHAPTER SEVEN

Contents: Contest with Pharaoh. First plague. Water turned to blood.

Characters: God, Moses, Aaron, Pharaoh, magician.

Conclusion: We see God's almighty power, the unstability of all things under the sun and the changes we may meet with in them. What is water today may be blood tomorrow. Sin turns man's comforts into crosses.

Key Word: Smitten (waters), vv. 1, 17.

Strong Verses: 1, 5, 17.

Striking Facts: Satanic resistance to God's testimony of His Son is often offered by those who have "a form of godliness without the power thereof." The magicians finally failed, proving (8:7) their tricks "lying wonders" (Rev. 13:15).

CHAPTER EIGHT

Contents: Plagues of frogs, lice, flies. Pharaoh's compromising offer.

Characters: God, Moses, Pharaoh, Aaron.

Conclusion: If God be against us, all creatures can be made to be at war with us. God can, as He pleases, arm the smallest parts of creation against men. He may choose contemptible instruments to defeat one, that He might magnify His own power.

Key Word: Smitten, v. 2.

Strong Verses: 1, 2, 19.

Striking Facts: Pharaoh's compromises are types of those Satan makes with the Christian. "Be a Christian but stay in Egypt, or at least, don't be so narrow as to come out entirely from the world." .

CHAPTER NINE

Contents: Plagues of murrain, boils and hail.

Characters: God, Moses, Pharaoh, Aaron.

Conclusion: The creature is made subject to vanity by reason of man's sins, liable to serve man's wickedness or share his punishment. When judgments are abroad, they may fall both on righteous and wicked but they are not the same to one as the other in the final reckoning.

Key Word: Smitten, vv. 27, 15.

Strong Verses: 5.

Striking Facts: v. 12. The Lord hardened his heart. Before this, Pharaoh hardened his own heart, resisting God's grace. There is a time when God gives one up to their own reprobate mind. Wilful hardness is sooner or later punished with judicial hardness. If men persist in shutting their eyes, God will close them.

CHAPTER TEN

Contents: Plagues of locusts and darkness.
Characters: God, Moses, Aaron, Pharaoh.
Conclusion: God's terms of reconcilliation are fixed and cannot be disputed or lowered. Men must meet the demand of God's will or God will permit their delusions and answer them according to their sin.
Key Word: Smitten, v. 21.
Strong Verses: 12, 17, 25.
Striking Facts: v. 11. Godly men make a subtle compromise if they desire for their children, a position in the world, or (v. 24) if they fail to consecrate all their possessions along with themselves to Christ.

CHAPTER ELEVEN

Contents: Last plague. Death of firstborn prophesied.
Characters: God, Moses, Aaron, Pharaoh.
Conclusion: Persistent enemies of God and His people will be made to fall under at last and those who have approved themselves, will look great in the eyes of those who have viewed them with contempt.
Key Word: Death, vv. 1, 5.
Strong Verses: 3, 7.
Striking Facts: In some way, God will always redress the injured, who in humble silence, commit their cause to Him, and in the end, they will not be losers by their adherance to Christ.

CHAPTER TWELVE

Contents: Deliverance for Israel through the Passover.
Characters: God, Moses, Aaron, Pharaoh.
Conclusion: Deliverance for the believer is based entirely upon the shedding of the blood of a divinely appointed substitute and its application to the heart once for all. If death has taken place for us, it cannot come to us.
Key Word: Passover, v. 13.
Strong Verses: 2, 13, 14. 27.
Striking Facts: v. 8. Secured by the blood, the believer feeds on the Person of the Lamb of God, roast with fire, not raw. If Christ is not seen as the One subjected to the fires of God's wrath against sin, one cannot feed upon Him. He cannot be an example if He is not first an atoning sacrifice.

CHAPTER THIRTEEN

Contents: Firstborn set apart for Jehovah. Directions for feast of unleavened bread and consecration of males.
Characters: God, Moses, Joseph.
Conclusion: The believer should retain remembrance of God's great deliverance and to impress it on the heart, should use the appointed means for preserving remembrance. So, under the Gospel, Christ said, "This do in remembrance of me."
Key Word: Remember, v. 3.
Strong Verses: 9, 16, 21, 22.
Striking Facts: That which by God's special mercy has in Christ been spared to us should be peculiarly dedicated to God's honor. God who is first and best should have our first and best.

CHAPTER FOURTEEN

Contents: God's power exerted to redeem Israel. Passing the Red Sea.
Characters: God, Moses, Pharaoh, angel.
Conclusion: The believer cannot go ahead in the strength of Christ until he has learned to stand still in his own helplessness. God can then place Himself between us and our circumstances and wonderfully deliver.
Key Word: Saved, v. 30.
Strong Verses: 13, 14, 19, 30, 31.
Striking Facts: By the blood, God comes between us and our sins. By His

presence, if we will permit, He will come between us and every overcoming circumstance. The cross separates from sin; the cloud from circumstances

CHAPTER FIFTEEN

Contents: The song of the redeemed.
Characters: God, Moses, Miriam.
Conclusion: Those who love God triumph in His triumphs and what is His honor is their joy. Our first thought should be to give glory to God.
Key Word: Triumph, v. 1.
Strong Verses: 2, 6, 7, 18.
Striking Facts: Bitter waters (v. 23) in the path of God's leading, remind us of the trials that come to God's people for their edification, not punishment. The tree (cross, Gal. 3:13) cast into the bitter waters, will make them all sweet.

CHAPTER SIXTEEN

Contents: Murmuring of the people. Manna and quails given by God.
Characters: God, Moses, Aaron.
Conclusion: The believer is apt to forget a thousand mercies in the presence of one trifling privation. God is longsuffering. Better to be in a desert with God than in the brick kilns of Egypt with Pharaoh.
Key Word: Murmuring, v. 2.
Strong Verses: 4, 7, 12.
Striking Facts: Jesus, the Bread of Life (John 6) is the true wilderness bread for believers, ministered by the Spirit through the Word. Christ may be partaken of unreservedly but we have no more of Him than faith appropriates. v. 16.

CHAPTER SEVENTEEN

Contents: Smitten rock at Meribah.
Characters: God, Moses, Joshua, Aaron, Hur.
Conclusion: Fed by the Bread of Life; refreshed by the Water of Life (John 7:37) means victory for the believer in every conflict with the world, the flesh and the devil.
Key Word: Jehovah-nissi (The Lord our banner), v. 15.
Strong Verses: 7, 15.
Striking Facts: Christ is the Rock (1 Cor. 10:4) He was smitten, and resulting from His finished work was the outpouring of the Holy Spirit giving power to all those who believe.

CHAPTER EIGHTEEN

Contents: Moses joined by his wife and children. Judges selected to solve the problems of the people.
Characters: God, Moses, Aaron, Jethro, Zipporah, Gershom, Eliezer.
Conclusion: Telling of God's wondrous works is good to the use of edifying What we have the joy of, let God have the praise of, thereby confirming others to faith and encouraging them to real worship.
Key Word: Told, v. 8 (testimony).
Strong Verses: 8, 9, 10.
Striking Facts: It will be noticed (Num. 11:14-17) that God ignored Jethro's counsel and his man-made organization, putting in its place, His own order (v. 18). We are not called to service on the ground of our ability, but Christ's ability. Phil. 4:13.

CHAPTER NINETEEN

Contents: Israel at Sinai and the preparation for receiving the law.
Characters: God, Moses, Aaron.
Conclusion: Humble reverence should possess the minds of those who draw near to God for we are sinners in the presence of a holy and righteous Judge; mean creatures before the Mighty Creator.
Key Word: Ready, vv. 11, 15.
Strong Verses: 5, 6.
Striking Facts: (Cp. 1 Pet. 2:9; Rev. 1:6; 5:10 with Ex. 19:5). Note that

what under law, was conditional, under Grace is freely given in Christ to every believer. Note also that God did not impose law until it was proposed and accepted by man.

CHAPTER TWENTY

Contents: Ten commandments delivered to Moses at Sinai.
Characters: God, Moses.
Conclusion: A holy and righteous God has holy and righteous standards. Those who love God will constantly endeavor to live as He requires, enabled by the Holy Spirit.
Key Word: Commands, v. 6.
Strong Verses: 3-17.
Striking Facts: Law proposes life and righteousness as the end to be attained by keeping it, but proves at the outset that man is in a state of death (Rom. 5:20; 7:7, 13; 3:20). Life and righteousness cannot come by that which only curses, but only through the grace of God in Christ.

CHAPTER TWENTY-ONE

Contents: Laws concerning servants. Injuries to the person.
Characters: God, Moses.
Conclusion: The great God of heaven stoops to take interest in the detail affairs between man and man and makes regulations even as to the loss of a tooth.
Key Word: Judgments, v. 1.
Strong Verses: 12.
Striking Facts: God who gives and maintains life, by His law would protect it.

CHAPTER TWENTY-TWO

Contents: Judgments on rights of property; crimes against humanity
Characters: God, Moses.
Conclusion: Man's attitude to his fellow man will be based on his attitude to God and His law.
Key Word: Judgments, 21:1.
Strong Verses: 29, 30, 31.
Striking Facts: One is struck by the number of things we are told NOT to do. These negative commands reveal human nature to itself. All is changed in the New Testament through Christ's sacrifice.

CHAPTER TWENTY-THREE

Contents: Judgments on the national feasts. Instructions concerning the conquest of Canaan.
Characters: God, Moses.
Conclusion: God's angels will keep the believer in the way, though it lay through the enemy's country and will bring him into the place God has prepared. A precept of obedience goes with every promise.
Key Word: Judgments, 21:1.
Strong Verses: 7, 12, 20, 22, 25.
Striking Facts: Familiarity with idolators is forbidden (32, 33). The believer by familiar converse with false worshippers, is often drawn into worship with them and his detestation of sin wears off.

CHAPTER TWENTY-FOUR

Contents: Order of worship prescribed, pending the building of the tabernacle.
Characters: God, Moses, Aaron, Nadab, Abihu, elders, Joshua, Hur.
Conclusion: The unapproachable glory of God tells a sinner to keep off, but the altar shows him how he can feast and worship in God's presence.
Key Word: Worship, v. 1.
Strong Verses: 8, 17.
Striking Facts: We never hear "draw near" (Heb. 10:22) from the shadows of the law. For Christ's work was not then done which entitled the sinner to draw near. Law always says "worship afar off."

CHAPTER TWENTY-FIVE

Contents: Moses in the mount; first directions concerning the tabernacle.
Characters: God, Moses.

Conclusion: The only way for God and man to meet is in the precise way and place which He has appointed (v. 22). When a righteous God and a ruined sinner meet on a bloodsprinkled platform, all is well. (1 Pet. 1:18, 19).
Key Word: Pattern, v. 9.
Strong Verses: 22.
Striking Facts: The tabernacle in every detail foreshadows Christ. Gold is a type of deity; silver of redemption; brass of judgment; blue of heavenly origin; purple of royalty; scarlet of atonement, etc.

CHAPTER TWENTY-SIX
Contents: Further directions regarding the tabernacle.
Characters: God, Moses.
Conclusion: The wonders of God's presence are known only to those, who by the proper ceremonies, have come inside the curtains of His grace. The natural man is screened out from the things of the Spirit.
Key Word: Fashion (pattern), v. 30.
Strong Verses: 30.
Striking Facts: We as Christ's followers have here no continuing city, being strangers and pilgrims through this world to a better land, having a moveable tabernacle. The presence of God is not tied to any place.

CHAPTER TWENTY-SEVEN
Contents: Directions about the brazen altar and the court.
Characters: God, Moses, Aaron.
Conclusion: Sinful man dare not approach God (at the ark) Heb. 9:8; but God approaches man as a sinner through Christ (brazen altar). There were blood prints all the way from the ark to the altar. Redeemed on that path, the sinner is safe in the courts of God.
Key Word: Pattern, 25:9.
Strong Verses: 20.
Striking Facts: In Jesus, God comes down in grace to the sinner. In Jesus the sinner is brought up in righteousness to God. These are our only grounds of standing before God.

CHAPTER TWENTY-EIGHT
Contents: Directions about the priesthood.
Characters: God, Moses, Aaron, Nadab, Eleazar, Ithmar.
Conclusion: The believer need never fear God has forgotten him for the Great High Priest bears the names of His own on His breast before God, presenting them as "those accepted in the beloved."
Key Word: Ministry, v. 1.
Strong Verses: 29, 41.
Striking Facts: Every true believer, through identification with Christ, is an earthly priest of God's family (Rev. 1:8) properly clothed for the work, (Rev. 19:7, 8), and should be duly consecrated and sanctified for his work of testimony.

CHAPTER TWENTY-NINE
Contents: Consecration of the priests and the offerings.
Characters: God, Moses, Aaron, Aaron's sons.
Conclusion: Those representing God should be set apart in solemn consecration. All their service must be based on the ground of the burnt offering.
Key Word: Consecration, v. 26.
Strong Verses: 18, 45, 46.
Striking Facts: Consecration means "to fill the hand." It is not the believer filling God's hand. In the arms of Aaron's sons were put the parts of the sacrifice which speak of the inherent richness and power of Christ. This was their acknowledgment that the power for service was not in themselves, but in another. This is consecration.

CHAPTER THIRTY
Contents: The altar of incense and the brazen laver.
Characters: God, Moses, Aaron.

Conclusion: (See Psa. 141:2). The prayer of a contrite believer ascends as a fragrant cloud to God. (Prov. 15:8).
Key Word: Incense (worship), v. 7.
Strong Verses: 30.
Striking Facts: Fire under the incense altar brought out the fragrance (Rom. 8: 26, 27). The fire was from the blood-sprinkled altar (Heb. 10: 19, 20). Their prayers were based on the intercession of a priest (Rom. 8:34).

CHAPTER THIRTY-ONE

Contents: The tabernacle and its workmen. Sabbath made a sign between God and Israel.   •
Characters: God, Moses, Bezaleel, Aholiab.
Conclusion: When God gives a commission, He will, in some measure give the qualifications according as the service is. When God has work to be done, He will not be without instruments.
Key Word: Workmanship, v. 3.
Strong Verses: 3, 17.
Striking Facts: When Christ sent His apostles to rear the Gospel tabernacle He poured out His Holy Spirit upon them to enable them to speak with power the wonderful works of God.

CHAPTER THIRTY-TWO

Contents: The broken law; Israel worships a golden calf. Intercession of Moses.
Characters: God, Moses, Aaron, Joshua.
Conclusion: It is a great sin to make gold, or anything else, a god, as those do who let it become a supreme object of their affections, taking the place of God in any degree.
Key Word: Great Sin, v. 30.
Strong Verses: 26, 29, 32.
Striking Facts: Moses typified Christ, who went above (Acts 1:9) telling the people to tarry. In His absence, some forget his promised return (John. 14:3; Acts 1:11) and make themselves gods (2 Tim. 3:1-4; 4:3-4; Matt. 24:12) denying His return (2 Pet. 3:3-4; Matt. 24:48, 49). Jesus will come unexpectedly (Matt. 25:13) punishing evil doers (2 Thess. 2:7, 8) who are naked (Rev. 6:16, 17) and gathering the true to Himself (1 Thess. 4:13-18).

CHAPTER THIRTY-THREE ˙

Contents: The journey to be resumed. God's presence assured.
Characters: God, Moses, Joshua.   .
Conclusion: God's special presence with us in the wilderness by His Spirit and grace to direct, defend and comfort, is the surest pledge of His acceptance of us. The bitter fruit of sin in the believer is the lost sense of His presence, which will cause any true believer to lament.
Key Word: Presence, v. 14.
Strong Verses: 11, 14, 20.
Striking Facts: Moses, as a prince who had power with God, was a type of Christ the great Intercessor whom the Father heareth always. Through His intercession, we obtain constant assurance of the blessings of salvation.

CHAPTER THIRTY-FOUR

Contents: Second tables of the law. The new vision and commission.
Characters: God, Moses, Aaron.
Conclusion: (12-17). We cannot expect the benefit of God's promises unless we make conscience of His precepts. God's name is "Jealous" and we cannot worship Him aright if we do not worship Him alone.
Key Word: Tables of testimony, v. 29.
Strong Verses: 6, 7, 14, 29.
Striking Facts: The shining of Moses' face was a great honor to him but nothing compared to the glory which excelled. We read of Jesus, that not only His face shone, but His whole body and His raiment was glistening (Luke 9:29).   )

CHAPTER THIRTY-FIVE

Contents: People instructed as to the tabernacle. The gifts of the people for the work.

Characters: God, Moses, Bezaleel, Aholiab.

Conclusion: God loves a cheerful giver and is best pleased with a free-will offering. Our gifts are our acknowledgment that we receive all from Him and dedicate all to Him.

Key Word: Gifts, v. 5.

Strong Verses: 21, 29.

Striking Facts: If we cannot do what others do for God, we are not to sit still and do nothing. Though our offering gains us no reputation with men, if given according to ability, it does not fail of acceptance with Him. (2 Cor. 8:12).

CHAPTER THIRTY-SIX

Contents: The tabernacle work begun. The curtains, coverings, sockets, bars, vail.

Characters: God, Moses, Bezaleel, Aholiab.

Conclusion: The talents with which God has entrusted the believer are not to be laid up but laid out. Have your tools ready and God will find you work.

Key Word: Work, v. 1.

Strong Verses: 1, 5, 6.

Striking Facts: Precious souls redeemed by Christ are the material of the Gospel tabernacle. (1 Pet. 2:5). Those called to the building of this house are those whom God has in some measure made fit for the work. Ability and willingness are the two things to be regarded in the call of the Christian worker.

CHAPTER THIRTY-SEVEN

Contents: Making of the ark, mercy seat, table, candlestick, altar.

Characters: Bezaleel.

Conclusion: As the workmen were to take great care to make all according to God's pattern, so the believer should have respect to all the light God gives, even to every iota and tittle of His commandments. God delights in sincere obedience and keeps exact account of it.

Key Word: Work, 36:1.

Strong Verses: 6, 9.

Striking Facts: Jesus Christ, the great propitiation, has made reconcilliation for the believer, restoring communion with God. From the mercy seat, He accepts us and teaches us, and under the shadow of the Spirit we are safe.

CHAPTER THIRTY-EIGHT

Contents: Altar of burnt offering, laver, court, gate.

Characters: God, Moses, Bezaleel, Aholiab, Ithamar.

Conclusion: Same as chap. 37.

Key Word: Work, v. 1. 36:1.

Strong Verses: 21.

Striking Facts: On the altar of burnt offering all the sacrifices were made. The altar is a type of Calvary's cross on which Christ, our whole burnt offering, offered Himself without spot to God (Heb. 9:14).

CHAPTER THIRTY-NINE

Contents: Garments for Aaron.

Characters: God, Moses, Aaron.

Conclusion: All believers are spiritual priests and their service-clothes are provided (Rev. 19:8). All who converse with them should be able to see that they are properly clothed as God's representatives.

Key Word: Garments, v. 1.

Strong Verses: 42, 43.

Striking Facts: Christ, our High Priest, in undertaking the work of man's restoration, wore the clothes of service—the gifts and graces of the Holy Spirit, which He had without measure.

CHAPTER FORTY

Contents: Tabernacle set up. God's glory manifested.

Characters: God, Moses, Aaron.

Conclusion: God will dwell with those who prepare Him a habitation. Where God has a throne and an altar in the heart, there is a living temple in which the Spirit will be manifested.

Key Word: Finished, v. 33.

Strong Verses: 17, 34, 38.

Striking Facts: What the glory cloud was to the tabernacle, the Holy Spirit is to the Church and the temple, which is the believer's body. (1 Cor.. 6:19).   •

LEVITICUS

Key Thought:	Number of Chapters:	Key Verse:	Christ seen as:
Atonement	27	16:34	High Priest

Writer of the Book:	Date:	Conclusion of the Book:
Moses	About 1500 B. C.	Access of the redeemed to God is only through the blood. Holiness of the redeemed is imperative.

SUMMARY

CHAPTER ONE

Contents: The burnt offering laws.

Characters: God, Moses, Aaron's sons.

Conclusion: Utter dependence upon the sacrifices, typifying the great sacrifice of Christ on which the iniquity of us all was laid is God's requirement. (The laying on of the offerer's hands signified identification of the believer with his offering).

Key Word: Burnt sacrifice, v. 3.

Strong Verses: 4.

Striking Facts: The burnt offering stands for Christ who offered Himself without spot to God in delight to do the Father's will even unto death. Fire, symbol of God's holiness, consumes the offering.

CHAPTER TWO

Contents: Meat offering and first-fruits laws.

Characters: God, Moses, Aaron's sons.

Conclusion: Leaven, typifying malice, wickedness and human pride is not accepted in spiritual sacrifices. Take heed of those sins which will certainly spoil the acceptableness of worship.

Key Word: Fine flour offering, v. 1. First-fruits, v. 12.

Strong Verses: 11.

Striking Facts: Fine flour speaks of the balance of the character of Christ; fire of His testing by suffering; frankincense of the fragrance of His life to God; absence of leaven, His character as "The Truth;" absence of honey—His life was not mere natural sweetness which may exist apart from God; oil mingled, Christ as born of the Spirit; oil upon, Christ baptized with the Spirit.

CHAPTER THREE

Contents: Peace offering laws.

Characters: God, Moses, Aaron's sons.

Conclusion: In Christ, God and the sinner meet in peace. God is propitiated and the sinner reconciled; both alike satisfied with Christ's work. "He is our peace."

Key Word: Peace offering, v. 1.

Strong Verses: 2.

Striking Facts: Details of the peace offering bring out the thought of fellowship, hence the peace offering is set forth as affording food for the priests, (7:31-34).

CHAPTER FOUR

Contents: Sin offering laws.

Characters: God, Moses.

Conclusion: Even sins done in ignorance need to be atoned for by sacrifice. To plead ignorance when charged with sin will not deliver. Our only hope is in acceptance of Him who "became sin for us."

Key Word: Sin offering, v. 3.

Strong Verses: 3.

Striking Facts: The sin offering is Christ seen laden with the believer's sins, absolutely in the sinner's place and stead, and not as in the sweet savor offerings, in His own perfections. Read Isa. 53.

CHAPTER FIVE

Contents: Trespass offering laws.
Characters: God, Moses.
Conclusion: Even when a man unwittingly breaks the laws of God, full restitution must be made, which is possible only through the presentation of the sacrifice.
Key Word: Trespass offering, v. 6.
Strong Verses: 17, 18.
Striking Facts: The chapter teaches us that we all have need to pray with David, "Cleanse thou me from secret faults." Psa. 19:12.

CHAPTER SIX

Contents: Further directions about offerings.
Characters: God, Moses, Aaron and sons.
Conclusion: Since Christ has "made His soul an offering for sin" we should seek to make restitution to any person we have injured or defrauded, and until we do, we will not enjoy the comfort of His forgiveness of our sins.
Key Word: Offerings.
Strong Verses: 6, 7.
Striking Facts: Trespass against our neighbor is trespass against God, because it is an affront to our Saviour who has redeemed us and the injury reflects upon God who has commanded that we should love our neighbor as ourselves.

CHAPTER SEVEN

Contents: Further directions concerning offerings.
Characters: God, Moses, Aaron and sons.
Conclusion: We are not left to our liberty in the solemn acts of religious worship, but are under obligation to perform them in the manner God directs in His Word.
Key Word: Offerings, v. 1.
Strong Verses: 37, 38.
Striking Facts: Use of leaven, v. 13, is significant. In v. 12, as the believer thanks God for his peace, he first of all presents Christ, Eph. 2:13, so leaven is excluded. In v. 13, he gives thanks for his participation in the peace, and the leaven signifies, that although having peace through Christ, the believer in himself is not perfect.

CHAPTER EIGHT

Contents: Consecration of Aaron and sons for the priesthood.
Characters: God, Moses, Aaron and sons.
Conclusion: All who minister about holy things must have an eye to God's commands as their rule and warrant, for only in the observance of these may they expect to be owned of God in their service.
Key Word: Sanctification, v. 12.
Strong Verses: 13, 36.
Striking Facts: Priests did not consecrate themselves. Moses was the appointed instrument of God to do this work. The sons of Aaron simply presented themselves for the work. See Rom. 12:1, where the believer presents himself unreservedly to Christ.

CHAPTER NINE

Contents: Priests begin their ministry before the Lord.
Characters: God, Moses, Aaron and sons.
Conclusion: God draws nigh to those who draw nigh to Him in the appointed way—the offering of faith in His Son, the Great Sacrifice being acceptable to Him.
Key Word: Offering presented, v. 12.
Strong Verses: 6, 23, 24.
Striking Facts: God does not ordain priests to be idle. Without a days

respite after their consecration, Aaron and his sons were immediately employed. God's spiritual priests have work laid out for them by Christ.

CHAPTER TEN

Contents: Strange fire of Nadab and Abihu.
Characters: God, Nadab, Abihu, Eleazer, Moses, Aaron, Ithamar, Michael, Elzaphan.
Conclusion: It is fatal to act in the things of God without seeking the mind of God (will worship, Col. 2:23.)
Key Word: Strange fire, v. 1.
Strong Verses: 9.
Striking Facts: Strange fire typifies any use of carnal means to kindle the fires of devotion and praise, which, if true, come only from Christ and the Holy Spirit.

CHAPTER ELEVEN

Contents: The proper food for God's people defined
Characters: God, Moses.
Conclusion: The body is the Lord's and it is sin against God to prejudice health for the pleasing of appetite.
Key Word: Eating, v. 2.
Strong Verses: 45.
Striking Facts: God's covenant people, Israel, by having a diet peculiar to themselves would be kept from familiar conversation with idolatrous neighbors. The laws, however, were probably primarily sanitary and necessary to the good of the people.

CHAPTER TWELVE

Contents: The law of motherhood.
Characters: God, Moses.
Conclusion: All are conceived and born in sin (Psa. 51:5) for, if the root be impure, so is the branch. It is only by Christ, the great sin offering, that the corruption of the child nature is done away
Key Word: Conceiving, v. 2.
Strong Verses: 8.
Striking Facts: Our Lord, though not conceived in sin—his mother accomplished the days of purification (Luke 2:22-24) and so poor were His parents that they could not bring a lamb.

CHAPTER THIRTEEN

Contents: Laws concerning those afflicted with leprosy.
Characters: God, Moses, Aaron.
Conclusion: Man is beset with troops of diseases on every side and all entered by sin. If not afflicted with any of these terrible sores, we are bound to praise God and glorify Him the more with our bodies.
Key Word: Leprosy, v. 2.
Strong Verses: 45, 46.
Striking Facts: Leprosy is a figure of the moral pollution of men's minds by sin, which is the leprosy of the soul, curable only through Christ's atoning work.

CHAPTER FOURTEEN

Contents: Laws concerning cleansing of lepers.
Characters: God, Moses.
Conclusion: As the leper was cleansed from his fearful malady through the water and the blood, so Christ comes into the soul for its cleansing "by water and blood" (1 John 5:6). See John 19:34.
Key Word: Cleansing, v. 2.
Strong Verses: 20.
Striking Facts: The leper did nothing toward his own cleansing. He was sought out by the priest and cleansed by him. Our cleansing is by Christ alone.

CHAPTER FIFTEEN

Contents: Imperative personal cleanliness.
Characters: God, Moses, Aaron.

Conclusion: Unclean diseases of the flesh are a wound and dishonor, the consumption of the body, and a sin which is often its own punishment more than any other.
Key Word: Unclean, v. 2.
Strong Verses: 30, 31.
Striking Facts: The chapter speaks to us of the contagion of sin and the danger of being polluted by conversing with those who are polluted. "Save yourselves from this untoward generation."

CHAPTER SIXTEEN

Contents: Day of atonement laws.
Characters: God, Moses, Aaron.
Conclusion: "Without the shedding of blood there is no remission for sin."
Key Word: Atonement, v. 6.
Strong Verses: 30, 34.
Striking Facts: As the priest entered the holiest with the blood, so Christ entered heaven itself with His own blood for us (Heb. 9:11, 12). His blood makes the throne of God a mercy seat which otherwise must have been a throne of judgment.

CHAPTER SEVENTEEN

Contents: The place of sacrifice and the sanctity of the blood.
Characters: God, Moses, Aaron.
Conclusion: God's people all meet at one altar in His appointed way, thereby preserving unity and family love among themselves.
Key Word: Blood, v. 11.
Strong Verses: 11.
Striking Facts: The worship of Christians is not now confined to one place (John 4:21; 1 Tim. 2:8) yet Christ is our altar and through Him, God dwells among us by His Spirit. It is in Him that our sacrifices are acceptable to God. 1 Pet. 2:5.

CHAPTER EIGHTEEN

Contents: Relationship and walk of God's people.
Characters: God, Moses.
Conclusion: Fleshly lusts war against the soul and will certainly be the ruin of it, if God's mercy and grace prevent not.
Key Word: Abominations, v. 26.
Strong Verses: 3, 4, 5, 24, 26, 30.
Striking Facts: There are many sins which level men with the beasts but these here mentioned sink men lower than beasts.

CHAPTER NINETEEN

Contents: Further laws concerning proper relationships.
Characters: God, Moses.
Conclusion: God's people being distinguished from all other people by a peculiar relationship with Him through Christ, should teach them real separation from the things of the world and flesh and entire devotedness to the will of God.
Key Word: Holy, v. 2.
Strong Verses: 2, 12, 18, 31.
Striking Facts: Notice the caution against having anything to do with spiritism. Seek not to them for discovery or advice and regard not their offers. It is an abomination to God.

CHAPTER TWENTY

Contents: Further laws on relationship and walk of God's people.
Characters: God, Moses.
Conclusion: God has distinguished His people from all others by a holy covenant with them through Christ, therefore they should distinguish themselves by consistent and holy living.
Key Word: Separated, v. 24.
Strong Verses: 6, 8, 22, 23, 24.
Striking Facts: Observe again the plain warning against spiritism. What greater madness than to go to an enemy for advice. Spiritualism is spiritual adultery, giving honor to the devil which is due to God.

CHAPTER TWENTY-ONE

Contents: Relationship and walk of the priests.
Characters: God, Moses, Aaron and sons.
Conclusion: Those whose office it is to instruct in God's truth must 'do it by example as well as precept.
Key Word: Holy, v. 6.
Strong Verses: 6, 8.
Striking Facts: We must honor those whom God has called as His ministers and every Christian should consider himself as concerned to be the guardians of their honor.

CHAPTER TWENTY-TWO

Contents: Separation of the priests; perfection of the sacrifices.
Characters: God, Moses, Aaron and sons.
Conclusion: Those contract great guilt who profane sacred things, doing in their own uncleanness, service which pretends to be hallowed to Him.
Key Word: Separate, v. 2.
Strong Verses: 3, 31, 32.
Striking Facts: v. 19 a law to make sacrifices fitter to be types of Christ, the great Sacrifice from which all these derive their virtue. He is called a "lamb without spot and without blemish" (1 Pet. 1:19).

CHAPTER TWENTY-THREE

Contents: The feasts of Jehovah.
Characters: God, Moses.
Conclusion: The Sabbaths of the Lord in our dwellings will be their beauty, strength and safety (by rising on the first day of the week and meeting His disciples again and again on that day, Christ appointed that day a holy convocation).
Key Word: Feasts, v. 2.
Strong Verses: 3, 22.
Striking Facts: As given to Israel, there were seven great religious festivals. Passover, feast of unleavened bread, feast of first-fruits, feast of Pentecost, feast of Trumpets, Day of Atonement, feast of Tabernacles,—all typical of Christ.

CHAPTER TWENTY-FOUR

Contents: Penalty of blasphemy.
Characters: God, Moses, son of Israelitish woman.
Conclusion: If those who profane the name of God escape punishment from men, yet the Lord our God will not suffer them to escape His righteous judgments.
Key Word: Blasphemy, v. 11.
Strong Verses: 15.
Striking Facts: v. 12. Those who sit in judgment should sincerely desire, and by prayer to Christ for wisdom, should endeavor to know, the mind of the Lord.

CHAPTER TWENTY-FIVE

Contents: Laws of the land. Sabbatic year and year of Jubilee.
Characters: God. Moses.
Conclusion: The blessing of God upon our provision will make a little go a long way and satisfy even the poor with bread. We can lose nothing by faith in God's promises and self-denial in our obedience.
Key Word: Sabbatic year, v. 4.
Strong Verses: 18, 19, 35, 36, 37.
Striking Facts: v. 25, the kinsman redeemer is an illustration of Christ who assumed our nature that He might be our kinsman, redeeming our inheritance which we by sin had forfeited. He made a settlement for all who become allied with Him by faith.

CHAPTER TWENTY-SIX

Contents: Conditions of blessing and warnings of chastisement.
Characters: God, Moses.

Conclusion: All adverse circumstances that come upon a people are God's servants, used often as a scourge wherewith He chastises a provoking people. If less judgments will not do their work, God will send greater, for when He judges a nation He will overcome.

Key Word: Punishment, v. 24.

Strong Verses: 8, 9, 40, 41, 42.

Striking Facts: If God's people faithfully observe His statutes they are assured that His hand (vv. 7, 8) will so signally appear with them that no disproportion of numbers could make against them.

CHAPTER TWENTY-SEVEN

Contents: Laws concerning dedicated persons and things.

Characters: God, Moses.

Conclusion: We should be cautious in making vows and constant in keeping those we have made. What is once devoted to the Lord should be His forever by a perpetual covenant.

Key Word: Vows, v. 2.

Strong Verses: 30.

Striking Facts: Let us not think because we are not tied to ceremonial laws that we are free of religious obligations. "Having boldness to enter into the holiest by the blood of Jesus, let us draw near with a true heart in full assurance of faith" saying "Blessed be God for the gift of His Son."

NUMBERS

Key Thought:	Number of Chapters:	Key Verse:	Christ seen as:
Discipline	36	33:1	Star of Jacob

Writer of the Book:	Date:	Conclusion of the Book:
Moses	About 1500 B. C.	The redeemed are saved to serve and must be on their guard against unbelief.

SUMMARY

CHAPTER ONE

Contents: Moses commanded to take census.

Characters: God, Moses, Aaron.

Conclusion: The Lord knows all those that are His (2 Tim. 2:19) by name (Phil. 4:3) and even the hairs of their heads are numbered. To all others He will say "I never knew you."

Key Word: Numbered, v. 2.

Strong Verses: 54.

Striking Facts: None under 20 years old were listed for military service. In compassion for their tender years God would not have them to bear arms. Nor were any to be numbered who were through any bodily infirmity, rendered unfit for war.

CHAPTER TWO

Contents: Order of the host and arrangement of the camp.

Characters: God, Moses, Aaron.

Conclusion: God is a God of order and not confusion, thus the camp of the saints should be compact, everyone knowing and keeping his God appointed place.

Key Word: Camp, v. 3.

Strong Verses: 34.

Striking Facts: The chapter furnishes an illustration of the movable state of Christ's people in the world, "strangers and pilgrims." At the same time it is a military state—our life is a warfare, as "good soldiers of Jesus Christ."

CHAPTER THREE

Contents: Order of the host; placing of the Levites

Characters: God, Moses, Aaron.

Conclusion: Having gifts differing according to the Grace given us—if ministry, let us wait on our ministering (Rom. 12:7). God has a place of definite service for each of His children.

Key Word: Levites, v. 6.

Strong Verses: 13.

Striking Facts: The Church is called "the church of the firstborn" which is redeemed not as the firstborn of the Israelites, with silver and gold, but ransomed with the precious blood of Christ.

CHAPTER FOUR

Contents: The service of the Kohathrites, Gershonites and Merarites

Characters: God, Moses, Aaron.

Conclusion: There is a service appointed to each of God's people in connection with His Church, and no matter how obscure the place it is important in God's program.

Key Word: Service, v. 4.

Strong Verses: 49.

Striking Facts: v. 3. They were not employed until 30 years old. This is not obligatory on Gospel ministers, but gives us a suggestion that ministers should not be novices but should be men of steadiness, and ripeness of judgment, knowing Christ well.

CHAPTER FIVE

Contents: Defilement of the camp.
Characters: God, Moses.
Conclusion: The purity of the church must be as carefully guarded as the order of it and it is for the edification of it that those who are openly and incorrigibly vicious should be cut off from communion until they repent.
Key Word: Defilement, v. 2.
Strong Verses: 3.
Striking Facts: All wives should learn from the "jealousy offering" to guard against giving any occasion for suspicions of their chastity—to abstain from all appearance of evil. Husbands should learn not to entertain causeless or unjust suspicions of their wives.

CHAPTER SIX

Contents: The Nazarite laws.
Characters: God, Moses, Aaron.
Conclusion: The Christian should be a true Nazarite, fully consecrated to God and separated from the things of this world, thus securing the special blessing of God.
Key Word: Separation, v. 2.
Strong Verses: 24, 25, 26.
Striking Facts: The Nazarite type found a perfect fulfillment in Jesus who was "holy, harmless, undefiled and separate from sinners" (Heb. 7:26) and allowed no mere natural claims to divert Him.

CHAPTER SEVEN

Contents: The gifts of the princes.
Characters: God, Moses, princes.
Conclusion: The great men should with their wealth and power uphold the work of God and should make conscience of being devout because of their great influence.
Key Word: Offering, v. 3.
Strong Verses: 89.
Striking Facts: Observe that the offerings of the princes were identical yet each is separately recorded by the pen of inspiration, showing how God takes notice of every whole-hearted gift. Mark 12:41-44.

CHAPTER EIGHT

Contents: Cleansing of the Levites for the ministry of the tabernacle.
Characters: God, Moses, Aaron.
Conclusion: All Christians, and especially ministers, should cleanse themselves from all filthiness of the flesh and spirit, perfecting holiness in the fear of the Lord. Those who bear the vessels of the Lord must be clean.
Key Word: Cleanse, v. 6.
Strong Verses: 21, 22.
Striking Facts: It is a great kindness to the Church that God has appointed overseers to go before the people in the things of God and religious worship. When Christ ascended, He supplied the gifts for His work (Eph. 4:8-12).

CHAPTER NINE

Contents: Law of the Passover; the guiding cloud.
Characters: God, Moses, Aaron.
Conclusion: Those who by circumstances are compelled to absent themselves from God's ordinances, may expect the favor of God's grace under their afflictions, and those who of choice absent themselves may justly expect the tokens of God's displeasure.
Key Word: Passover, v. 2.
Strong Verses: 8, 18.
Striking Facts: As it was safe and pleasant going for Israel when led by the cloud, token of God's presence, so there is peace for the Christian who has set Christ, the Great Shepherd, before him.

CHAPTER TEN

Contents: The first march of the camp.
Characters: God, Moses, Aaron's sons.
Conclusion: Those who have given themselves up to the leading of God's Word and Spirit, steer a safe course and so long as they walk in fellowship with their Guide, they need not fear losing the way.
Key Word: Journeying, v. 13.
Strong Verses: 33, 34.
Striking Facts: Those who through Christ, are bound for the heavenly Canaan should invite and encourage their friends to go along with them.

CHAPTER ELEVEN

Contents: Complaints about the manna and the consequences.
Characters: God, Moses, Eldad, Medad, Joshua.
Conclusion: Though God graciously gives us leave to complain to Him when there is cause, yet He is justly provoked if we are fretful when there is no cause and especially when we have been surrounded with His special favors.
Key Word: Complaining, v. 1.
Striking Facts: Unconverted church members with no healthy appetite for the Bread of God, the things of Christ, will clamor for things pleasing to the flesh in the work and way of the church.

CHAPTER TWELVE

Contents: Murmuring of Miriam and Aaron and the consequences.
Characters: God, Moses, Aaron, Miriam.
Conclusion: We have reason to be exceedingly cautious of saying or doing anything against the servants of God, for God will plead their cause if they are true servants and will reckon with the critic.
Key Word: Criticism, (speaking against), v. 1.
Strong Verses: 3, 8.
Striking Facts: There are seasons when it is decidedly out of place to criticize the leaders of the people. This affront was ill-natured and ill-timed, when the people were disposed to mutiny and had given Moses much vexation with their murmurings.

CHAPTER THIRTEEN

Contents: Spies sent into Kadesh-barnea, and their report.
Characters: God, Moses, Caleb, Joshua.
Conclusion: Faith looks at difficulties through God but unbelief looks through difficulties at God. All things are possible, if but promised, to him who believes.
Key Word: Searching, v. 25.
Strong Verses: 27, 30.
Striking Facts: Many Christians are forever getting frightened at these tremendous giants in the land who make them feel like grasshoppers. Giants cannot stand in the way of Christ's work if His people will be valiant in His strength.

CHAPTER FOURTEEN

Contents: Murmuring over the spies' reports and the consequences.
Characters: God, Moses, Aaron, Caleb, Joshua.
Conclusion. All the dangers that we are in are from our own distrust. We would succeed against all enemies if we did not make God our enemy. We are excluded from God's blessing only by excluding ourselves.
Key Word: Murmured, v. 2.
Strong Verses: 8, 9, 18.
Striking Facts: vv. 13-19. The best pleas in prayer are those taken from Christ's honor. The more danger there is of others reproaching Christ's power, the more desirous we should be to see it glorified.

CHAPTER FIFTEEN

Contents: Burnt and free will offerings.
Characters: God, Moses, man who broke Sabbath.

Conclusion: Sins committed ignorantly must have atonement made for them, for although God is very merciful with the ignorant, their ignorance cannot justify them. The presumptuous sinner invites severe judgments.
Key Word: Offerings, v. 3.
Strong Verses: 30.
Striking Facts: v. 35. God is jealous for the honor of His Sabbaths and will not hold men guiltless who profane them. God gave this exemplary punishment as a standing warning against presumptuous disregard of His holy day.

CHAPTER SIXTEEN

Contents: The gainsaying of Korah.
Characters: God, Moses, Aaron, Korah, Dathan, Abriam.
Conclusion: Proud and ambitious men projecting their own advancement by thrusting themselves into a place to which God has not appointed them, hurry on to a shameful fall.
Key Word: Murmur, v. 11.
Strong Verses: 26, 48.
Striking Facts: Men who have been true to Christ need not fear being slurred by others. Men who are most serviceable are often abused most shamefully.

CHAPTER SEVENTEEN

Contents: Aaron's rod that budded.
Character: God, Moses, Aaron.
Conclusion: Fruitfulness is the best evidence of a divine call. The plants of God's setting will flourish.
Key Word: Chosen, v. 5.
Strong Verses: 8.
Striking Facts: The budding rod is a type of Christ, who in His resurrection was owned of God as High Priest. All other authors of religion have died. Christ alone is exalted as High Priest.

CHAPTER EIGHTEEN

Contents: Regulations concerning maintenance of the priests.
Characters: God, Moses, Aaron.
Conclusion: We are to value as a great gift of divine bounty those called to be serviceable to us in the work of the church.
Key Word: Given, v. 6.
Strong Verses: 6, 12, 20.
Striking Facts: God orders that Christ's ministers should be well recompensed that they might be the more entirely addicted to their ministry and not be disturbed in it by worldly care.

CHAPTER NINETEEN

Contents: The ordinance of the red heifer.
Characters: God, Moses, Aaron, Eleazer.
Conclusion: The believer needs constant cleansing from defilement contracted in his pilgrim walk through the world.
Key Word: Unclean, v. 7.
Strong Verses: 2.
Striking Facts: Water typifies the Spirit and the Word. The Spirit uses the Word to convict the believer of some sin allowed. Thus convicted, he remembers that the guilt of his sin has been met by the sacrifice of Christ, therefore instead of dispairing, he judges and confesses the sin and is forgiven and cleansed. (1 John 1).

CHAPTER TWENTY

Contents: Water from the rock and Moses' sin.
Characters: God, Moses, Aaron, Miriam, Eleazar, King of Edom.
Conclusion: God is able to supply His people with necessaries even in their greatest straits and in the utmost failure of second causes.
Key Word: Complaint. v. 3.
Strong Verses: 12.

Striking Facts: cf. vv. 8 and 10. Moses and Aaron varied from their commission and assumed too much glory themselves. The nearer one is to God, the more offensive are their sins. God judges not as man judges.

CHAPTER TWENTY-ONE

Contents: Victories of Israel; the serpent of brass.
Characters: God, Moses, Aaron, Arad, Sihon, Og.
Conclusion: Those who cry without cause will be given just cause to cry and they will be compelled to receive their course from God in God's way.
Key Word: Sinned, v. 7.
Strong Verses: 9, 34.
Striking Facts: Serpent here, a symbol of sin judged; brass speaks of divine judgment. The brass serpent becomes a type of Christ "made sin for us" (2 Cor. 5:21; John 3:14-15) in bearing our judgment.

CHAPTER TWENTY-TWO

Contents: Balaam's visit to Balak and the strange warning on the way.
Characters: God, Balak, Balaam, Angel of Jehovah.
Conclusion The enemies of God's people are restless and unwearied in their attempts, but He who sits in heaven laughs at them and often uses "foolish things to confound the wise."
Key Word: Balaam, v. 5.
Strong Verses: 12, 38.
Striking Facts: When Satan tempted our first parents to sin he employed a subtle serpent, but when God would convince a hireling prophet, He employed a silly ass.

CHAPTER TWENTY-THREE

Contents: Balaam blesses instead of curses Israel.
Characters: God, Balaam, Balak.
Conclusion: Those who have the good will of heaven may expect the ill will of hell but God will not suffer real injury done to His people and what is done against them He takes as done against Himself and reckons accordingly.
Key Word: Blessed, v. 11.
Strong Verses: 8, 12, 21.
Striking Facts: He who made man's mouth knows how to manage it. God can extort a confession of his overruling power from wicked men to the confusion of many, if He chooses.

CHAPTER TWENTY-FOUR

Contents: Balaam foretells prosperity for Israel.
Characters: God, Balaam, Balak.
Conclusion: Those who oppose God and His people will sooner or later be made to see themselves wretchedly deceived.
Key Word: Latter days, v. 14.
Strong Verses: 13, 17.
Striking Facts: v. 17 is an illustrious prophecy of Christ who is coming to reign in great glory, not only over Israel but over all men.

CHAPTER TWENTY-FIVE

Contents: Sin of Israel with daughters of Moab.
Characters: God, Moses, Zimri, Phinehas, Cozbi.
Conclusion: God's people are more endangered by the charms of a smiling world than by the terrors of a frowning world. The daughters of Moab have conquered many strong men who could not be conquered by the sword.
Key Word: Whoredom, v. 1.
Strong Verses: 12, 13.
Striking Facts: Phinehas, v. 11, is pronounced his country's patriot and best friend. To be zealous for Jesus Christ is the best service we can do for the people.

CHAPTER TWENTY-SIX

Contents: The new generation of Israel numbered.
Characters: God, Moses, Eleazar, Caleb, Joshua.

Conclusion: God is faithful to His threatenings as well as to His promises. Millions may fall to the ground, but His Word cannot fall.
Key Word: Numbered, v. 64.
Strong Verses: 64, 65.
Striking Facts: v. 65. (Save Caleb and Joshua). The arrows of death, though they fly in the dark, do not fly at random but are directed to the mark intended, and no other.

CHAPTER TWENTY-SEVEN

Contents: The law of inheritance. Joshua appointed Moses' successor.
Characters: God, Moses, Eleazar, daughters of Zehophehad, Joshua.
Conclusion: The minister of Christ should concern himself in his prayers and endeavors for the rising generation, that work may flourish and the interest of the kingdom be maintained and advanced after he is gone.
Key Word: Appointment (set over), v. 16.
Strong Verses: 16, 17.
Striking Facts: Moses' attitude to his successor confirms his character as the meekest man on earth. He thought not for the advancement of his own family but yielded gladly to God's will in the matter.

CHAPTER TWENTY-EIGHT

Contents: The order of offerings.
Characters: God, Moses.
Conclusion: God asks of all His children continual offerings, v. 3, which intimates that we are to "pray without ceasing" on the ground of Christ's sacrifice, and at least, every morning and evening, v. 4, we are to offer solemn prayer and praise through Christ.
Key Word: Offering, v. 2.
Strong Verses: 2

CHAPTER TWENTY-NINE

Contents: Commands concerning the feast of Trumpets, Feast of Tabernacles, and Day of Atonement.
Characters: God, Moses.
Conclusion: We must not seek occasion to abate our zeal in God's service nor be glad of excuses to omit religious duties, but rather rejoice in the many privileges of worship. (Not omitting private worship on days we go to church. Not omitting secret prayer because of family devotions, etc.).
Key Word: Convocations, v. 1.
Strong Verses: 39.

CHAPTER THIRTY

Contents: The laws of vows.
Characters: God, Moses.
Conclusion: Our promises before God are bonds upon the soul and by them we must conscientiously consider ourselves bound out from all sin and bound up to the whole will of God.
Key Word: Vows, v. 2.
Strong Verses: 2.

CHAPTER THIRTY-ONE

Contents: The judgment of Midian.
Characters: God, Moses, Balaam.
Conclusion: Our worst enemies are those that draw us to sin. Over all such enemies there is absolute victory for those who take sides with God against them.
Key Word: Avenge, v. 3.
Strong Verses: 49.
Striking Facts: v. 2. Useful men are often removed when we think they can ill be spared from Christ's service, but it is clear that no one is removed until they have had full opportunity to do that which was appointed them.

CHAPTER THIRTY-TWO

Contents: The choice of the world-borderers.
Characters: God, Moses, Caleb, Joshua.

Conclusion: Would we choose our portion aright we must look above the things which are seen—otherwise we will be guided by the lust of the eye and the pride of life.
Key Word: Inheritance, v. 19.
Strong Verses: 11, 12, 23.
Striking Facts: v. 23. It concerns us to find our sins out that we may forsake them before they find us out to our confusion and ruin.

CHAPTER THIRTY-THREE

Contents: Summary of the journey from Egypt to Jordan.
Character: God, Moses, Aaron.
Conclusion: It is good for believers to preserve in writing an account of the providences of God concerning them, showing the series of mercies they have experienced, that deceitful memories might be helped and ground given for new faith.
Key Word: Journeys, v. 1.
Strong Verses: 53.
Striking Facts: vv. 51, 56. If we do not drive out sin, sin will drive us out. That which we are willing should tempt us will eventually vex us.

CHAPTER THIRTY-FOUR

Contents: Preparations to enter the land.
Characters: God, Moses, Eleazar, Joshua, prince of each tribe.
Conclusion: God sets bounds to our lot; let us therefore set bounds to our desires and bring our minds to our condition.
Key Word: Borders, v. 4.
Strong Verses: 2.
Striking Facts: God gives to Christ's people but a small share of this world. Those who have a portion in heaven have reason to be content with a small pittance of earth.

CHAPTER THIRTY-FIVE

Contents: The cities of refuge.
Characters: God, Moses.
Conclusion: God would teach us to conceive a dread and horror of the guilt of blood and to be very careful of life, lest even by negligence we occasion the death of any. (This is taught by confinement to the city of refuge, of those who killed even by accident.)
Key Word: Refuge, v. 6.
Strong Verses: 12, 30.
Striking Facts: Christ is the believer's refuge. In Him we are protected from the wrath of God and the curse of the law. Heb. 6:18; Phil. 3:9.
Wilful murder is to be punished with death and no commutation of the punishment was to be accepted.

CHAPTER THIRTY-SIX

Contents: Regulations concerning inheritance.
Characters: God, Moses, heads of families, Mahlah, Tirzah, Hoglah, Milcah, Noah.
Conclusion: It is the wisdom of those who have estates in this world to settle them and dispose of them so that strife and contention shall not arise about them among their posterity.
Key Word: Inheritances, v. 2.
Strong Verses: 7.
Striking Facts: Daughters can but marry well and to their satisfaction when they have looked to Christ to direct their choice of a husband.

DEUTERONOMY

Key Thought:	Number of Chapters:	Key Verse:	Christ seen as:
Obedience	34	10:12, 13	Prophet like Moses

Writer of the Book:	Date:	Conclusion of the Book:
Moses	About 1500 B. C.	Obedience to God is Imperative.

SUMMARY

CHAPTER ONE

Contents: Review of the failure at Kadesh-barnea.
Characters: God, Moses, Caleb, Joshua.
Conclusion: A sad pass it has come to with us when the God of eternal truth cannot be believed.   All disobedience to His laws and forgetfulness of His power and goodness flow from disbelief in His Word.
Key Word: Unbelief, v. 32.
Strong Verses: 17, 21, 30.
Striking Facts: Deuteronomy signifies "second law" or second edition, not with amendments, for there need be none, but with additions for further directions in divers cases not mentioned before.

CHAPTER TWO

Contents: The wanderings and conflicts in the wilderness.
Characters: God, Moses, Sihon.
Conclusion: It is a work of time to make souls meet for the heavenly Canaan and it must be done by many a long train of experiences.
Key Word: Journeys, v. 1.
Strong Verses: 7.
Striking Facts: vv. 25, 36.   Those who meddle with the people of Christ do it to their own hurt for God often ruins the enemies of His people by their own resolves.

CHAPTER THREE

Contents: Further review of journeyings.
Characters: God, Moses, Og, Joshua.
Conclusion: That cause cannot but be victorious for which the Lord of Hosts fights.   "If God be for us who can be against us?"
Key Word: Conquest, v. 22.
Strong Verses: 22, 24.
Striking Facts: vv. 25, 27.   If God does not by His providence give us what we desire, He can, by His grace in Jesus Christ, make us content with it. Be satisfied with this—Christ is all-sufficient.

CHAPTER FOUR   ⟩

Contents: The new generations taught the lessons of Sinai.   Cities of refuge designated.
Characters: God, Moses.
Conclusion: The review of God's providences concerning us should quicken us and engage us to duty and obedience.
Key Word: Keep (Obedience), v. 2.
Strong Verses: 2, 6, 9, 23, 24, 39.
Striking Facts: vv. 25, 31.   Moses forsees the Jewish apostasy and consequent scattering.   Those nations that cast off the duties of religion in their prosperity cannot expect the comforts of it when they come to be in distress.

CHAPTER FIVE

Contents: New generations taught the Mosaic covenant.
Characters: God, Moses.
Conclusion: Many have their consciences startled by the Law, who are not

purified (v. 29). Promises are made but the good principles are not rooted in them. Oh, to be sincere in our covenant with God.
Key Word: Covenant, v. 2.
Strong Verses: 6, 29, 33.
Striking Facts: v. 5. Moses stood between. Herein he is a type of Christ who stands between God and man, as the true mediator, so that we both hear from God and speak to Him without trembling.

CHAPTER SIX
Contents: Israel exhorted to observe all God's commandments.
Characters: God, Moses, Abraham, Isaac, Jacob, Pharoah.
Conclusion: The fear of God in the heart is the most powerful principle of obedience (v. 2, 5, etc.).
Key Word: Observe, v. 3.
Strong Verses: 3, 5, 7.
Striking Facts: Those who love the Lord Jesus Christ themselves should do all they can to engage the affections of their children to Him, to prevent the religion of the family from being cut off.

CHAPTER SEVEN
Contents: Command to be separate people and to destroy opposing nations.
Characters: God, Moses.
Conclusion: Those who are taken into communion with God must have no communication with the unfruitful works of darkness.
Key Word: 'Chosen, v. 6.
Strong Verses: 6, 9.
Striking Facts: The destruction of enemies furnishes an illustration of the Christian conflict. We are commanded not to let sin reign, nor to countenance it, but to hate it and strive against it. God has promised it shall not have dominion over us. Rom. 6:12, 14.

CHAPTER EIGHT
Contents: Israel reminded of God's gracious past dealings and warned to walk in His Way.
Characters: God, Moses.
Conclusion: It is good for us to remember all the ways both of God's providences and grace by which He has led us hitherto through this wilderness, that we may be prevailed with cheerfully to serve Him and trust Him.
Key Word: Remember, v. 2.
Strong Verses: 2, 5, 11.
Striking Facts: v. 4. Those who follow the Lord Jesus have the promise of not only being safe, but easy (Matt. 11:30). If we walk "in his steps," our feet will not swell. It is the "way of the transgressor" that is "hard" (Prov. 13:15).

CHAPTER NINE
Contents: Israel reminded of their unworthiness to possess the land in themselves.
Characters: God, Moses, Aaron, Abraham, Isaac, Jacob.
Conclusion: Our gaining of the heavenly Canaan must be attributed to God's power, not our might, and ascribed to His grace, not our merit. In Christ we have both righteousness and strength—in Him therefore we must glory, and not in ourselves. Gal. 6:14.
Key Word: Remember, v. 7 (stubbornness, v. 27).
Strong Verses: 4.
Striking Facts: It is good often to review the records conscience keeps of our past life of sin that we may see how much we are endebted to God's marvelous grace in Jesus Christ, and may humbly own that we never merited anything at God's hand but wrath and the curse.

CHAPTER TEN
Contents: Further warnings and exhortation and reminders of God's dealings.
Characters: God, Moses, Aaron, Eleazar.
Conclusion: Since we have received so many mercies from God, it becomes us to enquire what returns we shall make to Him. It should certainly

cause us to devote our lives to His honor and to lay ourselves out to advance the interest of His kingdom.

Key Word: Commandments, v. 13.

Strong Verses: 12, 17, 21.

Striking Facts: vv. 10, 11. Moses, Israel's intercessor, had the conduct and command of Israel. Herein he was a type of Christ, who ever lives to make intercession and who has all power in heaven and earth.

CHAPTER ELEVEN

Contents: Warnings and exhortations to obedience.

Characters: God, Moses.

Conclusion: The closer dependence we have had on God, the more cheerful should be our obedience to Him. In absolute obedience to Him is strength and true success.

Key Word: Obey, v. 27.

Strong Verses: 8, 16, 26

Striking Facts: v. 12. The Bible magnifies the land of Canaan above all others. God's eyes are still upon it for it is the center of much unfulfilled prophecy.

CHAPTER TWELVE

Contents: Statements of conditions of blessing in the land.

Characters: God, Moses.

Conclusion: We must not think that our religion is only for our years of servitude or our entertainment in the place of solitude, or our consolation in affliction. We must keep up devout worship in our Canaan experiences as well as our wilderness experiences.

Key Word: Observe, vv. 1, 28, 32.

Strong Verses: 32.

Striking Facts: The one precept pressed harder than any other by Moses is in regard to the necessity of bringing the sacrifice to one altar at the court of the tabernacle and there to perform all rituals. We are to offer up all spiritual sacrifices to God in the name of Jesus Christ, hoping for acceptance only on the ground of His mediation. 1 Pet. 2:5.

CHAPTER THIRTEEN

Contents: The test of false prophets.

Characters: God, Moses.

Conclusion: "Though we or an angel from heaven preach any other Gospel unto you than that which we have preached unto you, let him be accursed," Gal. 1:8. We are to be on our guard against imposition and lying wonders.

Key Word: Dreamers, v. 5.

Strong Verses: 4.

Striking Facts: Observe in v. 3 etc., that they were warned not even to patiently listen to false teachers and dreamers, but to instantly reject it with disdain as unscriptural. See Rom. 16:17, 18; 2 Tim. 3:5; 2 John 10.

CHAPTER FOURTEEN

Contents: Dietary laws.

Characters: God, Moses.

Conclusion: 1 Tim. 4:3-5.

Key Word: Eating, v. 3.

Strong Verses: 2.

Striking Facts: It is plain that the precepts concerning food belonged only to the Jews and were not moral or of perpetual use because of not universal obligation. What they might not eat themselves they might give to a stranger or a proselyte who had renounced idolatry or they might sell to an alien. It was evidently intended to keep them from mingling with and conforming themselves to idolatrous neighbors.

CHAPTER FIFTEEN

Contents: Laws concerning Sabbatic year and bondservants.

Characters: God, Moses.

Conclusion: That we who have received in abundance from God should be rigorous and severe in our demands from poor brethren, is displeasing to

God. His tender care of us obliges us to be kind to those who have a dependence upon us.
Key Word: Release, v. 1.
Strong Verses: 6, 7, 8, 10.
Striking Facts: The year of release typifies the grace of the Gospel in which is proclaimed the acceptable year of the Lord, by which we obtain the release of our debts, the pardon of our sins, teaching us to forgive others as we have been forgiven.

CHAPTER SIXTEEN

Contents: Laws concerning annual feasts.
Characters: God, Moses.
Conclusion: By frequent and regular meeting to worship God at appointed places and by recognized rules, we are kept faithful and constant in that holy religion which Christ has established among us.
Key Word: Feasts, v. 10.
Strong Verses: 17.
Striking Facts: See 1 Cor. 5:7. We are to keep this feast in holy conversation, free from the leaven of malice and hyprocisy and with the unleavened bread of sincerity and love.

CHAPTER SEVENTEEN

Contents: Laws concerning idolaters and obedience to authority and kings.
Characters: God, Moses.
Conclusion: God would possess men with a dread of that sin—worshipping false gods—which is a sin in itself exceedingly heinous and the highest affront that can be offered to Almighty God.
Key Word: Transgressing, v. 2.
Strong Verses: 18, 19, 20.
Striking Facts: v. 1. Old testaments sacrifices were required to be perfect because types of Christ, 1 Pet. 1:19, who was perfectly pure from all sin and all appearances of it.

CHAPTER EIGHTEEN

Contents: Laws concerning Levites, idolatrous practices and prophets.
Characters: God, Moses, Christ.
Conclusion: God has made Himself known to men through One above all prophets (Acts 3:22, 7:37; John 6:14). Hear ye Him.
Key Word: Prophet, v. 15
Strong Verses: 15, 18.
Striking Facts: vv. 9-14. Let those who give heed to fortune tellers or run to wizards for the discovery of things secret, that use spells for cures, are in league with familiar spirits or fellowship with those who are— know that they have no fellowship with God, but with demons.

CHAPTER NINETEEN

Contents: Cities of refuge; landmarks, witnesses.
Characters: God, Moses.
Conclusion: God would possess men with a great horror and dread of the sin of killing another, even by chance. If by willful violence, see 1 John. 3:15.
Key Word: Refuge (cities), v. 2.
Strong Verses: 9, 10.
Striking Facts: Cities of refuge were located in the center of districts so every corner of the land might have one in reach. Thus Christ is not a refuge at a distance (Rom. 10:8) but brings salvation through the Gospel, to our door.

CHAPTER TWENTY

Contents: Laws of warfare.
Characters: God, Moses.
Conclusion: Those enterprises which we undertake by a divine warrant and prosecute by divine direction, we may expect to succeed in. Those have no reason to fear in the battles of life who have God with them.
Key Word: Battle, v. 1.
Strong Verses: 1, 4.

Striking Facts: v. 14. A justifiable property is acquired in that which is won in lawful war. "The Lord thy God gives it thee." Therefore He must be owned in it.

CHAPTER TWENTY-ONE

Contents: Inquest for the slain. Domestic regulations.
Characters: God, Moses.
Conclusion: We are to have a dread of the guilt of blood, which defiles not only the conscience of the murderer but the land in which it is shed. When we hear of the wickedness of the wicked, we have need to cry earnestly for mercy for our land which groans and trembles under it.
Key Word: Guilt, v. 9 (wife, 10-17), rebellious son, (18-23).
Strong Verses: 8.
Striking Facts: vv. 18-23. Those who are bad members of families never make good members of the commonwealth. v. 23. Cf. Gal. 3:13; John 19:31. Christ underwent the curse of the law for us and was exposed to shame for us. In the evening, He was taken down, in token that now the law was satisfied.

CHAPTER TWENTY-TWO

Contents: Law of brotherhood, separation, unchaste wives and husbands.
Characters: God, Moses.
Conclusion: Christianity teaches us to be neighborly and to be ready to do all good offices as we have opportunity, to all men. Chastity should be as dear to us as our lives.
Key Word: Brotherly, v. 1, (whoredom, v. 21).
Strong Verses: 4.
Striking Facts: v. 25. We shall suffer for the wickedness we do, not for that which is done to us. That is not sin which has not more or less of the will in it.

CHAPTER TWENTY-THREE

Contents: Divers regulations.
Characters: God, Moses.
Conclusion: We must take care to keep the camp of the saints pure from moral, ceremonial and natural pollution.
Key Word: Holy, v. 14.
Strong Verses: 9, 14.
Striking Facts: Outward cleanliness is a reverence of the divine Majesty. Filthiness is offensive to the senses God has endued us with, is a wrong to human life and an evidence of slothful temper of mind.

CHAPTER TWENTY-FOUR

Contents: Law concerning divorce; miscellaneous regulations.
Characters: God, Moses.
Conclusion: It is of great consequence that love be kept up between husband and wife and that everything be carefully avoided which would estrange them. The changes made by discontent often prove for the worst.
Key Word: Divorce, v. 1.
Strong Verses: 22.
Striking Facts: The creditor who cares not though his debtor and his family starve, nor is at all concerned what becomes of them so he gets his money, goes contrary to both the law of Moses and of Christ.

CHAPTER TWENTY-FIVE

Contents: Divers regulations.
Characters: God, Moses.
Conclusion: Justice and equity will bring down upon us the blessing of God. Those who do unrighteously are an abomination to the Lord and miserable is the man who is distasteful to his God.
Key Word: Abominations, v. 16.
Strong Verses: 16.
Striking Facts: v. 3. See 2 Cor. 11:24. They always gave Paul as many stripes as ever they gave to any malefactor whatsoever.

CHAPTER TWENTY-SIX

Contents: Law of the offering of the firstfruits.
Characters: God, Moses.
Conclusion: We are to acknowledge God as giver of all good things which are the support and comfort of our natural lives and are therefore to give to God the first and best as those who believe Him to be the first and best.
Key Word: Firstfruits, v. 10.
Strong Verses: 10, 18.
Striking Facts: It is fitting that God who gives us all we have should by His Word direct the using of it and though we are not now bound by the tithing laws, we are commanded to give of such things as we have and to lay by in store as we are prospered, for the furtherance of Christ's work.

CHAPTER TWENTY-SEVEN

Contents: The blessing and cursing from Mt. Ebal and Gerizim.
Characters: God, Moses.
Conclusion: We are all compelled to say Amen to the law of God, owning ourselves justly under its curse and that we must certainly have perished had not Christ redeemed us from the curse of the law, being made a curse for us.
Key Word: Law, v. 8
Strong Verses: 9, 10.
Striking Facts: v. 5. Christ, our altar, is a stone cut out without hands (Dan. 2:34, 35) refused by the builders but accepted of God and made the headstone of the corner.

CHAPTER TWENTY-EIGHT

Contents: Conditions of blessing in the land and causes of chastisement.
Characters: God, Moses.
Conclusion: If we do not delight in God's will, we not only come short of the blessing promised but lay ourselves under chastisement, which is as comprehensive of all misery as His blessings are of all happiness.
Key Word: Obedience (keep commandments), v. 1.
Strong Verses: 2, 58.
Striking Facts: vv. 64, 65. Remarkably fulfilled in the present dispersion of the Jews. They have, through the centuries been continually on the move, either in hope of gain or in fear of persecution and so will continue until the King comes and they are restored by Him to the promised land.

CHAPTER TWENTY-NINE

Contents: Introductory words to the Palestinian covenant.
Characters: God, Moses.
Conclusion: We are bound in gratitude as well as duty and faithfulness to keep the words of the solemn covenant of God, through Christ.
Key Word: Covenant, v. 1.
Strong Verses: 9, 29.
Striking Facts: Moses concludes the prophecy of the Jews rejection, v. 29, as Paul concludes his discourse on the same subject. Rom. 11:33. God has kept back no truth that it is profitable for us to know about His counsels, but only that which it is good for us to be ignorant of.

CHAPTER THIRTY

Contents: The Palestinian covenant declared.
Characters: God, Moses.
Conclusion: Those shall have life who choose it. Those who come short of life and happiness must thank themselves. They would have had it, had they chosen communion with God.
Key Word: Choice, v. 19.
Strong Verses: 15, 19.
Striking Facts: Israel has never yet taken the land under the unconditional Abrahamic covenant, nor ever possessed the whole land promised. Gen. 15:18; Num. 34:1-12. The covenant awaits the coming of the King for its fulfillment.

CHAPTER THIRTY-ONE

Contents: Moses' last counsel to the priests and instruction to the Levites. Warning of Israelitish apostasy.

Characters: God, Moses, Joshua.

Conclusion: It is a great encouragement to God's people that in the place of some useful instrument of His whom He removes, He raises up others to carry on His work.

Key Word: Counsel, (spake these words) v. 1.

Strong Verses: 6, 8.

Striking Facts: v. 16. God has infallible foresight of all the wickedness of the wicked. How often He has conferred His favors upon those whom He knew would deal treacherously and ungratefully. "How unsearchable are His judgments and His ways past finding out."

CHAPTER THIRTY-TWO

Contents: The song and exhortation of Moses.

Characters: God, Moses, Joshua.

Conclusion: The warning and consoling words of God sent down from heaven should sink into our hearts and soften them as the rain softens the earth, so make us fruitful in obedience.

Key Word: Doctrine, v. 2. (He gave a song of praise, Ex. 15, but this is one of instruction).

Strong Verses: 4, 29, 43.

Striking Facts: vv. 49, 52. Those may die happily whenever God calls them, who have had a believing prospect through Christ and a foregleam of the heavenly Canaan as a well grounded hope of life beyond death.

CHAPTER THIRTY-THREE

Contents: Moses' blessing upon the tribes.

Characters: God, Moses.

Conclusion: It is a very desirable thing to have an interest in the prayers of those who are about to depart for heaven.

Key Word: Blessing, v. 1.

Strong Verses: 25, 27.

Striking Facts: Thrice happy is the people whose God is the Lord. They are in His hand, v. 3; at His feet, v. 3; at His side, v. 12; between His shoulders, v. 12; in His arms, v. 27; behind His shield, v. 29, and fitted with His sword, v. 29.

CHAPTER THIRTY-FOUR

Contents: Vision and death of Moses.

Characters: God, Moses, Joshua.

Conclusion: Those may leave this world with cheerfulness who have known God face to face through His Son, and who have had the vision of the heavenly Canaan in their eye.

Key Word: Death, v. 5.

Strong Verses: 10.

Striking Facts: It was reserved for Joshua (the Lord Jesus of whom Joshua was a striking type) to do for us that which the law could not do in that it was weak through the flesh. Through Him we are led into the land of rest—the rest of conscience and the rest of heaven.

We leave Moses, the great law giver, buried in the plains of Moab. We leave our Saviour, who came to fulfill the law, and bear for us its curse, seated at the right hand of God on high, awaiting the hour of His return, when of the increase and peace of His government, there shall be no end.

JOSHUA

Key Thought:	Number of Chapters:	Key Verse:	Christ seen as:
Possessions	24	· 1:3	Capt. of Lord's Hosts

Writer of the Book:	Date:	Conclusion of the Book:
Joshua	About 1425 B. C.	The faithfulness of Jehovah to His own has been fully demonstrated.

SUMMARY

CHAPTER ONE

Contents: Joshua's commission and command.

Characters: God, Moses, Joshua.

Conclusion: Those who make the Word of God their rule and conscientiously walk by that rule will both do well and make great progress. We will be animated and emboldened for God's work as we keep our eyes upon the divine warrant.

Key Word: Strong, vv. 6, 7, 9, 18

Strong Verses: 8, 9.

Striking Facts: Joshua, type of Christ as Captain of our Salvation. Heb. 2:10, 11. He comes after Moses, John 1:17. Leads to victory, Rom. 8:37. Our Advocate when we have met defeat, 1 John 2:1. Allots our portions, Eph. 1:11, 14.

CHAPTER TWO

Contents: Rahab and the Jericho spies.

Characters: Joshua, two spies, Rahab, king of Jericho.

Conclusion: Let not God's people be afraid of their most powerful enemies, for their God can, when He pleases make their worst enemies afraid of them.

Key Word: Spies, v. 1.

Strong Verses: 18, 24.

Striking Facts: v. 21. Rahab's scarlet line speaks, by its color, of the safety that comes to our households through the sacrifice of Christ if it be exhibited by faith in the believer. Heb. 9:19, 22.

CHAPTER THREE

Contents: The passing of Jordan.

Characters: God, Joshua, priests.

Conclusion: The believer is to go on in the way of duty, though foreseeing great difficulties, depending on the divine sufficiency for that which he finds himself not sufficient for. "Is anything too hard for Jehovah?"

Key Word: Pass-over, v. 6.

Strong Verses: 5, 17.

Striking Facts: The passing of the Jordan is a type of the believer's death with Christ (Rom. 6:6-11; Eph. 2:5, 6; Col. 3:1-3) in which we pass from an old world into a newness of life.

CHAPTER FOUR

Contents: The memorial stone.

Characters: God, Joshua, priests, 12 men.

Conclusion: God's works of wonder on our behalf ought to be kept in everlasting memory and means devised for preserving our memory of them.

Key Word: Memorial, v. 7.

Strong Verses: 22, 24.

Striking Facts: The Lord Jesus, our Joshua, passed through the Jordan of death, opening the Kingdom to all believers. He appointed his twelve apostles according to the tribes of Israel by the memorial of the Gospel to transmit the knowledge of this to the remote places and to the future ages.

CHAPTER FIVE

Contents: Reproach of Eg pt rolled away. New food for the new place. The unseen captain.

Characters: God, Joshua, Christ.

Conclusion: (Circumcision, the seal of the covenant in their flesh, was neglected in the wilderness wanderings. They were hereby owned as freeborn children of God, the reproach of the bondage in Egypt being removed.)

God is jealous for the honor of His people and is ready to roll away whatever reproach they may for a time lie under, if they become "circumcised in heart."

Key Word: Reproach (rolled away), 9.

Strong Verses: 14, 15.

Striking Facts: The N. T. uncircumcision is world conformity, the failure openly to take a believer's place with Christ in death and resurrection. Gal. 6:14-16; Rom. 6:2-11.

CHAPTER SIX

Contents: Conquest of Jericho.

Characters: God, Joshua, priests, Rahab, 2 spies.

Conclusion: The victories of faith are often to be won by means, and upon principles utterly foolish and inadequate in the view of human wisdom. If faith is obedient to God's precepts, He will certainly confound the mighty with the weak things.

Key Word: Fall (of Jericho), v. 5.

Strong Verses: 16, 27.

Striking Facts: By the foolishness of preaching, fitly compared to the sounding of the ram's horns, the devil's kingdom is thrown down and the weapons of our warfare, though not carnal, nor seeming to a carnal eye able to accomplish anything, are yet mighty, through God, to the pulling down of strongholds. 2 Cor. 10:4, 5.

CHAPTER SEVEN

Contents: Sin of Achan and the defeat at Ai.

Characters: God, Joshua, Achan.

Conclusion: Let all men know that it is nothing but sin that separates them from God and if it be not sincerely repented of and put away, will bring disaster, not only upon themselves, but those associated with them.

Key Word: Accursed, v. 13.

Strong Verses: 12, 13, 19.

Striking Facts: The story illustrates the truth of the oneness of the church in Christ. 1 Cor. 5:1-7; 12:12, 14, 26. The whole cause of Christ is injured by the unspirituality of one believer.

CHAPTER EIGHT

Contents: Conquest of Ai. The blessings and cursing of Ebal.

Characters: God, Joshua, king of Ai.

Conclusion: The believer, clad in the whole armor of God, meeting the enemy of God as God directs, will see the scale easily and quickly turned against those who have not God on their side.

Key Word: Victory (took the city), v. 19.

Strong Verses: 26, 35.

Striking Facts: Achan, caught with forbidden spoil, lost it, his life and all. The people who had conscientiously refrained from the accursed thing were given the spoil of Ai. The way to have the comfort of what God allows us through Christ is to forbear what He forbids us.

CHAPTER NINE

Contents: The league with the Gibeonites.

Characters: God, Joshua, ambassadors of the Gibeonites.

Conclusion: We make more haste than good progress in any business when we do not stop to take God along with us and by the Word and prayer to ascertain His will.

Key Word: League, v. 15.

Strong Verses: 14, 25.

Striking Facts: vv. 4, 5, 12, 13. ¡God's people have often been deceived and imposed upon with a show of antiquity. Those who will be caught with the Gibeonitish strategem prove that they have not consulted God.

CHAPTER TEN

Contents: Victory at Gibeon, Makkedah, etc. Sun's action halted.

Characters: God, Joshua, Adonizedek, king of Makkedah.

Conclusion: When enemies set themselves in array against us and threaten to swallow us up, we may by faith and prayer, apply to Christ, our Joshua, for strength and succor and will assuredly receive the answer of victory and faith.

Key Word: Delivered, vv. 8, 30, 32.

Strong Verses: 8, 14, 25.

Striking Facts: v. 25. A figure of Christ's victories over the powers of darkness and the believer's victories through Him. All enemies shall be made His footstool. Psa. 110:1. All things will be put under Him, Heb. 2:8, and principalities and powers made a show of. Col. 2:15.

v. 12. Astronomy demands this day and histories of several countries declare it took place. Astronomical calculations have shown a period of 23 1/3 hours to be accounted for somewhere in this period of time.

v. 13. (About a whole day). See 2 Kings 20:11—ten degrees, 40 minutes, the exact balance wanted to make up another 24 hours.

CHAPTER ELEVEN

Contents: Final conquest of Canaan.

Characters: God, Joshua, Jabin, Jobab.

Conclusion: Those who, through obedience to His precepts, have God on their side, need not be disturbed as to the number and power of their enemies. "More are those that are with us than those that are against us."

Key Word: Delivered, vv. 6, 8.

Strong Verses: 6, 23.

Striking Facts: As Israel, at first forwarded by miracles, and now left to make their own way, so the war carried on against Satan's kingdom was at first advanced by special miracles, but being sufficiently proved by them to be of God, we are now left to the ordinary assistance of divine Grace in Christ in the use of the Sword of the Spirit and need not look for hailstones nor the standing still of the sun.

CHAPTER TWELVE

Contents: The roster of the kings of Canaan.

Characters: God, Moses, Joshua.

Conclusion: Fresh mercies must not drown the remembrance of former mercies, nor must the glory of present servants of God be allowed to diminish the honor due those who have gone before them, paving the way for later victories. (v. 6).

Key Word: Kings, v. 1.

Strong Verses: 6.

Striking Facts: vv. 6, 7. The triumphs and grants of the law were glorious but those of the Gospel far exceed in glory. Jesus, the true Joshua, has provided for all the children of promise, spiritual blessings—the privilege of His presence and heaven hereafter.

CHAPTER THIRTEEN

Contents: Joshua instructed concerning the division of the land.

Characters: God, Moses, Joshua.

Conclusion: All people, and especially old people, should set themselves to do that quickly which must be done before they die, lest death prevent them. vv. 1, 7.

Key Word: Divide (the land), v. 7.

Strong Verses: 1.

Striking Facts: Joshua had the honor of dividing the land as Christ, the true Joshua, who has conquered for us the gates of hell and opened to us the gates of heaven, purchasing an eternal inheritance for all believers, will in due time, have the honor of putting them in possession.

ɪ **CHAPTER FOURTEEN**
Contents: Land divided, the portion of Caleb.
Characters: God, Joshua, Caleb, Eleazar.
Conclusion: Whatever we undertake, God's favorable presence with us is all in all to our success, therefore we should make sure of it by conformity to His will and an eye to His favor. vv. 8, 9.
Key Word: Divided (land), v. 5.
Strong Verses: 10, 11, 12.
Striking Facts: v. 12. Because it was formerly in God's promise, Caleb shows how he values the promise and insists on the mountain the Lord had spoken of. The man of faith values that which is given by promise far above that given by providence only.

CHAPTER FIFTEEN
Contents: Land divisions; the portion of Judah.
Characters: God, Joshua, Caleb, Othniel, Achsah.
Conclusion: It is no breach of God's law moderately to desire those comforts and conveniences of life which are attainable in a fair and regular way and will make us more efficient workmen for God.
Key Word: Borders.
Strong Verses: 19.
Striking Facts: v. 10. The blessings of the upper springs illustrate those which relate to our souls, and those of the nether springs speaks of those which relate to the body and the life that now is.

CHAPTER SIXTEEN
Contents: Land divisions; portions of Manasseh and Ephriam.
Characters: None mentioned.
Conclusion: It is a brand of failure upon the Christian, when through carelessness, cowardice or want of faith in God, he fails to drive out the Canaanite (world) as commanded. Coveteousness often brings us into compromise and leads eventually to being infected with the world's idolatry.
Key Word: Borders, v. 5.
Strong Verses: 10.

CHAPTER SEVENTEEN
Contents: Land divisions; portion for Manasseh.
Characters: God, Joshua, Eleazar, Moses, Zoplehad's daughter.
Conclusion: (v. 14). Many covet larger possessions who do not cultivate and make the best of what they have. If we would have more talents bestowed upon us, we should trade with those with which we are entrusted.
Key Word: Portions, v. 5
Strong Verses: 13, 15, 18.
Striking Facts: v. 13. Many Christians try to serve their own ends by conniving with the Canaanites, whom Christ has distinctly commanded must be driven out. To thus court compromise with the world is to court failure.

CHAPTER EIGHTEEN
Contents: Tabernacle set up; apportionment of land to seven tribes.
Characters: God, Joshua, three surveyors.
Conclusion: Many Christians stand in their own light and forsake their own mercies for the sake of lying vanities. With the title to a good land, given us by the sacrifice of Christ, we must not allow ourselves to be slack in possessing it all, because of seeming difficulties that are in the way.
Key Word: Borders, v. 12.
Strong Verses: 1, 3.
Striking Fact: The setting up of the tabernacle (v. 1) in Shiloh, gives a hint that in the coming Shiloh (Christ) of whom Jacob had spoken, all the ordinances of the worldly sanctuary would have their accomplishment in a greater and more perfect tabernacle. Heb. 9:1, 11.

CHAPTER NINETEEN

Contents: Land divisions for six more tribes.
Characters: God, Joshua, Eleazar.
Conclusion: (v. 49.   The last served was the eldest and greatest man of Israel).   Men in great public places should learn to prefer the common welfare before their own private satisfaction.
Key Word: Inheritance, v. 11.
Strong Verses: 47, 49.
Striking Facts: v. 10.   Within the lot of Zebulun were places made illustrious in the N. T.   Within it was Nazareth where the Saviour spent so much of His time and mount Tabor on which He was transfigured and the coast of the Sea of Galilee on which He preached so many sermons and wrought so many miracles.

CHAPTER TWENTY

Contents: Cities of refuge.
Characters: God, Joshua.
Conclusion: Other refuge have we none, in any trouble, save Him in whom our trust is stayed.
Key Word: Refuge, v. 2.
Strong Verses: 9.
Striking Facts: Cities of refuge typify the relief which the Gospel provides for poor, penitent sinners and their protection from the curse of the law and the wrath of God, in our Lord Jesus Christ, to whom believers flee for refuge.   Heb. 6:18.

CHAPTER TWENTY-ONE

Contents: Land divisions; portions for Levites.
Characters: God, Joshua.
Conclusion: God performs His promises to the utmost (v. 45) and if in anything the promise seems to come short, the saint must confess that upon himself rests all the blame.
Key Word: Inheritance, v. 3.
Strong Verses: 44, 45.
Striking Facts: There is an inheritance provided for all the saints, God's royal, priesthood (Levites) for which they must petition through the true Joshua, Christ who has said, "Ask, and it shall be given you."

CHAPTER TWENTY-TWO

Contents: Two and a half tribes dismissed to their homes.   Altar of Reuben and Gad.
Characters: God, Joshua, Phinehas.
Conclusion: Unhappy strifes will be prevented or soon healed by an impartial and favorable inquiry into that which is the matter of the offense.   God, does, and men MUST often overlook the weakness of an honest zeal.
Key Word: Witness, v. 27.
Strong Verses: 5, 18, 29.
Striking Facts: v. 28.   Those who have found the benefits of God's ordinances cannot but desire to perpetuate them upon their children and use all precaution lest their children cease from following the Lord Jesus.   To this end the believer should set up a constant witness of Christ in the home.

CHAPTER TWENTY-THREE

Contents: Last counsels of Joshua.
Characters: God, Joshua.
Conclusion: As all good things come upon the believer according to the promise, so long as we have kept close to God, so all evil things will befall, according to His threatenings, if we forsake Him.
Key Word: Counsel (said unto them), v. 2.
Strong Verses: 3, 6, 8, 10, 14.
Striking Facts: v. 16.   The goodness of the heavenly Canaan and the thought

of the possession they might have had, will aggravate the misery of those who shall be shut out from that which they might have enjoyed through God's free grace in Christ.

CHAPTER TWENTY-FOUR

Contents: Last charge of Joshua and his death. Eleazar's death.

Characters: God, Joshua, Eleazar.

Conclusion: v. 15. It is the will of God that all should make religion their serious and deliberate choice and to resolve upon a life of godliness because upon honest investigation, it is found to be the best way.

Key Word: Counsel, v. 2.

Strong Verses: 15, 16, 20, 24.

Striking Facts: The book which began with triumphs here ends with funerals by which all the glory of man is stained.

JUDGES

Key Thought:	Number of Chapters·	Key Verse:'	Christ seen as:
Failure	21	21:25	Messenger of Jehovah

Writer of the Book:	Date:	Conclusion of the Book:
		Man is prone to wander from God. God's grace
Samuel	About 1410 B. C.	ever pursues and seeks to restore the backslider.

SUMMARY

CHAPTER ONE

Contents: The incomplete victories of Judah, Benjamin and Manasseh.

Characters: God, Judah, Simeon, Adoni-bezek, Caleb, Achsah, Othniel.

Conclusion: God appoints service according to the strength He has given (v. 2) but distrust of His power and promise, lose for us our advantages and run us into a thousand troubles.

Key Word: Partial victory, (vv. 19, 21, 27, 29, 30, 31, 33).

Strong Verses: 2, 7.

Striking Facts: v. 2. Judah was the tribe out of which the Saviour sprang. Christ, the Lion of the tribe of Judah, engaged the powers of darkness and in Him we are more than conquerors.

CHAPTER TWO

Contents: Review of Israelitish invasion of Canaan up to Joshua's death. Results of incomplete obedience. Judges instituted.

Characters: God, angel of Jehovah (Jesus) Joshua.

Conclusion: God never designed defeat for His own; let them be faithful to Him and they will find Him unchangeably constant to them. His covenants never break except on our side.

Key Word: Sold, v. 14.

Strong Verses: 18, 20, 21.

Striking Facts: The Angel of Jehovah, v. 1, was none other than Christ Himself. He seemed to come up from Gilgal, the place where their covenant had been renewed, of which they would be reminded. The remembrance of what we have received and heard from God, prepares us for special messages from Christ to hold fast. (Rev. 3:2, 3).

CHAPTER THREE

Contents: Apostasies of Israel. Deliverances through Othniel, Ehud and Shamgar.

Characters: God, Othniel, Chushan-rishathian, Eglou, Ehud, Shamgar.

Conclusion: Man's memory is treacherous in that it easily forgets God and he must be repeatedly tested that God might be kept in sight. It often takes affliction to make him cry to God with importunity, when before he would scarcely think of Jehovah. A deliverer is always ready to answer the prayer of a contrite heart.

Key Word: Proved (tested), vv. 1, 4.

Strong Verses: 9, 15.

Striking Facts: vv. 1, 2. War is sometimes God's will. When a country is exceedingly rich and fruitful, abounding with dainties of all sorts, if the people are not sometimes brought to know hardship, they are in danger of sinking into the utmost degree of luxury and effeminacy.

CHAPTER FOUR

Contents: Victories of Deborah and Barak.

Characters: God, Jabin, Deborah, Barak, Sisera, Jael.

Conclusion: Those who slight God in their prosperity, will find themselves under a necessity of crying mightily to Him when they are in trouble. He

is faithful in spite of our unfaithfulness, and when we sincerely turn to Him, He will give the victory.
Key Word: Prevailed, v. 24
Strong Verses: 14.
Striking Facts: It is a sure mark of apostasy in a nation when a woman is found in the place of leadership.

CHAPTER FIVE

Contents: Song of Deborah and Barak.
Characters: God, Deborah, Barak, Jael, Sisera, Shamgar.
Conclusion: When we have received mercy from God, we should be speedy in our returns of praise while the impressions of the mercy are fresh. Song is a good expedient for perpetuating the memory of God's special favors.
Key Word: Song of praise, vv. 2, 12.
Strong Verses: 31.
Striking Facts: v. 20. "Stars fought"—the elements were against Sisera. Those to whom God is an enemy because of rejection of His Son and His Gospel are at war with the whole creation.

CHAPTER SIX

Contents: More apostasy in Israel. Call of Gideon.
Characters: God, Angel of Jehovah (Jesus), Holy Spirit, Gideon, prophet, Joash.
Conclusion: In times of apostasy, God often calls His mightiest servants from places of obscurity, and inspiring them with the assurance of the divine presence, He works through them great deliverances for His people.
Key Word: Valour, v. 12, (in God's hands).
Strong Verses: 34.
Striking Facts: v. 24. Jehovah-shalom (God our peace). See Eph. 6:15. The peace of God, found alone in Christ who "is our peace," is the only preparation for intense conflict. In the midst of strife, one who has Christ for his peace, may be possessed of perfect tranquility within. If the Christian is called to battle, let him set up the altar of Jehovah-Shalom.

CHAPTER SEVEN

Contents: Gideon's three hundred and the victory over Midian and Amalek.
Characters: God, Gideon, Phurah, Oreb, Zeeb.
Conclusion: God wants prepared men to fight God's battles with God's weapons in God's way. A Christian's unfitness for the battle is often seen in the unconscious and trifling acts of his life, which betray his utter lack of faith. (v. 5).
Key Word: Victory, v. 15.
Strong Verses: 2, 7.
Striking Facts: Empty pitchers (v. 16) type of earthly body, emptied of self (2 Cor. 4:7) but filled with God's Word, the lamp (Psa. 119:105). The pitcher was not to be spared in the advance, and the lamp was to be held forth (v. 20 Phil. 2:16). With the trumpet, the tidings of victory were sounded (Mark 16:15).

CHAPTER EIGHT

Contents: Jealousy of Ephriam. Events to the death of Gideon. Apostasy.
Characters: God, Gideon, Zebah, Zalmunna, Abimelech, Jerubbaal, Jether.
Conclusion: Many are led into false ways by one false step of a good man (v. 27). False worship soon makes way for false deities.
Key Word: Snare, v. 27 (whoring, 27,33).
Strong Verses: 23, 34.
Striking Facts: v. 22. The Lord Jesus has delivered us out of the hands of our dangerous spiritual enemies, and it is fitting that He should rule over us. See Luke 1:24, 25.

CHAPTER NINE

Contents: Conspiracy of Abimelech.
Characters: God, Abimelech, Jerubbaal, Jocham, Gaal, Zebul.
Conclusion: Evil pursues sinners and sometimes overtakes them when they

are apparently triumphant. The mighty things of the world may be confounded by the weakest, if God so wills.

Key Word: Vengeance, vv. 24, 56.

Strong Verses: 56.

CHAPTER TEN

Contents: Further apostasy; servitude to Philistines and Amorites.

Characters: God, Tola, Jair.

Conclusion: The pleasures of sense, the gods of this world, cannot be our satisfaction (v. 14). True happiness and safety are only in God, to whom a true penitent will refer himself for correction as God may see fit, owning that his sin is highly malignant in its deserts (v. 10).

Key Word: Vexed, oppressed, v. 8.

Strong Verses: 10, 14, 16.

CHAPTER ELEVEN

Contents: Jeptha's awful vow and the victory over the Ammcrites.

Characters: God, Holy Spirit, Jeptha, his daughter.

Conclusion: A Christian in the hands of the Spirit is assured of success in the undertaking to which God has called him. v. 29.

Key Word: Subdued (enemy), v. 33.

Strong Verses: 35, 36.

Striking Facts: v. 30. One should be cautious and well advised in the making of vows, lest by indulging a present emotion even of pious zeal, they involve themselves in a great mistake.

Jeptha's sacrifice is a figure of the great sacrifice of Christ. The daughter was a chaste sacrifice, devoted to death by the father and so made a curse. She submitted after a period of agony, to her father's will.

CHAPTER TWELVE

Contents: Second jealousy of Ephriam.

Characters: God, Jeptha, Ibzan, Elon, Abdon.

Conclusion: Proud men think all the honors wasted that they themselves did not win. Envy brings serious contentions in the ranks of those who should be as one to fight God's battles.

He who rolls the stone of reproach unjustly upon another, let him expect that it will justly return upon himself.

Key Word: Envy, v. 1.

Strong Verses: 3.

CHAPTER THIRTEEN

Contents: Parents of Samson and Samson's birth.

Characters: God, Angel (Jesus), Holy Spirit, Manoah.

Conclusion: A promise is given to try our faith and a precept to try our obedience—for God requires both faith and obedience from those on whom He would bestow special favors.

(It is desirable that our children be devoted to God even before their birth.)

Key Word: Conceive, 3, 24.

Strong Verses: 18, 23.

Striking Facts: v. 18. "Secret" is lit. "Wonderful," the name applied to Christ in Isa. 9:6. v. 22 declares they were face to face with God who is manifested only in His Son. As the flame ascended from the altar He ascended. We owe the acceptance of all our praises and prayers to His mediation. It is Christ in our hearts by faith that makes our offering a sweet smelling savour.

CHAPTER FOURTEEN

Contents: Samson as Judge. His victory over a lion; his riddles; his wife.

Characters: God, Holy Spirit, Samson, parents, woman of Timnah.

Conclusion: He that in the choice of a wife is guided only by his eye and governed by his fancy must afterward thank himself if he finds a Philistine in his arms. (v. 3). We should not be "unequally yoked with unbelievers."

(God often overrules our mistakes to take occasion against the enemies of His Truth).
Key Word: Wife, v. 2.
Strong Verses: 6, 19.
Striking Facts: When God, by His providences, brings good out of evil to the followers of Christ—when that which has threatened their ruin turns to their advantage and the wrath of men turns to His praise—then comes meat out of the eater and sweetness out of the strong.

CHAPTER FIFTEEN

Contents: Samson takes vengeance on the Philistines.
Characters: God, Holy Spirit, Samson, his family and friends.
Conclusion: There is nothing too hard or too much for him to do on whom the Holy Spirit comes in power, even though there are only the most contemptible instruments at hand with which to work (foxes, jawbone).
Key Word: Avenged, v. 7.
Strong Verses: 16, 18.
Striking Facts: In the bursting of Samson's bands, we find an illustration of the way the Lord Jesus was loosed from the cords of death and came forth from the tomb and graveclothes. Thus, He triumphed over the powers of darkness that shouted against Him.

CHAPTER SIXTEEN

Contents: Samson and Delilah; his fatal error and his death.
Characters: God, Holy Spirit, Samson, Delilah.
Conclusion: Beware of Satan who ruins men by rocking them to sleep, flattering them into a good opinion of their own safety, then robbing them of their strength and honor, leading them captive at his will.
(God often leaves men to do foolish things to punish them for indulging in the lusts of uncleanness.)
Key Word: Strength, v. 6, (departed, v. 20).
Strong Verses: 20, 28.
Striking Facts: Samson's strength was not in his hair but in his Nazarite consecration, of which his long hair was but a badge. By losing the badge, he forfeited the strength. What was real in Samson was his great faith in times of awful apostasy and God honored this faith. Heb. 11:32.

CHAPTER SEVENTEEN

Contents: Micah's worship in self will.
Characters: Micah, his mother, a Levite.
Conclusion: The love of money makes much mischief; destroys the duty and comfort of every relation and frequently leads to the setting up of a false worship.
Key Word: Graven image, v. 3.
Strong Verses: 6.
Striking Facts: v. 13. Apostates who please themselves with their own delusions infer, if providence brings anything to their hands that helps them in their way, that God is pleased with them. With all false worship there is usually an exaltation of false priesthood, usurping the place of Christ.

CHAPTER EIGHTEEN

Contents: The Danite invasion. Civil and religious confusion.
Characters: Micah, Jonathan, priests.
Conclusion: Many seek to justify themselves in their idolatrous impiety by the prosperity that seemingly attends them, not knowing that many are brought to destruction by their false security and that departing from the revealed will of God concerning worship is a dangerous move for a people to make.
Key Word: Seeking inheritance, v. 1.
Strong Verses: 9, 10.
Striking Facts: v. 24. An excellent definition of idolatry. Anything put in place of God, which man is concerned about as if life and comfort, hope and happiness were bound up in it, is an idol.

CHAPTER NINETEEN

Contents: The Levite and his concubine. Wickedness of Gibeonites.

Characters: Levite, concubine, her father.

Conclusion: Because men like not to retain God in their knowledge, God gives them up to vile affection through which they dishonor themselves and turn His glory into shame. Rom. 1:24, 28.

Key Word: Abused, 25.

Strong Verses: 30.

Striking Facts: In the miserable end of this woman, we see the hand of God punishing her for her uncleanness. v. 2.

CHAPTER TWENTY

Contents: Civil war in which the Benjamites are punished.

Characters: God, a Levite, Phinehas.

Conclusion: We cannot expect the presence of God with us in our enterprises unless we seek it by humbling ourselves before Him. (v. 26). He is not under obligation to prosper us. Men are often so confident that God owes them His favor because they think their cause a good one, that they think it needless to humble themselves before God in penitence.

Key Word: Vengeance, vv. 9, 28.

Strong Verses: 11, 18, 26.

CHAPTER TWENTY-ONE

Contents: Mourning for the lost tribe of Benjamin.

Characters: God.

Conclusion: There may be overdoing in well doing. Great care must be taken in the government of our zeal, for even necessary justice must be rendered with compassion. Many a war is ill-ended which was well begun. (2, 6, 13).

Key Word: Depleted tribe, vv. 3, 6.

Strong Verses: 2, 13.

Striking Facts: v. 25. Men should learn to be thankful for magistrates, both supreme and subordinate for they are ministers for God unto us for good. Any government is better than no government or anarchy.

ʹ RUTH

Key Thought: Kinsman	Number of Chapters· 4	Key Verse: 4:14	Christ seen as: Kinsman Redeemer

Writer of the Book: Unknown	Date: About 1300 B. C.	Conclusion of the Book: True rest comes only through redemption and union.

SUMMARY

CHAPTER ONE

Contents: Naomi departs from Moab and returns with Ruth to Bethlehem.

Characters: God, Naomi, Ruth, Orpah, Elimelech, Mahlon, Chilion.

Conclusion: When we take God for our Father we must take His people for our people though they be poor and despised. Those who forsake the communion of saints and return to the people of Moab will sooner or later break all communion with God and embrace the idols of Moab.

Key Word: Fidelity, v. 17.

Strong Verses: 16, 17.

Striking Facts: Many have a value and affection for Christ yet come short of salvation by Him because they cannot find it in their hearts to forsake other things and attach themselves to Him. If we resolve that nothing shall separate us from our duty to Christ, we may be sure that nothing can ever separate us from happiness in Him.

CHAPTER TWO

Contents: Ruth serves Boaz who exercises a great kindness toward her.

Characters: God, Ruth, Naomi, Boaz.

Conclusion: God wisely orders small events and those that seem altogether contingent serve His own glory and supply the needs of His trusting people.

Key Word: Favour, v. 13.

Strong Verses: 12, 20.

Striking Facts: vv. 22, 23. If we would benefit through Christ, we must adhere closely to Him, His fields and His servants. Has the Lord dealt bountifully with us? Let us not be found in any other field seeking happiness and satisfaction in the world.

CHAPTER THREE

Contents: Ruth rests at the feet of Boaz.

Characters: God, Ruth, Boaz, Naomi.

Conclusion: The married state should be a state of rest, when wandering affections are fixed in one who is fit, both temporally and spiritually to be a good husband.

Key Word: Rest, v. 1.

Strong Verses: 10, 11.

Striking Facts: The Lord Jesus is our Kinsman Redeemer. Through His incarnation He became kin to us as human beings that we, through the Spirit, might become betrothed to Him.

CHAPTER FOUR

Contents: Ruth finds reward in her marriage to Boaz.

Characters: God, Boaz, Ruth, Naomi, kinsman, Obed.

Conclusion: Fair and square dealings in all matters of contract and business is what all those must make conscience of who would approve themselves as "Israelites indeed without guile."

Key Word: Kinsman redeemer, v. 1.

Strong Verses: 14.

Striking Facts: At vast expense, our Lord Jesus, the Bethlehemite Redeemer purchased the heavenly inheritance for us which by our sin was mortgaged and forfeited, and which of ourselves we could never have redeemed.

I. SAMUEL

Key Thought: Kingdom	Number of Chapters: 31	Key Verse 10:25	Christ seen as: Seed of David

Writer of the Book: Uncertain, Samuel, Nathan or Gad	Date: About 1155 B. C.	Conclusion of the Book: Prayer should have a great place in our lives that the power of God may work for and through us.

SUMMARY

CHAPTER ONE

Contents: The vow of Hannah and the birth of Samuel.

Characters: God, Eli, Elkhanah, Hannah, Samuel, Peninnah.

Conclusion: Prayer is heart's ease to a gracious soul. If we seek on the basis of God's glory (v. 11) we shall be confident that we do not seek in vain. Prayer smoothes the countenance (v. 18).

Key Word: Bitterness, v. 10.

Strong Verses: 17, 27, 28.

Striking Facts: True prayer may only be offered on the grounds of the sacrifice (v. 3). By Christ's offering, not only is atonement made for sin, but the audience and acceptance of our prayers is obtained for us. In all our supplications, we must have an eye to the Great Sacrifice.

CHAPTER TWO

Contents: Hannah's prophetic prayer. Evil sons of Eli. Samuel in the tabernacle. The warning to Eli.

Characters: God, Hannah, Eli, Samuel, Hophni, Phinehas, Elkanah, a prophet.

Conclusion: Nothing is more provoking to God than the profanation of sacred things and men serving their lusts with the offerings of the Lord. Those who allow and countenance their children in an evil way by not using their authority to restrain and punish them, involve themselves in their guilt and may be expected to be cast off from God's service.

Key Word: Evil sons, v. 23.

Strong Verses: 2, 3, 6, 7, 8, 9, 10, 30.

Striking Facts: v. 35. This had its full accomplishment in the priesthood of Christ, that faithful High Priest raised up of God when the Levitical priesthood was cast aside, who in all things did His Father's mind, and for whom God builds a sure house, built on a rock so that the gates of hell cannot prevail against it.

CHAPTER THREE

Contents: Samuel becomes Jehovah's prophet-priest.

Characters: God, Samuel, Eli.

Conclusion: A child may have an ear for God's call; a mind for God's service and a message for God's bidding, for God will not be without a mouthpiece even though the ordained priesthood be deaf to His voice.

Key Word: Called, v. 4.

Strong Verses: 10, 18, 19.

Striking Facts: God's ministers must nourish a holy sensitiveness to sacred things, or callousness will lead them to some sin for which God will be compelled to lay them aside. (v. 13).

CHAPTER FOUR

Contents: Ark taken by Philistines.

Characters: God, Eli, Hophni, Phinehas, his wife, Ichabod.

Conclusion: One may go forth with a Bible under the arm and a shout upon the lips and yet not have God Himself. Many who have estranged themselves from the vitals of religion putting their confidence in the rituals of religion, find themselves with only a form of godliness without the power thereof.

Key Word: Ark taken, vv. 11, 17.

Strong Verses: 22.

Striking Facts: Farewell, all in this world, if the ark, the token of Christ's presence with us, be lost.

CHAPTER FIVE

Contents: Ark of God a curse to Philistines.

Characters: God.

Conclusion: Sacred signs are not things that God is tied to or that man can trust to for blessing. His presence may be a savour of life unto life or of death unto death.

Key Word: Hand of the Lord, vv. 6, 9, 11.

Strong Verses: 6.

Striking Facts: Those who contend with God, His ark and the followers of His Beloved Son will invariably be ruined at last.

CHAPTER SIX

Contents: Ark brought to Joshua.

Characters: God.

Conclusion: The Word of God in the hands of the world brings them condemnation (v. 2) causing them to seek to get rid of it. By refusing to part with their sins, sinners but lengthen out their own miseries (v. 4).

Key Word: Ark, v. 1.

Strong Verses: 13, 20.

Striking Facts: v. 13. The return of the ark (token of God's presence) and the revival of holy ordinances after days of restraint and trouble must be a matter of great joy to Christians. We must reverently use the tokens of God's grace through Christ or we will be made to sink under the tokens of His displeasure (v. 19).

CHAPTER SEVEN

Contents: Ark brought to house of Abinadab. Revival of Mizpah. Victory at Eben-ezer.

Characters: God, Samuel, Eleazar, Abinadab.

Conclusion: When we are truly sensible that by sin we have provoked God to withdraw from us and that we are undone if we continue in that state, if we make a solemn business of returning to God we may be assured we are on the way to a renewed prosperity and deliverance.

Key Word: Return, v. 3.

Strong Verses: 3, 8, 12.

Striking Facts: v. 12. The Christian should, as he passes along, set up his Ebenezers by which he will be reminded that "hitherto the Lord hath helped him" and by which he will give all the glory of his victories to God and His Son Jesus Christ.

CHAPTER EIGHT

Contents: Israel demands a king; theocracy rejected.

Characters: God, Samuel, his sons, Joel, Abiajah.

Conclusion: When God's people will not accept His best for them, they will get the best they can be persuaded to take and, with the answer to their selfish prayers, will receive also an added judgment.

Key Word: King, vv. 5, 19.

Strong Verses: 7, 9, 18.

Striking Facts: v. 20. For a professed Christian to want to live like the world means not only that he is displeasing Christ, but will at last find himself a dupe.

It was God's will that Israel should have a king but in His own time. He must come of the tribe of Judah (Gen. 49:10). Because of Judah's sin (Gen. 38, Deut. 23:2) his line was prohibited from office for ten generations. David is found to be the first one to satisfy these conditions. (Matt. 1).

CHAPTER NINE

Contents: Saul chosen king.

Characters: God, Samuel, Saul, his servant, Kish.

Conclusion: The wise God serves very great and certain purposes by seemingly small and casual affairs. Let us therefore remember that promotions come not by chance and that faithfulness and humility on-the-path of present duty are the key to exaltation at the hands of God.

Key Word: Saul, v. 2.

Strong Verses: 21, 25, 27.

Striking Facts: v. 24. Note the suggestiveness of the dish set before Saul. The shoulder denotes strength; the breast which went with it denotes affection. Let all who are called to minister to Christ's people be reminded that a great responsibility is upon their shoulders and that the people should be dear to their bosom.

CHAPTER TEN

Contents: Saul annointed king.

Characters: God, Holy Spirit, Samuel, Saul, his uncle.

Conclusion: Whom God calls He qualifies. When God works in us by His Spirit, it serves to confirm faith and furnish proof of a divine commission, v. 9.

Key Word: Annointed, v. 1.

Strong Verses: 6, 7, 24.

Striking Facts: The sacred unctions point to the Great Messiah, the annointed One who was annointed with the oil of the Spirit without measure, above all priests or princes of earth.

v. 19. Their obstinacy was a pressage of their rejecting Christ, in the rejecting of whom they cast off God that He should not reign over them.

CHAPTER ELEVEN

Contents: Saul's victories at Jabesh-gilead. Kingdom renewed at Gilgal.

Characters: God, Holy Spirit, Saul, Samuel, Nahash.

Conclusion: Unless the Christian has forsaken his covenant with God, there is no occasion for his courting a covenant with the world by compromise. Through our King, we may have the victory.

Key Word: Compromise (covenant) rejected, vv. 1, 13.

Strong Verses: 6, 13.

Striking Facts: The right eye is the eye of faith. The left eye was covered with the shield. By the compromise they would be unfitted to fight. Thus Satan seeks to cripple the follower of Christ in service. A compromising saint is always blind in one eye.

CHAPTER TWELVE

Contents: Samuel's proclamation of the kingdom. Deliverances of God rehearsed. The sign of thunder and rain.

Characters: God, Samuel.

Conclusion: Religion has reason on its side (v. 7) which demonstrates that obedience to God is the happiness of men and disobedience to God is the ruin of men.

Key Word: Reason (counsel), v. 7.

Strong Verses: 14, 15, 22-25.

Striking Facts: v. 22. Had God chosen us on our good merits, we might fear He would cast us off for our bad merits, but choosing us in Christ before the foundation of the world, for His name's sake, He cannot lose us.

CHAPTER THIRTEEN

Contents: The self-will of Saul. He intrudes into the priests office. His divine rejection announced.

Characters: God, Samuel, Saul, Jonathan.

Conclusion: Some lay great stress upon the external performances of religion, thinking thereby to excuse their ignorance of God Himself. Though enemies press, we are powerless to engage them without God Himself. We will make progress if we wait upon Him and become assured of divine power.

Key Word: Disobedience, v. 13.

Strong Verses: 14.
Striking Facts: v. 11. Scoffers of the latter days think the promise of Christ's return is broken because He does not come in their time, though it is certain that He will come "in such an hour as we think not."

CHAPTER FOURTEEN

Contents: Jonathan's great victory over the Philistines.
Characters: God, Jonathan, armor-bearer, Saul, Ahiah, Abner.
Conclusion: Let this strengthen the weak and encourage the timid, that no matter how few and feeble those are who seek to Him for direction and acknowledge Him in all their ways, God will give the victory. God can not only save us, but save by us, therefore let faith venture.
Key Word: Delivered, v. 12.
Strong Verses: 6, 45.
Striking Facts: To fail to feed upon the honey (Christ in the Word) vv. 25-30, is not time gained but strength lost, unfitting one for the conflicts.

CHAPTER FIFTEEN

Contents: Saul's incomplete obedience and his rejection as king
Characters: God, Samuel, Saul, Agag.
Conclusion: Some judge many things in their lives, but spare one Agag which the Lord has condemned. Partial obedience spells disobedience and in the absence of perfect obedience, our sacrifices are worthless, v. 22.
Key Word: Disobedience, vv. 11, 19, (rejected, v. 23).
Strong Verses: 22, 24, 25.
Striking Facts: v. 20. We see how hard it is to convict the children of disobedience of their sin and strip them of their fig leaves, for they ever seek to justify themselves on the ground of their good intentions. Ceremonial observances cannot take the place of humble, sincere obedience to the will of God which requires full yieldedness to Jesus Christ.

CHAPTER SIXTEEN

Contents: Choice of David as king. His annointing and visit to Saul.
Characters: God, Holy Spirit, Samuel, David, Jesse, Saul, Eliab, Abinadab, Shammah.
Conclusion: Whom God appoints, He annoints, and whom He annoints is truly qualified for service.
Key Word: Chosen, v. 1, (annointed, v. 17).
Striking Facts: David means "beloved" for he was a type of the Beloved Son. As David was called from the place of obscurity and contempt, so Christ came from a humble walk of life. David was first annointed by God and later by the people. (2 Sam. 2:4, 5:3). Christ was annointed at His baptism, and at His coming again, it will be ratified by His brethren, the Jews and all nations.

CHAPTER SEVENTEEN

Contents: Defiance of Israel by Goliath and David's victory over him.
Characters: God, David, Saul, Goliath, Eliab, Abinadab, Shammah.
Conclusion: The battle is God's battle. If our confidence is purely in the power of God, rather than in any armor or sufficiency of our own, we may be certain the world's utmost might cannot withstand. God resists the proud and pours contempt upon those who bid defiance to His people, humiliating them by a defeat with the meanest of instruments.
Key Word: Prevailed, v. 50.
Strong Verses: 37, 47.
Striking Facts: David's victory over Goliath is a type of the triumph of the Son of God over Satan. Goliath is also a remarkable type of the anti-Christ (note 6 pieces of armor, vv. 5-7). David annointed for the kingship but not yet in power is defied by the boastful champion whom he overcomes in the name of the Lord of Hosts. When Jesus comes as Lord of Hosts, anti-Christ will be destroyed by the brightness of His coming.

CHAPTER EIGHTEEN

Contents: Love covenant of Jonathan and David. Saul's jealousy and attempts on David's life. Saul's daughter given to David.

Characters: God, David, Saul, Jonathan, Merab, Michal, Adriel.
Conclusion: The weeds of envy will grow if one thinks more of reputation than of duty. (vv. 7, 8). It is is a sign that the Spirit of God has departed from men, if they be continually envious and suspicious of those about them and cannot endure to hear anyone praised but themselves. v. 12.
Key Word: Envy (displeased), vv. 8, 29.
Strong Verses: 14.
Striking Facts: vv. 3, 4. Jonathan's love is an illustration of the love the Lord Jesus has shown to us. He stripped Himself to clothe us; He even clothed Himself with our rags that we might be clothed upon with His glory. Phil. 2:5-7.
v. 23. We should magnify the honor of being sons to the King of Kings. "Behold what manner of love the Father has bestowed upon us "

CHAPTER NINETEEN

Contents: Saul's murderous hate pursues David.
Characters: God, Holy Spirit, David, Saul, Jonathan, Michal, Samuel.
Conclusion: God always raises up a friend for us in time of need. Envy allowed its way becomes murderous. Cut the claws of the tiger pup, lest it become a full grown tiger, when it is too late.
Key Word: Murderous envy, vv. 1, 10, 15.
Strong Verses: 12.
Striking Facts: The murderous attempts on the life of the annointed king by the usurping king, remind us of the repeated attempts of the usurper, Satan, against the life of God's Anointed One, Christ, when He was upon earth.

CHAPTER TWENTY

Contents: Jonathan protects David. Their parting.
Characters: God, David, Jonathan, Saul.
Conclusion: Though the believer be despised of many, compelled to leave all comforts and part with best friends for Christ's sake, be this our comfort, that we have made an everlasting covenant with Jehovah who will exalt us in due time.
Key Word: True friend, v. 17, (loved as his own soul)
Strong Verses: 17, 42.
Striking Facts: v. 15. The covenant of Jonathan and David is an illustration of that between God and the Son on behalf of believers. John 10:28; Rom. 8:32-39.

CHAPTER TWENTY-ONE

Contents: David flees to Ahimelech and Achish.
Characters: David, Ahimelech, Doeg, Achish.
Conclusion: If we would but trust God aright, we would not have to resort to miserable and dishonoring devices for our preservation in times of testing.
Key Word: Afraid, v. 12.
Strong Verses: 9.
Striking Facts: v. 6. Jesus showed from this in Matt. 12:3 that ritual observances must at times give way to moral duties in case of urgent necessity, thus He justified His disciples in plucking corn on the Sabbath day.

CHAPTER TWENTY-TWO

Contents: David in rejection gathers mighty men. His wanderings and dangers.
Characters: David, Saul, Gad, Ahimelech, Doeg, Abiathar.
Conclusion: Those who give way to jealousy are in a continual agitation and torment and show that the Spirit of God is not with them.
Key Word: Suffering with David, v. 22.
Strong Verses: 14, 23.
Striking Facts: v. 23. Those who honor Christ, the true David, must expect to share in His rejection and suffering. As He has been promised that the Father will hide Him in the shadow of His hand (Isa. 49:2) so we, with Him, may be confident of being safeguarded.

CHAPTER TWENTY-THREE

Contents: Wanderings and adventures of David.

Characters: God, David, Saul, Jonathan, Abiathar.

Conclusion: Whatever befalls us, if we acknowledge God in all our ways and seek direction from Him, God will baffle the designs of the enemy and turn their counsels in our favor.

Key Word: Hunted (search him out), vv. 14, 23.

Strong Verses: 14, 16.

Striking Facts: As David might justly claim that his enemies rewarded him evil for good and that for his love they were his adversaries, so Christ was basely used. John 10:32.

CHAPTER TWENTY FOUR

Contents: David's mercy to Saul in En-gedi.

Characters: God, David, Saul.

Conclusion: Be not overcome of evil but overcome evil with good.

Key Word: Mercy (dealt well), v. 18.

Strong Verses: 12, 17.

Striking Facts: As David rendered good for evil to him from whom he had received evil for good, he was a type of Christ who saved His persecutors.

CHAPTER TWENTY-FIVE

Contents: Samuel's death; David and Nabal. Abigail becomes David's wife, and also Ahinoam.

Characters: God, David, Samuel, Nabal, Abigail.

Conclusion: Let the believer be encouraged to commit his cause to God when in any way injured, being assured that in His own good time God will redress the wrongs in His own way if we but sit still and leave the matter to Him.

Key Word: God avenges (returned the wickedness), v. 39.

Strong Verses: 28, 29.

Striking Facts: v. 44. Saul's defrauding David of his only rightful wife led him into the irregularity of having several wives. When the marriage knot is once loosed, it is seldom ever tied fast again. See Matt. 19:4, 5.

CHAPTER TWENTY-SIX

Contents: Saul spared by David a second time.

Characters: God, David, Saul, Abishai, Abner, Ahimelech.

Conclusion: No questionable means need be employed to help out God's plans for our advancement (v. 10) God can weaken the strongest and befool the wisest on our behalf. Wait His time.

Key Word: Spared, v. 11.

Strong Verses: 9, 10, 24.

Striking Facts: v. 24. As David's way to the throne lay through multiplied sorrows and difficulties, so does Christ's, who, though the anointed King with undisputed title, yet remains "meek and lowly" awaiting the set time.

CHAPTER TWENTY-SEVEN

Contents: David down in the dumps.

Characters: David, Schish, Ahmoan, Abigail.

Conclusion: Unbelief is a sin that besets those who have been undergoing long trials. It is no advantage to us when we are in the dumps, to cross over the borders into the world for comfort, for we cannot expect God's protection when we are out of His will.

Key Word: Discouragement (I shall perish), v. 1.

Strong Verses: 1.

Striking Facts:

CHAPTER TWENTY-EIGHT

Contents: David among Israel's enemies. Saul consults the witch.

Characters: God, David, Saul, Samuel, Achish, witch.

Conclusion: Seek the Lord while He may be found-for there is a time when He will not be found (v. 6). To think that any spiritualistic medium can be of help when God has frowned upon us, is to heap contempt upon God, who has expressly forbidden all such recourse.

Key Word: Spiritism, v. 7.

Strong Verses: 15, 16.

Striking Facts: v. 8. Never did Saul look so mean as when he went sneaking to a spiritist at night. Such works are of the darkness and cannot bear the light. Either Satan had Samuel impersonated, or else God on this occasion, actually sent back the spirit of Samuel, that Saul might get an answer to his design and should be given up to strong delusions.

CHAPTER TWENTY-NINE

Contents: David saved from fighting against Israel.

Characters: David, Achish.

Conclusion: God's providence orders wisely and graciously for His children even when they have sadly erred. Even the ill favor of men may turn out to be for our good that a door might be opened for deliverance out of straits our own folly have brought us into.

Key Word: Ill favor, v. 6.

Strong Verses: 6.

CHAPTER THIRTY

Contents: David avenges the destruction of Ziglag.

Characters: God, David, Abiathar, an Egyptian.

Conclusion: When we go abroad to tarry for a while with the enemies of God's people, we may expect to be met with evil tidings when we return home again. In the mercy of God, we can even then, if called according to His purpose, encourage ourselves in God and be assured that He will overrule and bring light out of darkness and peace out of trouble.

Key Word: Recovered, vv. 8, 18.

Strong Verses: 6.

CHAPTER THIRTY-ONE

Contents: Death of Saul and Jonathan.

Characters: Saul, Jonathan, Abinadab, Melchi-shua.

Conclusion: As men live, so will they die. Those are indeed in a deplorable condition, who, despairing of the mercy of God, would leap into a hell before them thinking to escape the hell within them. We all need to pray, "lead us not into temptation."

Key Word: Defeat, v. 8.

Strong Verses: 11, 12.

Striking Facts: The book which began with the birth of a godly man ends with the burial of a wicked man. Let the two lives teach us to prefer the honor that comes from God rather than that which Satan pretends to bestow.

II. SAMUEL

Key Thought:	Number of Chapters:	Key Verse:	Christ seen as:
Kingdom	24	1 Sam. 10:25	Seed of David

Writer of the Book:	Date:	Conclusion of the Book:
Uncertain	About 1155 B. C.	Be sure your sin will find you out.

SUMMARY

CHAPTER ONE

Contents: David mourns the death of Saul and Jonathan.

Characters: God, David, Saul, Jonathan, an Amalekite.

Conclusion: He that is deeply concerned for the honor of God cannot rejoice in the afflictions that come upon his enemies. In the disgrace that comes upon them, let us not forget their former successes and real service.

Key Word: Mourned, vv. 12, 17.

Strong Verses: 26, 27.

Striking Facts: v. 13. The killing of the Amalekite who brought the message was just. David made him own a second time that he was an Amalekite and in slaying him, David did what his predecessor should have done and was rejected for not doing.

CHAPTER TWO

Contents: David received as King of Judah. Abner makes Ish-bosheth king over eleven tribes. Civil war.

Characters: God, David, Abner, Ish-bosheth, Joab, Abishai, Asahel.

Conclusion: We may expect, one upon another, trials of our faith in the promises of God and of our patience, whether we can wait God's time for the performances of the promises.

Key Word: Annointed, v. 4.

Strong Verses: 1.

Striking Facts: v. 4. Jesus first presented Himself to Judah. Thus, like David, His kingdom is set up by degrees. He is Lord of all by divine designation but we see not yet all things put under His feet.

CHAPTER THREE

Contents: Abner deserts to David. Joab's murder of Abner.

Characters: God, David, Joab, Abner, Ish-bosheth, Michal, Phaltiel, Rizpeh, Abishai, Asahel.

Conclusion: Evil pursues sinners and will overtake them at the last in one way or another. (Illustrated both in the case of Abner and that of Joab, v. 29).

Key Word: Great man fallen, v. 38.

Strong Verses: 39.

Striking Facts: v. 37. The servants of the King of Kings do many things thinking to further His Kingdom, that have not His sanction and will bring trouble upon the heads of those who do them in His name without His leading.

CHAPTER FOUR

Contents: Murder of Ish-bosheth.

Characters: David, Ish-bosheth, Mephibosheth, Baanahm, Rechab.

Conclusion: The guilt of blood brings a curse, and if men do not avenge it, God will.

Key Word: Murder, v. 11.

Strong Verses: 11.

Striking Facts: v. 9. God had hitherto helped him in his difficulties and in coming to the throne, David would therefore depend upon Him and not the devices of men to complete His purpose. Let this teach us that Jesus Christ is coming to the throne, not by man dragging in the millenium but by the hand of God Himself.

CHAPTER FIVE

Contents: David becomes king over Israel. War with Philistines.
Characters: God, David, Hiram.
Conclusion: Those who have the Lord of Hosts for them need have no fear what hosts of men or demons can do against them. If we grow great and win many victories, we can only ascribe our advancement to God's favor with us.
Key Word: Annointed, v. 3, (victory, v. 25).
Strong Verses: 10, 19.
Striking Facts: David was recognized as king on three counts. (1) Of their flesh, v. 1. Christ, Matt. 25:40. (2) Their leader in battle, v. 2. Christ, Josh. 5:13-15. (3) Designated by God, v. 2. So also Christ, Rom. 3:25. As David had three annointings; one by God, one by Judah and one by all tribes, so Christ was annointed at His baptism, will be received of the Jews and later of all nations.

CHAPTER SIX

Contents: David seeks to bring the ark to Jerusalem.
Characters: God, David, Michal, Uzzah, Obed-edom, Abinadab.
Conclusion: God will have His work done in His own way and cannot bless us if we carry it on under wrong principles. We need to seek His directions continually lest we do good things in a wrong way.
Key Word: Ark, v. 2.
Strong Verses: 11.
Striking Facts: Careful directions had been given how the ark must be borne. Num. 4:1-15. David adopted a Philistine method. 1 Sam. 6:7, 8. We cannot expect God's blessing if we employ heathen methods in doing the work of Christ's church.

CHAPTER SEVEN

Contents: David's desire to build the Lord's house. The Davidic covenant.
Characters: God, David, Nathan.
Conclusion: We need no more to make us happy than to have God for a Father to us. If He is our Father, we must be dutiful children, or expect His chastisements, which are an article of the covenant and which flow from His father-love.
Key Word: Established (kingdom), v. 16, (confirmed, v. 24).
Strong Verses: 14, 22, 25.
Striking Facts: The covenant confirmed to David by the oath of Jehovah and renewed to Mary by the angel Gabriel, is immutable, and God will yet give to the thorn-crowned King the throne of His Father David forever. Luke 1:31-33; Acts 2:29-33, 15:1-17.

CHAPTER EIGHT

Contents: Full establishment of David's kingdom.
Characters: God, David, Hadadezer, Joram, Toi.
Conclusion: After the long and frequent struggles which the Christian has with the powers of darkness, he shall at last be made more than conqueror and shall reign with Christ.
Key Word: Reigning, v. 15.
Strong Verses: 14.
Striking Facts: The Son of David shall at length put down all principality and power and take the throne. He has, as David had, a line to kill and a line to save. The Gospel is to some a savor of life unto life and to others a savor of death unto death.

CHAPTER NINE

Contents: David's kindness to Mephibosheth.
Characters: God, David, Mephibosheth, Ziba, Machir, Micha.
Conclusion: Kindness is one of the laws of Christianity and the Christian should seek opportunity of doing good. The most necessitous are generally the least clamorous and the best objects of our kindness and charity are such as will be discovered only through our inquiry.
Key Word: Kindness, v. 7.
Strong Verses: 7.

Striking Facts: The story gives us a picture of salvation by God's grace in Christ. Grace comes to the helpless, those "sold under sin;" invites us to the place of peace and satisfaction; feasts us at God's table; keeps our lame feet out of sight.

CHAPTER TEN

Contents: The Ammonite-Syrian war.
Characters: David, Joab, Abishai, Hanun, Hadarezer, Shobach.
Conclusion: False men are ready to think all others as false as themselves. There is nothing so well meant but that it may be misinterpreted, and is likely to be so by men who love nobody but themselves. "Love thinketh no evil."
Key Word: Kindness misinterpreted, vv. 2, 3.
Strong Verses: 12.
Striking Facts: v. 5. The Christian may learn not to lay too much to heart the reproaches he receives for Christ's sake, for they will soon wear off and turn eventually to the shame of their authors. "God will bring forth thy righteousness as the light—wait patiently for Him."

CHAPTER ELEVEN

Contents: David's great sin.
Characters: David, Uriah, Bathsheba, Joab.
Conclusion: A Christian with natural tendencies to sensuality may have cravings even when the general bent of his mind is to live in God's will. The devil finds work for idle hands to do (v. 1) and we should therefore be warned of the danger of having nothing in particular to do. Sin started leads to more sin to hide it. After all, the atmosphere of trial and difficulty is the occasion of highest strength.
Key Word: Adultery, v. 4, (murder, v. 15).
Strong Verses: 11, 27.
Striking Facts: We need to bear in mind that as the chosen seed through which Messiah was to come, David and others of the direct line had the combined forces of evil against them to accomplish, if possible their downfall. Of all men, they should have walked in hourly dependence on God.

CHAPTER TWELVE

Contents: David's rebuke and repentance. Birth of Solomon. Ammonite victory.
Characters: God, David, Nathan, Bathsheba, Joab.
Conclusion: If the believer, brought face to face with his sins sincerely confesses and repents of them, he may be restored to fellowship, although God will not interfere with the consequences in this life, v. 1.
Key Word: Confession and restoration, v. 13.
Strong Verses: 13, 22, 23.
Striking Facts: God always has His man for His work and while it may cost the man nights of pain and prayer to deliver the message of Christ he may be sure that if God sent him, his message will accomplish its purpose. A dogmatic message is truer and more tender than soft speeches that do not arouse conscience.

CHAPTER THIRTEEN

Contents: Ammon's crime. Absalom's vengeance for Tamar's wrong.
Characters: David, Absalom, Ammon, Tamar, Jonadab.
Conclusion: Fleshly lusts are their own punishment and not only war against the soul but against the body also, and are the rottenness of the bones. The sin of adultery makes awful mischief in families and the sinner serves a hard master.
Key Word: Shame, v. 13, (avenged, v. 32).
Strong Verses: 39.
Striking Facts: v. 1. Those who are peculiarly beautiful have no reason, on that account to be proud, but great reason to stand upon their guard.

CHAPTER FOURTEEN

Contents: The recall of Absalom and David's forgiveness.
Characters: God, David, Joab, Absalom, woman of Tekoah, Tamar.

Conclusion: If we let private affections stand in the **way** of public duty (See Gen. 9:6) we may justly expect that God will make the one whom our foolish pity spares, a scourge upon us.

Key Word: Forgiven, v. 33.

Strong Verses: 14.

Striking Facts: v. 33. If the compassion of a father prevails to reconcile him to an impenitent son, shall penitent sinners doubt the compassion of God, in His Son, when they truly come to Him?

CHAPTER FIFTEEN

Contents: Absalom steals the love of ten tribes. David's flight.

Characters: God, David, Absalom, Ittai, Zadok, Abiathar, Hushai, Ahimaaz, Jonathan, Ahitophel.

Conclusion: He who steals one heart away from another by means of innuendos is the vilest of robbers, and especially when professed devotion to God is used as a pretext to carry out the design. (v. 7).

Key Word: Conspiracy, v. 12.

Strong Verses: 25, 26.

Striking Facts: The mother of this rebellious son was the daughter of a heathen king. David, in this unhappy issue of the marriage, has to smart for being unequally yoked with an unbeliever.

CHAPTER SIXTEEN

Contents: False servant of Mephibosheth. Shimea curses David. Absalom takes Jerusalem.

Characters: God, David, Abishai, Ziba, Shimei, Absalom, Hushai, Ahitophel.

Conclusion: A humble and tender spirit will turn reproaches into reproofs and so get good by them instead of being provoked at them. The world's smiles are more dangerous than its frowns.

Key Word: Cursed, v. 5.

Strong Verses: 11, 12.

Striking Facts: v. 9. David is herein a type of Christ who rebuked his disciples, who in zeal for His honor, would have used their miraculous powers on the heads of those who affronted Him. (Luke 9:55).

CHAPTER SEVENTEEN

Contents: Conflicting counsel of Ahitophel and Hushai.

Characters: God, David, Absalom, Ahitophel, Hushai, Shobi, Machir, Barzillai, Ahimaaz, Jonathan, Amasa, Joab.

Conclusion: It is to the comfort of all who fear God that He has an overruling hand in all counsels and a negative voice in all resolves, and laughs at men's projects against His annointed ones.

Key Word: Counsel, v. 15.

Strong Verses: 27, 28, 29.

Striking Facts: Absalom is a type of the false Messiah, who will gather an army against Christ the Greater David (Rev. 19:19), meeting his defeat in the brightness of Christ's coming.

CHAPTER EIGHTEEN

Contents: Battle of Mount Ephriam. Slaying of Absalom.

Characters: God, David, Absalom, Joab, Abishai, Ittai, Ahimaaz, a Cushite.

Conclusion: Those who exalt themselves shall be abased. It never pays to take counsel against the Lord and His annointed.

Key Word: Avenged, v. 31.

Strong Verses: 31, 33.

Striking Facts: As the false king was cast into a pit, so anti-Christ will be thrown into the bottomless pit at the coming of Christ, and then every tongue shall confess that Christ is King of Kings.

CHAPTER NINETEEN

Contents: Joab reproaches David's return to the throne.

Characters: David, Joab, Zadok, Abiathar, Shimei, Ziba, Abishai, Mephibosheth, Barzillai, Chimham, Amasa.

Conclusion: A good man and a good cause will again recover their credit and interest, though, for a time, they may seem to have lost them. The good services done will still be remembered when men come to their right minds.

Key Word: Return, v. 14.

Strong Verses: 22, 23.

Striking Facts: vv. 14, 15. Our Lord Jesus will rule in those who invite Him to the throne of their hearts, and not until He is invited

CHAPTER TWENTY

Contents: Joab murders Amasa. Suppression of Sheba's revolt.

Characters: David, Joab, Amasa, Sheba, Abishai.

Conclusion: We must not think it strange while in this world if the end of one trouble be the beginning of another, but God will bring us victoriously through them all, if we but trust in His wisdom.

Key Word: Traitor, v. 1.

Strong Verses: 20.

Striking Facts: vv. 12, 13. Wicked men think themselves safe if they can just conceal it from the eye of the world. The covering of blood with a cloth cannot stop its cry for vengeance in God's ears.

CHAPTER TWENTY-ONE

Contents: Three years famine. Saul's sons slain. War with Philistines.

Characters: God, David, Rizpah, Ishbi-benab, Abishai, Sebechai, Saph, Elhanan, Jonathan.

Conclusion: When we are under God's judgments, we should enquire the grounds of the controversy, and when the cause is revealed, should go to all lengths to make right the wrongs of the past, that God's full blessing may be renewed upon us.

Key Word: Recompense (atonement) v. 3.

Strong Verses: 3, 7.

Striking Facts: vv. 9, 13, 14. Through Christ who was hanged and made a curse for us to expiate our guilt, though He was Himself guiltless, God is entreated for us. In token of the completeness of the sacrifice they took Him down from the cross and laid Him in the sepulchre.

CHAPTER TWENTY-TWO

Contents: David's song of deliverance.

Characters: God, David.

Conclusion: No believer has so little from God but there is ground for praise, nor so much but that he has need to call upon God. Praise is the blossom of prayer.

Key Word: Praise, vv. 4, 50.

Strong Verses: 2, 3, 4, 31, 33, 48.

CHAPTER TWENTY-THREE

Contents: Last words of David. Deeds of his mighty men.

Characters: God, Holy Spirit, David, Joshebbasheth, Adino, Eleazar, Shammah, Abishai, Benaiah, other great men.

Conclusion: Those who have ventured themselves for the good of the public are worthy of double honor, both to be respected by their fellow citizens and to be remembered by their posterity. Though our deeds be not recorded by men, they are recorded in heaven.

Key Word: Mighty men, v. 8.

Strong Verses: 2.

Striking Facts: vv. 3, 5. The verses have a prophetic application to Christ who is to be the just ruler, ordering all things according to His Father's will, and who will be as the light of the morning.

CHAPTER TWENTY-FOUR

Contents: David's sin in numbering the people. His choice of punishment.

Characters: God, angel (Jesus), Joab, David, Gad, Araunah.

Conclusion: God does not judge of sin as we do.   What appears to us to be but a small offense, may be a great sin in the eyes of God who knows men's principles, being a discerner of the thoughts and intents of the heart.   His judgments are according to the truth.

Key Word: Sinned, v. 10.

Strong Verses: 10, 24.

Striking Facts: v. 25.   Christ is our altar and sacrifice.   Through Him alone may we expect to get favor with God and to escape His wrath for our sins.

I. KINGS

Key Thought:	Number of Chapters:	Key Verse:	Christ seen as:
Royalty	22	2:12	King of Kings

Writer of the Book:	Date:	Conclusion of the Book:
Uncertain	About 560 B. C.	Jehovah is the sovereign ruler of Israel blessing the obedient, punishing the disobedient, and forgiving the penitent.

SUMMARY

CHAPTER ONE

Contents: David's declining strength. Adonijah plots to seize kingdom. Counter plot of Nathan and Bath-sheba. Solomon annointed.

Characters: God, David, Solomon, (Adonijah), Joab, Nathan, Bath-sheba, Zadok, Benaiah, Abiathar, Jonathan, Abishag, Shimei, Rei.

Conclusion: When men exalt themselves, God very often leaves them to themselves until they are corrected with a scourge of their own making. He that in the morning grasps at a crown, may before night be forced to hold to the horns of the altar and beg for life. God will be consulted.

Key Word: Self-exalted, v. 5 (humbled, v. 50).

Strong Verses: 29, 30.

Striking Facts: v. 39. Solomon is a type of Christ as Prince of Peace, (Isa. 9: 6; 1 Chron, 22:9) Jesus will not fulfill the Solomon type until He has fulfilled the David type. Chosen before born (Isa. 42:1) Rode into Jerusalem on a mule (Jn. 12:14-16) Annointed (Acts 10:38) Peace filled the earth when His reign was finally set up (Zech. 14:9).

CHAPTER TWO

Contents: David's charge to Solomon, David's death. Execution of Adonijah. Abiathar removed. Execution of Shimei.

Characters: God, David, Solomon, Bath-sheba, Adonijah, Abishag, Joab, Abiatha, Benaiah, Shimei.

Conclusion: The punishment of sin may be slow of foot but it is sure of nose and will at length find the offender. Even a hoary head, ought not to be any man's protection from justice.

Key Word: Punishment, vv. 5, 8.

Strong Verses: 2, 3.

CHAPTER THREE

Contents: Alliance of Solomon and Pharoah. Marriage with Pharoah's daughter. Loses at Gibeon. Solomon's prayer. His wisdom.

Characters: God, Solomon, two women.

Conclusion: The wisdom of God is laid up for those who have the spirit of a child (Lk. 10:21) vv. 8, 9. A knowledge of our own limitations is very essential to true success, if we have learned that the power of the omnipotent God is at our disposal.

Key Word: Wisdom, vv. 9, 28.

Strong Verses: 7.

Striking Facts: Wisdom: Its beginning, Psa. 111:10. Its source, Dan. 2:20-22. Its quality, Jas. 3:17. Way to it, 1 Cor. 3:18. Personification of it, 1 Cor. 1:30. How to obtain it, Jas. 1:5. Who is it for, Mt. 7:24-25.

CHAPTER FOUR

Contents: Princes and commissaries of Israel. Solomon's reign and wisdom.

Characters: God, Solomon.

Conclusion: There is spiritual peace and joy and a holy security for all faithful subjects of God's Annointed One.

Key Word: Safety, v. 25.

Strong Verses: 25.
Striking Facts: Solomon was a type of Christ in whom are hidden all the treasures of wisdom and knowledge—hidden for a use—for "He is made unto us wisdom."

CHAPTER FIVE

Contents: Preparation for building the temple.
Characters: God, Solomon, Hiram.
Conclusion: Satan does all he can to hinder the work of God's temple, but when he is withheld for a time, we should be extra zealous in that which is good that we might carry it forward to completion. (Acts 9:31).
Key Word: Temple, v. 5.
Strong Verses: 5, 17.
Striking Facts: v. 17. The costly stones speak of Christ who was laid for the foundation of the spiritual temple, an elect and precious stone.

CHAPTER SIX

Contents: Work on the temple begun. Dimensions and materials.
Characters: God, Solomon.
Conclusion: We should not mistake noise and notoriety for spiritual progress (v. 7). Quietness and order both become and befriend the carrying on of spiritual work.
Key Word: Finished, v. 14.
Strong Verses: 12.
Striking Facts: Christ is the true Temple (Jn. 2:21). God Himself prepared Him. (Eph. 1:4; Heb. 10:5). In Him all God's spiritual children meet and through Him have access to God.

CHAPTER SEVEN

Contents: Work on the temple and Solomon's house.
Characters: God, Solomon, Hiram.
Conclusion: God who is best should be served and honored with our best.
Key Word: Work ended, v. 51.
Strong Verses: 51.
Striking Facts: The temple is not only a type of Christ but of the believer who is also spoken of as a temple, or habitation of God. (1 Cor. 3:16-17; 6:19). It should be as beautiful as the Holy Spirit can make it, therefore we should be yielded to His master strokes.

CHAPTER EIGHT

Contents: Ark brought in; Skekinah glory fills the temple. Solomon's sermon.
Characters: God, Solomon.
Conclusion: All cost and pains are lost on stately structures unless God has been in the work, and if He fails to manifest His glory in them, they are after all but a ruinous heap. A temple without the ark and the glory are like a candlestick without a candle.
Key Word: Dedicated (filled with glory) v. 11.
Strong Verses: 10, 27, 57, 58, 61.
Striking Facts: It is a great thing when a nation's ruler can be led of the Spirit in prayer and when he realizes that all answer to prayer is only on the ground of the shed blood of Christ. vv. 22, 62. (Heb. 9:22; 10:19-20).

CHAPTER NINE

Contents: Jehovah appears to Solomon. Covenant made. Solomon's fame
Characters: God, Solomon, Hiram.
Conclusion: God deals plainly with men and, sets before them blessing or cursing. God never fails to perform His part of a covenant and if we improve the grace He is willing to give, He will confirm us to the end.
Key Word: Covenant, v. 4.
Strong Verses: 9, 25.
Striking Facts: v. 7. (Israel shall be a byword) lit. a "sheninah." Some have thought that the epithet "sheeney" used in speaking disgustingly of Jews throughout the centuries, came from this prophecy.

CHAPTER TEN

Contents: Solomon and the queen of Sheba. His revenue and splendor.
Characters: God, Solomon, queen of Sheba.
Conclusion: That fame is true fame which has associated with it the name of the Lord and which challenges inquiry into the means of God's grace.
Key Word: Fame, vv. 7, 23.
Strong Verses: 8, 24.
Striking Facts: Mt. 12:42. Christ mentions this queen's inquiry after God through Solomon as showing the stupidity of those who would not enquire after God through Jesus Christ who was God manifest in the flesh and therefore better able to instruct them than anyone else.

CHAPTER ELEVEN

Contents: Solomon's heart turned. Chastened of God. Rise of Jeroboam. Death of Solomon.
Characters: God, Solomon, Hadad, Pharaoh, Rezon, Jeroboam, Adoram, Ahijah.
Conclusion: The way of sin is down hill and those who get into it cannot easily get untangled. God at first appointed one woman for one man, and he who thinks one not enough, will not be satisfied with two. When our love is set on the things of the flesh, we may be sure we have lost our love for God and are on the way to trouble.
Key Word: Backslidden, v. 9 (heart turned).
Strong Verses: 9.
Striking Facts: v. 32. The house of David must, in spite of everything be kept intact, because out of it was to come the Messiah. As it was spared on account of the promise to David, so all God's favors shown to us are for Christ's sake and the covenant made with Him.

CHAPTER TWELVE

Contents: Accession and folly of Rehoboam. Kingdom divided.
Characters: God, Rehoboam, Jeroboam, Adoram, Shemiah.
Conclusion: Taking the counsel of unspiritual men always spells blunder and a rough answer never fails to bring division. If we make God the source of our counsel (Jas. 3:15) we will avoid all folly.
Key Word: Counsel forsaken, vv. 8, 13.
Strong Verses: 7.
Striking Facts:—The golden calf was set up where the first altar to God had been placed (v. 29 Gen. 12:8). All isms originate in man's heart (v. 26), have a selfish purpose back of them (v. 27-29) and are launched on a pretense that it is for the people's good; yet always tend to sin and idolatry.

CHAPTER THIRTEEN

Contents: Warning of punishment for idolatry. Disobedience and death of the prophet.
Characters: God, Jeroboam, disobedient prophet, lying prophet.
Conclusion: If we offer to God that which is an abomination to Him (the worship of the flesh) the offerer will certainly fall under the wrath of God.
Key Word: Warning, v. 2.
Strong Verses: 4, 8.
Striking Facts: v. 9. God would teach His servants not to have fellowship with the works of darkness, lest they fall under their contagion and give them encouragement. The devil always has his snares ready to entrap one who bears Christ's message.

CHAPTER FOURTEEN

Contents: Prophecy against Jeroboam and partial fulfillment. Judah's apostacy under Rehoboam and his death.
Characters: God, Ahijah, Jeroboam, Rehoboam, Shishak, wife and son of Jeroboam.
Conclusion: Be not deceived; God is not mocked and often He makes quick work of sinners. If men of prominence do wickedly they involve many

others who follow their pernicious ways (v. 16) and he who leads many others to hell must answer eternally for it.
Key Word: Cut off, v. 10.
Strong Verses: 9, 16.

CHAPTER FIFTEEN

Contents: Accession of Abijam and Asa over Judah.   War with Baasha. League with Syria.   Accession of Nadab over Israel and Baasha over Israel.
Characters   God, Abijam, Asa, Nadab, Baasha, Ben-hadad.
Conclusion   Divine threatenings are not bugbears, for no word of God shall fall to the ground.   The harboring of evil **MUST** eventuate in open defeat and ruin.
Key Word: Wars, vv. 6, 16, 20, 29, 32.
Strong Verses: 4, 11.
Striking Facts: v. 14 (Cp. v. 18) A heart perfect with the Lord is not sinless perfection, nor flawless obedience, but sincerity of intent and desire to do Christ's will.

CHAPTER SIXTEEN

Contents: Evil reigns of Baasha, Elah, Zimri, Omri, Ahab—kings of Israel.
Characters: God, Baasha, Jehu, Elah, Zimri, Omri, Ahab, Jezebel, Tibni, Hiel, Segub.
Conclusion: Destruction, when it comes, whoever is the instrument of it, is the act of God's justice and the result of sin.   Those who resemble others in their sins may expect to get similar plagues.
Key Word: God provoked, v. 2.

CHAPTER SEVENTEEN

Contents: Elijah's ministry and prediction of drought.   Elijah fed.   Raising of the widow's son.
Characters: God, Elijah, Ahab, Sarephath woman, her son.
Conclusion: God can wonderfully raise up servants and suit them to the work He designs them for.   He can, if He chooses, use one man to arrest the downward movement of a nation, and with no weapon but the Word of God and prayer.
Key Word: Man of God, v. 24.
Strong Verses: 1, 24.
Striking Facts: God marvelously provides for His true servants in times of sore testing.   He may be called upon at times to live from hand to mouth, but if it be from God's hand, each day's need will be supplied.
v. 13. "Bring it to me." Cp. Mt. 14:18. Herein Elijah is a type of Christ as our provider.

CHAPTER EIGHTEEN

Contents: Elijah goes to meet Ahab and gives challenge.   Contests with the priests of Baal.
Characters: God, Elijah, Jezebel, Obadiah, Baal,—priests.
Conclusion: The man of faith need not be afraid to risk his all on the honor of God (v. 23).   Let opposers who talk of the failure of Christianity, do what it does—bring down the consuming, cleansing, illuminating power of God into the lives of men.
Key Word: Challenge, v. 24.
Strong Verses: 21, 37, 39.
Striking Facts: Those who are given great power for public service for God, need to constantly humble themselves before God and give Him all the glory.   He who bows lowest in the presence of God will be able to stand straightest in the presence of sin.

CHAPTER NINETEEN

Contents: God's care of His overwrought prophet.   Call of Elisha.
Characters: God, Elijah, Jezebel, Elisha.
Conclusion: Even though we faint in our faith, God abideth faithful.   The best thing for a discouraged man is to get where he can see from God's

viewpoint (v. 11) which he can do only by coming before God in prayer.
Key Word: Discouragement, v. 4.
Strong Verses: 7, 18.
Striking Facts: v. 12. Under law God spoke to His people with terror, but in the Gospel of Christ, which was introduced in the spirit and power of Elias, He speaks by a still small voice which makes none afraid. Heb. 12:18.

CHAPTER TWENTY

Contents: Ahab's Syrian campaigns and victories. His sin in sparing Ben-hadad.
Characters: God, Ahab, Ben-hadad, two prophets.
Conclusion: Enemies are more than a match for us, but no match for Jehovah. God often uses one wicked man to scourge another.
Key Word: Victory, (vv. 13, 28); Disobedience, (v. 42)
Strong Verses: 13.
Striking Facts: v. 42. There are times when keeping back the sword from blood is doing the work of God deceitfully. Foolish pity spoils many a victory.

CHAPTER TWENTY-ONE

Contents: Ahab covets Naboth's vineyard. Elijah announces Ahab's doom.
Characters: God, Elijah, Ahab, Naboth, Jezebel.
Conclusions: One may covet and get what it is not God's will for them to have, but he may be sure that with it, he will get a curse. Coveteousness opens the door for all sin.
Key Words: Coveting, v. 4.
Strong Verses: 3, 29.
Striking Facts: Coveteousness was the first sin in Eden (Gen. 3:6) first on entering the promised land (Josh. 7:21) first in the early church (Acts 5:1-3).

CHAPTER TWENTY-TWO

Contents: Alliance of Ahab and Jehosophat. Ahab's ultimate defeat.
Characters: God, Jehoshaphat, Ahab, Micaiah, Zedekiah, Syrian king, false prophets, Ahaziah.
Conclusion: He who joins himself in affinity with vicious men, rejects the counsels of God and hates the preachers of God's Word, will find that no masquerade will hide him from God's judgment and that no armor is proof against His vengeance.
Key Word: Alliance, v. 4. (Defeat, v. 37).
Strong Verses: 14.
Striking Facts: v. 14. The greatest kindness possible to a person going on a dangerous path is to tell them God's truth, as it is in Christ. Through self-styled prophets multitudes are led on their way to destruction.

II. KINGS

Key Thought:	Number of Chapters:	Key Verse:	Christ seen as:
Rolalty	25	10:10	Kings of Kings

Writer of the Book:	Date:	Conclusion of the Book:
		God's Word is certain
Uncertain (Ezra)	About 560 B. C.	of fulfillment to saint and sinner.

SUMMARY

CHAPTER ONE

Contents: Elijah's message to Ahaziah. Elijah's deliverance.
Characters: God, angel (Jesus), Elijah, Ahaziah.
Conclusion: Those who will not inquire of the Word of God for their comfort will be made to listen to it, whether they wish it or not. To consult with the devil's agents as to fortune means departure from God.
Key Word: Prediction, v. 4.
Strong Verses: 15.
Striking Facts: v. 15. All heaven is interested in Christ's true servants. Who can harm those whom God will shelter?

CHAPTER TWO

Contents: Translation of Elijah. Faith of Elisha. Theological students and their unbelief. Elisha's miracle.
Characters: God, Holy Spirit, Elisha, Elijah.
Conclusion: Those who know they are soon going to heaven should be concerned for those they are leaving behind to carry on God's service and to leave with them their experiences, testimonies, counsels and prayers.
Key Word: Translated, v. 11.
Strong Verses: 9.
Striking Facts: Those who ask for the mantle of and walk in the steps of their godly and faithful predecessors will certainly experience the same grace. Jordan means "judgment" Christ and the believer go together (v. 8) through the judgment of the cross. Gal. 2:20; Rom. 6:3.

CHAPTER THREE

Contents: Accession of Jehoram over Israel. Moab rebels against Israel. Elisha's reproof of alliance between Jehoshaphat and Jehoram. Defeat of Moabites.
Characters: God, Jehoram, Jehoshaphat, Mesha, king of Moab, king of Edom, Elisha.
Conclusion: It would often go hard with us if God did not take more care of us, both for body and soul, than we take for ourselves. For reasons which He alone knows, God sometimes puts victories in the hands of those who are not faithful to Him.
Key Word: Victory, v. 18
Strong Verses: 18.

CHAPTER FOUR

Contents: Increase of the widow's oil. Woman of Shunom and her son restored to life. Noxious pottage healed. A hundred men fed.
Characters: God, Elisha, widow, Shunanmite woman, Gehazi, sons of prophets, man of Baalshalishah.
Conclusion: Be a man of God and God will give you His work to do, He who has power from God to satisfy the deepest needs of man will never want for applicants.
Key Word: Man of God, vv. 7, 9, 16, 21, 22, 40, 42.
Strong Verses: 6, 7, 40, 41.
Striking Facts: v. 41. When the theological student feeds on the wild

gourds of the world, he will find himself in the grip of spiritual death. The meal, made of bruised corn, speaks of Christ in the Gospel. If the results of the cross are put in the pot, it will take away its poison.

CHAPTER FIVE

Contents: Naaman the Syrian healed by obeying Elisha's word.

Characters: God, Elisha, Naaman, maid, Syrian king, king of Israel, Gehazi.

Conclusion: There is little hope for one who is more concerned about his dignity than his disease, but full blessing is assured to one who will humble himself as a little child and walk in the light of God's commands.

Key Word: Leper cleansed, vv. 1, 14.

Strong Verses: 13, 15.

Striking Facts: Leprosy is an intense symbol of sin. 1. Circulates in the blood, hereditary. 2. Contagious. 3. Subtle, at first concealing its presence. 4. Unclean, a state of living death. 1 Tim. 5:6. 5. Banishing, Rev. 21:27. 6. Incurable by human power, Jer. 13:23. 7. Its only cure, the power of Christ.

CHAPTER SIX

Contents: Elisha recovers the lost axe. Seige of Samaria by Syrians.

Characters: God, Elisha, Ben-hadad, Jehoram, nameless woman.

Conclusion: The Christian on his knees can see more than the philosopher on his tiptoes. They who fight against God are given up to delusions, not knowing that the believer has God, (Rom. 8:13) Christ, (Mt. 28:20) the Holy Spirit, (Jn. 16:16-17) and angels (Heb. 1:14) on his side.

Key Word: Man of God, v. 9 (Prayer, v. 17).

Strong Verses: 16.

Striking Facts: v. 6. The God of nature is not tied up to its laws. As He raised the iron against the natural laws, so His grace can raise the iron heart which has sunk into the mud of this world and raise up affections naturally earthly to things above.

CHAPTER SEVEN

Contents: Jehovah's terror upon the Syrians.

Characters: God, Elisha, Jehoram, captain of Israel, four lepers.

Conclusion: Faith expects from God what is beyond all human expectation. They who cannot find it in their hearts to take God at His Word, forfeit all benefits of His promises.

Key Word: Promise fulfilled, vv. 1, 16.

Strong Verses: 6, 7.

Striking Facts: vv. 6, 7. The wicked flee when no man pursues. God can, if He wills, dispirit the boldest and most brave enemy of Christ's cause, and make the stoutest heart to tremble at the shaking of a leaf.

CHAPTER EIGHT

Contents: Famine predicted. Jehoram restores the Shunanmite land. Reigns of Jehoram and Ahaziah of Judah and Joram of Israel.

Characters: God, Elisha, Gehazi, Jehoram, Ben-hadad, Hazael, Ahaziah, Shunanmite woman.

Conclusion: God through His ministers, calls for reformation and obedience, and if the calls be not regarded, men may expect plagues and evil days to come, for He WILL be heard. (vv. 1, 12).

Key Word: Prediction, vv. 1, 10.

Strong Verses: 19.

Striking Facts: v. 13. Men often think themselves sufficiently armed against those sins by which they are afterward entirely overcome.

CHAPTER NINE

Contents: Jehu annointed king of Israel. Slays Jehoram, Ahaziah and Jezebel.

Characters: God, Elisha, a prophet, Jehu, Jezebel, Jehoram, Ahaziah, Ahab.

Conclusion: God doesn't always pay up for sin every week, but in the end, He pays. He is known by His judgments.

Key Word: Sin requitted, vv. 26, 36.

Strong Verses: 26.

Striking Facts. v. 11. Men who have no religion commonly look upon followers of Christ as mad. Of the Savior they said, "He is beside himself."
Of John, "He has a devil." Of Paul, "Much learning hath made thee
mad."

CHAPTER TEN

Contents: Judgment on house of Ahab. Princes of Judah slain. Baal worship put out. Jehu's reign and death.
Characters: God, Jehu, Jehonadab, Hazael.
Conclusion: God is not the author of any man's sin, but even by that which
men do from bad principles, He serves His own purposes and takes vengeance on those who have defied Him.
Key Word: Judgment, vv. 10, 17.
Strong Verses: 10.
Striking Facts: v. 16. If we aim at the applause of men and make their
praise our highest aim, instead of the honor of Christ, we are upon a false
bottom. An upright heart approves itself to God and covets no more
than His acceptance.

CHAPTER ELEVEN

Contents: Royal seed of Judah destroyed. Joash becomes king. Execution
of Athaliah. Revival through Jehoida.
Characters: God, Joash, Jehoida, Athaliah, Jehoshaba.
Conclusion: All attempts to frustrate God's revealed purpose are foolish and
bound to be fruitless. Who can disannul what God has purposed? Though
the promise be bound up in one life, yet will it not fail
Key Word: Preserved, v. 3.
Strong Verses: 17.
Striking Facts: Three times the royal line was all extinct except for one
babe. Moses, Heb. 11:23; Joash, v. 3. Christ, Mt. 2:12-16.

CHAPTER TWELVE

Contents: Reign of Joash over Judah and his death. Repair of the temple.
Characters: God, Joash, Jehoida, Hazael.
Conclusion: Those who are entrusted with public money for the carrying on
of God's work should learn to deal faithfully, as those who know God
will reckon with them, if men do not. Loose financial methods in the
church dishonor God.
Key Word: Repairing temple, v. 5.
Strong Verses: 2, 15.
Striking Facts: v. 9. This is the first mite box mentioned in the Bible.
The last one is in Mk. 12:4.

CHAPTER THIRTEEN

Contents: Reign of Jehoahaz over Israel and his death. Accession of Jehoash
and his death. Elisha's death and the miracle at his tomb.
Characters: God, Elisha, Jehoahaz, Jehoash, Hazael.
Conclusion: The slowness of God's processes against sinners must be con-
strued to the honor of His mercy, not to the impeachment of His justice
(v. 23). It is of the Lord's mercies, that they are not consumed.
Key Word: Gracious, v. 23.
Strong Verses: 4, 23.
Striking Facts: v. 14. It is much to our spiritual advantage to attend the
death beds of Christlike men that we might hear their last counsels.

CHAPTER FOURTEEN

Contents: Reign of Amaziah over Judah. War between Israel and Judah.
Reign of Jeroboam in Jerusalem.
Characters: God, Amaziah, Jehoash, Jeroboam, Jonah, Azariah.
Conclusion: Those who are too eager, through pride, to fight, may get enough
of it in quick order. Many would have honor and wealth enough, if they
but knew when they had enough.
Key Word: Defeat, v. 12.
Strong Verses: 26, 27.

CHAPTER FIFTEEN

Contents: Reign of Azariah and Jotham over Judah and Zechariah, Shallum, Menahem, Pekahiah, Pekah over Israel.

Characters: God, Azariah, Jotham, Zechariah, Shallum, Menahem, Pul, Pekahiah, Pekah, Rezin, Ahaz.

Conclusion: God may for a time suffer wickedness to prosper that it may of itself carry away the wealth and honors that might have been kept if God had been recognized. One wicked man is made the scourge of another and every wicked man sooner or later ruins himself.

Key Word: Reigns.

Strong Verses: 12.

CHAPTER SIXTEEN

Contents: Reign of Ahaz over Judah. Assyrians take Damascus.

Characters: God, Ahaz, Tiglath-pileser, Urijah, Rezin, Pekah.

Conclusion: That religion is of no worth which is guided by fancy instead of faith (v. 10). The hearts of idolaters walk after their eyes.

Key Word: Abominations, v. 3.

CHAPTER SEVENTEEN

Contents: Reign of Hoshea in Israel. Israel becomes tributary to Assyrians. The sins of Israel.

Characters: God, Hoshea, Shalmaneser, So.

Conclusion: Those who forget God may themselves expect to be forgotten. Those who try to be like the world may expect to be swallowed up by the world. Those who will not serve God in their own land need not be surprised if they are forced to serve enemies in a strange land.

Key Word: Carried away, vv. 6, 18.

Strong Verses: 13, 14, 37, 39.

Striking Facts. v. 7. From this captivity, Israel has never been restored to Palestine. See Deut. 28:15-68. A remnant of Judah returned but the national restoration is yet to be fulfilled.

CHAPTER EIGHTEEN

Contents: Reign and revival of Hezekiah over Judah. Victory over Phillistines. Invasion of Sennacherib. Insolence of Rab-shekeh.

Characters: God, Hezekiah, Hoshea, Shalmaneser, Sennacherib, Eliakim, Shebnah, Tartan, Rabsaris, Rab-shakeh, Joah.

Conclusion: Santanic suggestions are always artful and cleverly managed and well sprinkled with pride, malice, falsehood and blasphemy. Thus Satan steals a man's watch and explains it so well, the victim gives him his coat and vest.

Key Word: Seducers, v. 30.

Strong Verses: 6, 7.

CHAPTER NINETEEN

Contents: Hezekiah's message to Isaiah and the answer. Sennacherib defies God. Hezekiah's prayer and the answer through Isaiah.

Characters: God, angel (Jesus), Hezekiah, Isaiah, Sennacherib, Eliakim, Shebna, Rab-shakeh.

Conclusion: Prayer changes things. If the motive of our prayer is the honor of God, we may be sure He will graciously and copiously answer, being able to do exceeding abundantly above all that we ask or think.

Key Word: Prayer answered, vv. 19, 34.

Strong Verses: 15, 34.

Striking Facts: v. 30. The remnant shall yet again be planted in their own habitations and shall take root there and grow rich. That soul is indeed prosperous who takes root downward by faith in Christ, and then becomes fruitful upward in righteousness.

CHAPTER TWENTY

Contents: Hezekiah's illness and recovery.

Characters: God, Hezekiah, Isaiah, Berodach-baladan.

Conclusion: Neither greatness nor goodness can exempt us from sickness, yet often when the death sentence has apparently been received within the body, it is reversible through Spirit-born, faith-filled prayer.

Key Word: Healed, v. 5.

Strong Verses: 5.

Striking Facts: v. 7. It is duty to make use of legitimate means to assist nature when we are sick, unless God has by a special revelation made it clear that He intends to heal entirely by miraculous power. Medicines are God-given and He has graciously made them serviceable to man in consideration of the poor.

CHAPTER TWENTY-ONE

Contents: Evil reigns of Manasseh and Amon in Judah.

Characters: God, Manasseh, Amon.

Conclusion: Those have much to answer for who not only are wicked themselves but help to make others so. v. 16.

Key Word: Evil reigns, vv. 2, 20.

Strong Verses: 11, 12.

CHAPTER TWENTY-TWO'

Contents: Reign of Josiah. Repairing temple and finding of the book of the law.

Characters: God, Josiah, Hilkiah, Shaphan, Huldah, Ahikam, Achbor, Asahiah.

Conclusion: An unread Bible is a lost Bible and a lost Bible always means spiritual degeneracy and its accompanying curses. When man finds the Word, the Word is quick to find him and convict him of sin. Either sin keeps one from the Book or the Book keeps one from sin.

Key Word: Bible found, v. 13.

Strong Verses: 13, 19.

CHAPTER TWENTY-THREE

Contents: Law read to the people. The king's covenant and reformations.

Characters: God, Josiah, Hilkiah, Pharaoh-neche, Jehoahaz, Jehoikim, Eliakim.

Conclusion: We should put ourselves heartily into God's hands for service and as far as our influence goes, our endeavors should go to do good and bring the wickedness of the wicked to an end.

Key Word: Covenant, v. 3.

Strong Verses: 3, 25.

CHAPTER TWENTY-FOUR

Contents: Jehoikim tributary to Nebuchadnezzar. Reigns of Jehoikim, Jehoichin and Zedekiah. Deportation to Babylon.

Characters: God, Jehoiakim, Jehoiachin, Zedekiah.

Conclusion: Time will not wear out the guilt of sin. Threatenings will be fulfilled as certainly as promises if the sinner's repentance prevent not.

Key Word: Judgment, vv. 3, 14.

Strong Verses: 3.

CHAPTER TWENTY-FIVE

Contents: Seige of Jerusalem and final deportation.

Characters: God, Zedekiah, Nebuchadnezzar, Gedaliah, Ishmael, Evil-merodach, Jehoiachin.

Conclusion: Those who have by sin provoked God to leave them may expect ultimately to be encompassed about with innumerable evils.

Key Word: Broken up, v. 4.

Striking Facts: v. 30. Let none say they shall never see good again because they have so long seen nothing but evil, for we know not what good turn providence may yet give to our affairs according to the days wherein we have been afflicted. Psa. 90:15.

I. CHRONICLES

Key Thought: Temple	Number of Chapters: 29	Key Verse: 2 Chron. 15:2	Christ seen as: God's true King

Writer of the Book: Uncertain (Ezra)	Date: About 1000 B. C.	Conclusion of the Book: Jehovah is the sovereign Lord blessing the obedient and punishing the disobedient.

SUMMARY

CHAPTER ONE

Contents: Genealogy: Adam to dukes of Edom. The patriarchal line.
Characters: Adam, Noah, Shem, Abraham, Isaac, Ishmael, Esau, Israel.
Conclusion: We are all by nature the seed of Adam. Let us see to it that by faith we become the spiritual children of Abraham. Rom. 4:11-12.
Key Word: Genealogy.

CHAPTER TWO

Contents: Genealogy, sons of Judah.
Characters: Jacob, Judah, Boaz, Jesse, David.
Conclusion: The best and most honorable families may have those belonging to them who are black sheep.
Key Word: Genealogy.

CHAPTER THREE

Contents: Genealogy of David's line.
Characters: David, Solomon, Rehoboam, Jehoshaphat, Hezekiah, Manasseh, Josiah, Zerrubabbel.
Conclusion: Since piety and devotion are not hereditary, it behooves all parents to consecrate their children to God long before they are born and to do their best to bring them up in the nurture and admonition of the Lord, praying for the coming generations.
Key Word: Genealogy.
Striking Facts: From David's line our Lord came, as regards the flesh, as appears from Lk. 3:31.

CHAPTER FOUR

Contents: Posterity of Judah and Simeon.
Characters: God, Jabez, Caleb.
Conclusion: If we set ourselves to acknowledge God in all our ways we put ourselves under the divine blessing and protection and will be prospered accordingly. (v. 10).
Key Word: Genealogy.
Strong Verse: 10.

CHAPTER FIVE

Contents: Line of Reuben, Gad, half of Manasseh. Captivity for their sins.
Characters: Reuben, Judah.
Conclusion: In all conflicts we must look up to heaven for strength and it is believing prayer that will be prevailing prayer.
Key Word: Genealogy
Strong Verses: 20, 22.
Striking Facts: v. 22. If we depend upon a commission from God to wage war upon another country we may depend upon His providence to give success.

CHAPTER SIX

Contents: Sons of Levi. Cities of the priests and Levites.
Characters: Gershom, Kohath, Merari, Aaron, Moses and Miriam.
Conclusion: There is always abundance of service to be done by God's children

in His house. As everyone has received the gift, therefore let him minister according to all that God has commanded.

Key Word: Genealogy.

Strong Verses: 49.

CHAPTER SEVEN

Contents: Sons of Issachar, Benjamin, Naphtali, Manasseh, Ephriam, Asher.

Characters: As above, Joshua.

Conclusion: (v. 22). It is often the burden of those who live to be old that they see their children go before them. It is a brotherly and friendly office on the part of the Christian, to comfort such in their afflictions with the Word of God.

Key Word: Genealogy.

Striking Facts: v. 21. Ephriam had been promised a seed that should become a multitude (Gen. 48:19) and here the promise seems defeated. God's providences many times seem to contradict His promises, but eventually God makes the promise more illustrious by wonderfully fulfilling it.

CHAPTER EIGHT

Contents: Sons of Benjamin. The stock of Saul and Jonathan.

Characters: Ehud, Saul, Jonathan.

Conclusion: (v. 40). It is much to a man's praise that he is qualified to serve his country being mighty in valor, even though not a child of God.

Key Word: Genealogy.

CHAPTER NINE

Contents: Record of the Israelites. The charge of certain Levites.

Characters: God, Eleazar, Saul, Jonathan.

Conclusion: God's work is likely to be done well when each knows the duty of his place and makes a business of it. That which is everybody's work in the church will generally be nobody's work.

Key Word: Inhabitants.

CHAPTER TEN

Contents: Saul's overthrow and death. Triumph of the Philistines. Saul's sin.

Characters: God, Saul, Jonathan, David.

Conclusion: Those who abandon themselves to the devil's leading will be abandoned by God and their doom will be according to their transgressions.

Key Word: Retribution, v. 13.

Strong Verse: 13.

Striking Facts: v. 6. Those who love their children will avoid sin lest they bring ruin on their children with themselves or entail a curse upon them in later years.

CHAPTER ELEVEN

Contents: David becomes King of Israel. Catalog of his mighty men.

Characters: God, David, Joab, Jashobeam, Eleazar, Abishai, Benaiah.

Conclusion: God's counsels will be fulfilled at last, whatever seeming difficulties lie in the way.

Key Word: Anointed (king). v. 3.

Strong Verse: 9.

Striking Facts: v. 10. The honors of Christ's kingdom are prepared for those who fight the good fight of faith and are willing to venture even life itself for Christ's sake.

CHAPTER TWELVE

Contents: David's army at Ziglag. The leaders who made David king.

Characters: Holy Spirit, David, Amasai, Jehoiada.

Conclusion: It is good to take sides with those who take sides with God and have God with them. Let us therefore testify our allegiance to the Lord Jesus and make ourselves His helpers without reservation.

Key Word: Helpers, vv. 1, 21.

Strong Verses: 22, 38.

Striking Facts: vv. 38-39. When Christ is enthroned in a soul, there is bound to be great joy, and a great feast begins, to last not merely for a few days but throughout eternity.

CHAPTER THIRTEEN

Contents: David's attempt to bring the ark to Jerusalem. The ark left at the house of Obed-edom.
Characters: God, David, Uzzah, Obed-edom, Abinadab, Ahio.
Conclusion: Beware of presumption, rashness and irreverence in dealing with holy things and think not that a good intention will always justify a rash action. We must not trifle in our approaches to God.
Key Word: Ark. v. 3.
Strong Verses: 14.
Striking Facts: There are preachers who lay hands on the doctrines of God's Word, thinking to save Christianity from overthrow. It is dangerous to put unsanctified hands on the person of Christ, His virgin birth, atonement, resurrection, etc.

CHAPTER FOURTEEN

Contents: The prosperity of King David. Double defeat of the Philistines.
Characters: God, David, Hiram.
Conclusion: David's frequent inquiry of God should direct us in all our ways to acknowledge Him and in all our perplexities to fly to Him that we might perceive God to go before us.
Key Word: Kingdom exalted, v. 2.
Strong Verse: 16.
Striking Facts: v. 17. God has highly exalted our Redeemer, David's greater Son and given Him a name above every name.

CHAPTER FIFTEEN

Contents: Ark brought to Jerusalem in the appointed way.
Characters: God, David, Zadok, Abiathar, Michael, Uriel, Asaiah, Joel, Shemaiah, Eliel.
Conclusion: It is not enough that we seek God in a due ordinance, but we must seek Him in due order. When those who have suffered for their irregularity learn from God's Word to be obedient in all details, the correction is well bestowed.
Key Word: Ark brought, vv, 15, 25.
Strong Verses: 13, 28.
Striking Facts: v. 26. Those who bear the vessels of the Lord have great need of divine help in their ministrations, that Christ may be glorified in them and the churches edified through them.

CHAPTER SIXTEEN

Contents: David's festival and psalm of thanksgiving. The ark established in Jerusalem.
Characters: God, David, Zadok, Asaph, Obed-edom, Heman, Jeduthun.
Conclusion: Though God's Word may be clouded and eclipsed for a time, it will at length shine out of obscurity, wherefore let us encourage ourselves to triumph and trust in God and glorify Him continually by our praises.
Key Word: Praise, v. 4.
Strong Verses: 8, 15, 31, 34.
Striking Facts: v. 10. Ceremonial worship was a divine institution containing the types of the mediation of Christ and could not therefore be omitted. So the church should keep up the appointed ordinances in which Christ is remembered, until He comes.

CHAPTER SEVENTEEN

Contents: David's desire to build the temple. The Davidic covenant and David's prayer.
Characters: God, David, Nathan.
Conclusion: Thrice happy is that people whose God is Jehovah, for He will be to them a God all-sufficient (v. 27). Whom He blesses are truly and eternally blessed, therefore let our desires and hopes be for things eternal.

Key Word: Covenant, v. 23.
Strong Verses: 20, 27.
Striking Facts: v. 7. David is here a type of Christ in the flesh, the Shepherd King. At His first coming He took the Shepherd's place. At His return He will take the place of ruler over Israel.

CHAPTER EIGHTEEN

Contents: David's kingdom fully established.
Characters: God, David, Hadarezer, Tou, Hadoram, Abishai, Joab, Jehoshaphat, Benaiah.
Conclusion: Those who take God along with them whithersoever they go may expect to prosper and be preserved whithersoever they go.
Key Word: Judgment and justice, v. 14.
Strong Verses: 6, 13.
Striking Facts: All opposing rule will eventually be put down by the Son of David and the most inveterate enemies shall fall before Him, acknowledging that He is Lord to the glory of the Father.

CHAPTER NINETEEN

Contents: Ammonite-Syrian war.
Characters: God, David, Joab, Abishai, Hanun, Shophach, Hadarezer.
Conclusion: Those who design ill themselves are apt to be jealous and to suspect ill of others without cause, but the hearts of such are marked for ruin. Right will prevail at last.
Key Word: Misjudged, v. 3.
Strong Verses: 13.
Striking Facts: v. 19. Let those who in vain have stood out against Christ be wise for themselves and agree with Him quickly while they are in the way.

CHAPTER TWENTY

Contents: Joab and David take Rabbah. War with Philistines.
Characters: David, Joab, Sibbechai, Sippai, Jonathan, Elhanan.
Conclusion: The power and pride of great men against us need not terrify us if we have the power and peace of God with us. God takes pleasure in abasing lofty looks and mortifying the giants who array themselves against Christianity.
Key Word: War, v. 4.

CHAPTER TWENTY-ONE

Contents: David's sin in numbering the people. Joab's faithful protest. David's choice of punishment.
Characters: God, Satan, David, Joab, Gad, Ornan, angel (Jesus)
Conclusion: God does not judge of sin as we do. What appears to man to be but a small offense may be a great sin in the eyes of God who knows men's principles, being a discerner of the thoughts and intents of the heart. His judgments are according to the truth.
Key Word: Sin, v. 8.
Strong Verses: 8, 13.
Striking Facts: v. 18. If we have sinned, the safest thing to do is to flee to Christ, who is an altar and sacrifice, for through Him alone there is hope of winning back the joy of salvation and getting favor with God.

CHAPTER TWENTY-TWO

Contents: Material prepared for the temple. David instructs Solomon in God's promises. Princes charged to assist Solomon.
Characters: God, David, Solomon.
Conclusion: Nothing is more powerful to engage us in any service for God than to know that hereunto we were appointed by God. Where God gives rest He expects work (v. 9-10) let us therefore be invigorated for Christian service.
Key Word: Temple, v. 10.
Strong Verses: 13, 19.

Striking Facts: Everything about the temple was to be stately and magnificent, being a type of Christ in whom all fullness dwells and in whom are hid all treasures.

CHAPTER TWENTY-THREE

Contents: Number and distribution of the Levites.
Characters: God, David.
Conclusion: There is a place in the service of God for every Christian and God would have each at his own post, for of all men an idle Christian makes the worst figure. No place in God's service is commonplace unless it be made so by an unworthy spirit.
Key Word: Service, v. 4.
Strong Verse: 25.

CHAPTER TWENTY-FOUR

Contents: The divisions of the priests and Levites for the temple service.
Characters: God, David, Zadok, Ahimelech, Eleazer, Ithamar.
Conclusion: God was, and is still, the God of order, particularly in the things of His worship. Every Christian should therefore pray to know his place in the work of God and should keep to it.
Key Word: Service, vv. 3, 19.
Striking Facts: In the mystical body of Christ every member has its use for the good of the whole. Rom. 12:4-5; 1 Cor. 12:12.

CHAPTER TWENTY-FIVE

Contents: The offices of the temple singers.
Characters: God, David, Asaph, Jeduthun, Heman.
Conclusion: The glory and honor of God should be extolled in the music of the church whether vocal or instrumental, making melody from the heart as to the Lord. (Eph. 5:19.)
Key Word: Sacred song, v. 6.

CHAPTER TWENTY-SIX

Contents: The division of the temple porters. Levites as treasurers. Officers and judges
Characters: God, Shelemiah, Zechariah, Shuppin, Hozah, Obed-edom.
Conclusion: Whatever service God wishes men for, He either finds them fit or makes them so. All service for God is honorable, and happy will be that man who is faithful to his appointed part.
Key Word: Ministry, v. 12.
Striking Facts: The temple treasuries illustrate the plenty there is in our Father's house, enough and to spare. In Christ, the true Temple, are hid all treasures of wisdom and knowledge and riches to supply all the believer's needs.

CHAPTER TWENTY-SEVEN

Contents: The captains for each month. Princes of the twelve tribes. David's several officers.
Characters: God, David, Joab, Jonathan, Jeluel, Ahitophel, Hushai, Jehoiada, Abiathar.
Conclusion: It is the wisdom of rulers in providing for public safety to seek to make it effectual and yet easy and as little as possible burdensome to the people.
Key Word: Officers, v. 1.
Striking Facts: v. 24. A good man cannot, if he stops to reflect, be pleased with that which he knows displeases Christ nor take comfort in that which is obtained through unbelief in God's promises.

CHAPTER TWENTY-EIGHT

Contents: David counsels Israel and Solomon concerning the temple.
Characters: God, David, Holy Spirit (v. 12), Solomon.
Conclusion: As the time apparently draws nigh for God's servants' to die,

they should put forth every effort to counsel and encourage their successors, calling attention to the patterns God has given in His Word.

Key Word: Counsel, v. 2.

Strong Verses: 8, 9, 20.

Striking Facts: The Gospel temple of Christ, being builded of living stones, is all being framed according to the divine counsels, ordained before the foundation of the world for God's glory. In bringing it to completion we should cling to the plans given in the New Testament.

CHAPTER TWENTY-NINE

Contents: David exhorts the people. The princes and people willingly offer. David's thanksgiving and prayer. Solomon made king. David's death.

Characters: God, David, Solomon, Zadok.

Conclusion: Those whose affections are set upon the service of God will think no pains nor cost too much to bestow upon it and God loveth a cheerful giver.

Key Word: Willing offerings, v. 6.

Strong Verses: 9, 11, 12.

Striking Facts: v. 25. Solomon's glorious and peaceful kingdom is a type of the coming kingdom of the Messiah on earth. His will be indeed "the throne of the Lord" (v. 23) for the Father will commit all judgment to Him.

II. CHRONICLES

Key Thought:	Number of Chapters:	Key Verse:	Christ seen as:
Temple	36	15:2	God's true King.

Writer of the Book:	Date:	Conclusion of the Book:
Uncertain (Ezra)	About 530 B. C.	Seeking and serving the Lord is the secret of a vital religion and a life of victory. *

SUMMARY

CHAPTER ONE

Contents: Solomon's sacrifices at Gibeon. His vision and prayer and God's answer.

Characters: God, Solomon.

Conclusion: Those who make this world their end come short of the other and are never satisfied with this. Those who make the other world their end and seek spiritual gifts, not only obtain these with full satisfaction, but enjoy much of this world on their way there.

Key Word: Prayer, v. 7.

Strong Verses: 11, 12.

Striking Facts: The Christian's real character appears in his choices and desires. "What wouldst thou have?" tries a man as much as "What wouldst thou DO?" v. 7.

CHAPTER TWO

Contents: Preparation to build the temple.

Characters: God, Solomon, Hiram, King of Tyre.

Conclusion: (vv. 4-6) It becomes us to go about every work for God with a due sense of our utter insufficiency for it and our incapacity in ourselves to do anything adequate to the divine perfections.

Key Word: Temple, v. 4.

Strong Verses: 6.

Striking Facts: The artificer was a Gentile, a good omen of uniting Jew and Gentile in the Gospel temple, which is Christ, v. 14

CHAPTER THREE

Contents: Temple begun. The materials and dimensions.

Characters: God, Solomon.

Conclusion: God's Word prescribes all the details of how His work is to be carried on. Nothing can be added to or subtracted from God's perfect plans.

Key Word: Temple, v. 1.

Striking Facts: The temple was built at Jerusalem (v. 1). As it typified Christ it was fitly built there; since it was there He raised up the temple of His body.

CHAPTER FOUR

Contents: Further details about the temple.

Characters: God, Hiram the artificer.

Conclusion: Everything in the temple directed the worshipper to the great propitiation. So should we in all our devotions keep the eye of faith upon Jesus Christ who was the fulfillment of all.

Key Word: Temple.

CHAPTER FIVE

Contents: The ark brought in. The glory fills the house.

Characters: God, Solomon.

Conclusion: When God's work is carried out according to His revealed will and done in the spirit of unity with praise, He is certain to own it and to give a special manifestation of His presence.

Key Word: Glory, v. 14.
Strong Verses: 14.
Striking Facts: The ark was a type of Christ, and as such a token of the presence of God. The temple would be a desolate place indeed if Christ was not in it to glorify it.

CHAPTER SIX

Contents: Solomon's sermon and prayer.
Characters: God, Solomon.
Conclusion: Those who set God before them and walk before Him with all their hearts, will find Him as good as His word and better. He will both keep covenant with them and show mercy to them. (v. 14.)
Key Word: Dedication, v. 12.
Strong Verses: 14, 41.
Striking Facts: v. 20. We may with confidence pray to God to be well pleased with us because we are in Jesus Christ in whom God is well pleased. He says not now of any house "this is my beloved place," so there is but one safe shelter—Christ.

CHAPTER SEVEN

Contents: Divine acceptance. Sacrifice and rejoicing. God appears to Solomon.
Characters: God, Solomon.
Conclusion: The surest evidence 'of God's acceptance of our prayers is the descent of His holy fire upon us. The heart to which God manifests Himself is thereby owned as a living temple.
Key Word: Accepted, vv. 1, 12.
Strong Verses: 1, 14.
Striking Facts: v. 1. Christ, our sacrifice, was made sin and a curse for us and the sacrifice was consumed by the fire of God's wrath against sin that we might escape, and inherit His perfect righteousness.

CHAPTER EIGHT

Contents: The energy and fame of Solomon.
Characters: God, Pharaoh's daughter, Solomon, King of Tyre.
Conclusion: When our hearts are truly set on God's work, we find our Father in heaven ready to indulge us in many innocent desires and to give us success in our undertakings.
Key Word: Solomon's work, v. 16.

CHAPTER NINE

Contents: Solomon and the queen of Sheba. His revenue and splendor.
Characters: God, Solomon, queen of Sheba.
Conclusion: Those who honor God, He will honor. The best way to get the credit of our endowments as well as the full enjoyment of them is to consecrate them to God and use them for Him.
Key Word: Fame, v. 1.
Strong Verses: 8.
Striking Facts: The lustre of Solomon's kingdom was typical of the glory of the coming kingdom of Christ and a faint representation of His throne to be set up when He returns.

CHAPTER TEN

Contents: Accession and folly of Rehoboam. Division of the kingdom. Accession of Jeroboam over Israel.
Characters: God, Rehoboam, Jeroboam, Ahijah, Hadoram.
Conclusion: Taking counsel of men who know not God is sure to mean serious blunders, and a rough answer never fails to bring division. Good words cost nothing and purchase great things.
Key Word: Foolish counsel, v. 8.

CHAPTER ELEVEN

Contents: Rehoboam returns to Jerusalem. Jeroboam rejects the worship of God
Characters: God, Rehoboam, Jeroboam, Abijah, Shamaiah.

Conclusion: It is dangerous to undertake anything contrary to the will of God, and he is wise who, when he finds himself going contrary to God's plans, lets his own plans drop.
Key Word: Deterred, v 4.
Striking Facts: v. 14. Christ's representatives should never allow a secular advantage to keep them among worshippers of the devil or in any place where they are in danger of making shipwreck of faith and conscience.

CHAPTER TWELVE

Contents: Rehoboam defeated by Shishak. Death of Rehoboam.
Characters: God, Rehoboam, Shishak, Shemaiah.
Conclusion: It becomes us, when we are under the rebukes of providence, to justify God (v. 6) and humble ourselves (v. 12), thereby we may be saved from total ruin, though we have to bear a part of God's judgment.
Key Word: Humbled, v. 7.
Strong Verses: 12.

CHAPTER THIRTEEN

Contents: War between Abijah and Jeroboam. Death of Jeroboam.
Characters: God, Abijah, Jeroboam.
Conclusion: Right may indeed go by the worst for a time, but it will prevail at last. The battle is ours, if God be for us.
Key Word: Reliance (on God), v. 18.
Strong Verses: 10, 12.
Striking Facts: v. 18. The prayer of faith is the prevailing prayer and it is by faith in Christ's mediation that we overcome the world. 1 John 5:4.

CHAPTER FOURTEEN

Contents: Death of Abijah. Accession of Asa. Asa's victory over Zerah.
Characters: God, Asa, Zerah.
Conclusion: He who has sought God in the day of peace and prosperity can with holy boldness cry to Him in the day of testing and God will have delight in giving him a great victory.
Key Word: Rest (on God) v. 11.
Strong Verses: 11.
Striking Facts: v. 7. Those have rest indeed who have the peace of Christ, for He gives not as the world gives. John 14:27.

CHAPTER FIFTEEN

Contents: Warnings of Azariah. Reform under Asa.
Characters: God, Holy Spirit, Azariah, Asa, Oded, Maachah.
Conclusion: If we turn aside from God and His ordinances, He is not tied to us, but will certainly cease to act for us, when we will discover that present triumphs are no security to us. If we keep praying we will keep prevailing.
Key Word: Reform v. 8.
Strong Verses: 2, 7, 15.
Striking Facts: v. 8. Attachment to Christ means detachment from idols. 1 Thes. 1:9.

CHAPTER SIXTEEN

Contents: War between Asa and Baasha. Asa's rebuke and death.
Characters: God, Asa, Hanani, Baasha, Ben-hadad.
Conclusion: God is much displeased when He is distrusted and when the arm of flesh is relied on more than His power and goodness. Since we have the Rock of Ages to rely upon, let us not lean upon broken reeds.
Key Word: Unbelief, vv. 7, 12.
Strong Verses: 9.
Striking Facts: v. 12. (Physicians) Egyptian healers whose methods were demonical, answering to spiritualism, Christian Science, New Thought, clairvoyancy, etc., of our own time. The help of physicians is good if we trust not to the physician but to Christ the Great Physician.

CHAPTER SEVENTEEN

Contents: Accession of Jehoshaphat and his growing power.
Characters: God, Jehoshaphat.
Conclusion: True religion and obedience to God are the best friends to outward prosperity.
Key Word: Obedience, v. 4.
Strong Verses: 3, 4
Striking Facts: v. 3 (ways of David) Note that Jehoshaphat followed David as far as David followed God. Paul exhorts us to be followers of him, but only as far as he followed Christ. 1 Cor. 11:1.

CHAPTER EIGHTEEN

Contents: Jehoshaphat's alliance with Ahab. Ahab's lying prophets. Micaiah's true prophecy. Defeat and death of Ahab.
Characters: God, Jehoshaphat, Ahab, Micaiah, Zedekiah, king of Syria, lying spirits.
Conclusion: Some men's kindnesses are dangerous and their society infectious. There can be no surety of being in familiar converse with wicked people and yet getting no hurt by them.
Key Word: Ungodly alliance, v 1.
Strong Verses: 13.
Striking Facts: v. 21. One evil spirit can make use of 400 prophets to deceive those who will not receive the love of the truth. Beware of the false prophets who speak in Satanic energy.

CHAPTER NINETEEN

Contents: Jehu rebukes Jehoshaphat's alliance with Ahab.
Characters: God, Jehoshaphat, Jehu, Amariah, Zebadiah.
Conclusion: Rebuke a wise man and he will take warning (Prov. 9:8-9) and if he truly repents, he will be particularly concerned to recover those who have fallen into sin or been hardened in it by his example.
Key Word: Returned, v. 4.
Strong Verses: 7.

CHAPTER TWENTY

Contents: Jehoshaphat's prayer for deliverance and its answer. Invading armies stricken.
Characters: God, Holy Spirit, Jehoshaphat, Jahaziel, Ahaziah.
Conclusion: Faith takes God's bonds, knowing they are as good as ready money (v. 19). If the battle is God's and we are on God's side, we may be certain of shortly being made more than conquerors through Him that loved us. This is the victory, even our faith.
Key Word: Believing, v. 20.
Strong Verses: 9, 17
Striking Facts: v. 26 The valley of Berachah, lit. "blessing" (modern Bible class name—Baraca) was perpetuated for the encouragement of succeeding generations to trust in God and to remind us that our praises should be as oft repeated as our prayers.

CHAPTER TWENTY-ONE

Contents: Jehoram's wicked reign over Judah and its accompanying disasters.
Characters: God, Jehoram, Elijah, Libnah.
Conclusion: Bad men bring judgment upon themselves and all about them. Wickedness makes men despicable even in the eyes of those who have little religion, and the name of the wicked shall rot. (v. 19.)
Key Word: Evil, v. 6.
Strong Verses: 7.

CHAPTER TWENTY-TWO

Contents: Accession of Ahaziah over Judah. Athaliah's wicked plot.
Characters: God, Ahaziah, Athaliah, Joram, Jehu, Jehoshaphat, Joash, Jehoshabeath.
Conclusion: The counsel of the ungodly is the ruin of many. Those who forsake the divine guidance of the Holy Spirit and the Word debase and destroy themselves.

Key Word: Evil, v. 4.
Striking Facts: Three times the royal seed was extinct except for a single babe whom God preserved. 1. Moses, Heb. 11:23. 2. Joash. 3. Jesus, Matt. 2:12, 16.

CHAPTER TWENTY-THREE

Contents: Joash becomes king of Judah. Execution of Athaliah. Revival through Jehoiada.
Characters: God, Jehoiada, Athaliah, Joash.
Conclusion: Some who are themselves most guilty are commonly most forward to cry "treason" at others. Evil doers will surely be cut down like the grass and wither as the green herb, then shall the righteous shine forth as the noonday.
Key Word: Execution, v. 15.
Strong Verses: 16.
Striking Facts: v. 21. When the Lord Jesus is enthroned upon the heart and the usurper of the life put down, all is quiet and springs of joy are opened.

CHAPTER TWENTY-FOUR

Contents: Reign of Joash. Temple repaired. Zechariah stoned. Judah defeated by Syrians.
Characters: God, Holy Spirit, Joash, Jehoiada, Zechariah, Zabad, Jehozabad, Amaziah.
Conclusion: It is easier to build temples than to be a temple of the Holy Spirit. Outward religious zeal is no substitute for inward spiritual vision. (vv. 4, 24.)
Key Word: Repaired (temple), v. 6; judgment, v. 24.
Strong Verses: 10, 20.
Striking Facts: vv. 24-26. If vengeance pursues men, the end of one trouble will be but the beginning of another.

CHAPTER TWENTY-FIVE

Contents: Reign of Amaziah over Judah. War between Judah and Israel.
Characters: God, Amaziah, Joash, man of God, Obed-edom.
Conclusion: Trust in God means to be willing to venture the loss of anything for Him, knowing that He can more than make up any damage we sustain in obeying His commands. A firm belief in God's all-sufficiency to bear us out in our duty, will make His yoke easy and His burden light.
Key Word: Counsel despised, v. 16.
Strong Verses: 8.
Striking Facts: v. 2. Amaziah is an illustration of many today, who live moral lives, yet not enemies to Christ. He that is not with Christ is counted against Him.

CHAPTER TWENTY-SIX

Contents: Accession of Uzziah. His successes and fame.
Characters: God, Uzziah, Zechariah, Jotham, Isaiah.
Conclusion: The world's smiles are the devil's darts and prosperity ruin as many as adversity. It is dangerous to be strong except in the Lord and the power of His might.
Key Word: Pride, v. 16.
Strong Verses: 5.
Striking Facts: Humility is always the safest plan for it brings Christ's successes into our lives. Psa. 105:4.

CHAPTER TWENTY-SEVEN

Contents: Reign of Jotham in Judah and his death.
Characters: God, Jotham.
Conclusion: The more steadfast we are in religion, the mightier we shall be for the resistance of evil and the performance of good
Key Word: Mighty, v. 6.
Strong Verses: 6.

CHAPTER TWENTY-EIGHT

Contents: Reign of Ahaz. War with Rekah. Intercession of Oded. Edomite and Philistine invasion.

Characters: God, Ahaz, Syrian king, Tiglath-pileser, Zechri, Pekah, Oded.

Conclusion: If men will not be humbled by God's judgments, God will find means to bring them low and will make them as despicable as they have been formidable.

Key Word: Brought low, v. 19.

Strong Verses: ¯, 8,

Striking Facts: v. 16. Estrangement from Christ is generally followed by seeking protection from the enemies of Christ, v. 20, but no enemy of Christ can strengthen the people of God.

CHAPTER TWENTY-NINE

Contents: Hezekiah's reign in Judah and the revival. Temple restored.

Characters: God, Hezekiah.

Conclusion: Those who begin with God begin at the right end of their work and will prosper accordingly. Let us do our part to revive the work of God and ascribe to Him all the glory of what is done.

Key Word: Cleansed, v. 15.

Strong Verses: 11, 27.

Striking Facts: v. 22. Even repentance and reformation will not obtain pardon but through Christ who was made our sin offering we may find peace. With our offering, our praises should ascend, because Christ has been made unto us righteousness.

CHAPTER THIRTY

Contents: Preparations for the passover and its observance.

Characters: God, Hezekiah.

Conclusion: In every true reformation, the doctrine of the atonement must be emphasized. God's grace will meet us in our deepest difficulties if they are felt and confessed and if we approach Him by the blood-sprinkled way.

Key Word: Passover, v. 1.

Strong Verses: 8, 9.

Striking Facts: v. 15. Christ our passover was sacrificed for us. 1 Cor. 5:7. When He is trusted as the Lamb of God who heareth away sin, God is in a position to heal us and to give us the joy of salvation.

CHAPTER THIRTY-ONE

Contents: Idols destroyed and other reforms of Hezekiah.

Characters: God, Hezekiah, Azariah, Cononiah, Kore.

Conclusion: Vital communion with God on the ground of the shed blood will kindle in us a holy zeal and an indignation against sin and all that is offensive to God.

Key Word: Prospered, v. 21.

Strong Verses: 10, 21.

Striking Facts: v. 10. If one has tasted the sweetness of the passover Lamb, which is Christ, he will never grudge the expenses of carrying on His work, but will freely give as he has freely received.

CHAPTER THIRTY-TWO

Contents: Invasion of Sennacherib. His army defeated in answer to prayer.

Characters: God, Hezekiah, Isaiah, angel.

Conclusion: A believing confidence in God will raise us above the prevailing fear of man. The good soldier of Jesus Christ can always say "If God be for us, who can be against us?"

Key Word: Trust, v. 8.

Striking Facts: Satan is ever determined to destroy the believer's faith in Christ's all-sufficiency, knowing that if he can but scare him, his point is won. When thus tempted, we should betake ourselves immediately to Christ who will instantly give the victory.

CHAPTER THIRTY-THREE

Contents: Manassah's accession and evil ways. Reign and death of Amon. Accession of Josiah.

Characters: God, Manasseh, Assyrian king, Amon, Josiah.

Conclusion: In prosperity men forget God, but in adversity they can find no other refuge. Blessed be the affliction that brings one to his knees, for the divine mercy far exceeds the divine vengeance.

Key Word: Sin, v. 2; repentance, v. 12.

Strong Verses: 12, 13.

Striking Facts: v. 16. God is ever ready to accept and welcome returning sinners who entreat Him on the grounds of Christ's atoning sacrifice.

CHAPTER THIRTY-FOUR

Contents: Reign of Josiah. Book of the law found and read.

Characters: God, Josiah, Hilkiah, Shaphan, Huldah, Maaseiah, Joah, Ahikam, Abdon, Asaiah.

Conclusion: When man finds the Word, the Word finds man and reveals to him his true condition. If heartily received, it will lead to cleansing, consecration and continuance in the ways of God.

Key Word: Reform, v. 33.

Strong Verses: 27.

Striking Facts: A Bible may be lost through disregard, disobedience or distortion. It may be found again by recognizing it, receiving it and ransacking it.

CHAPTER THIRTY-FIVE

Contents: The passover kept. Death of Josiah.

Characters: God, Josiah, Pharaoh-Necho, Jeremiah.

Conclusion: Religion cannot flourish if the passover is neglected. Christ, our passover, is sacrificed for us and it is well for us to be continually put in mind of His atoning death through the ordinances of the church.

Key Word: Passover, v. 1.

Striking Facts: v. 13. The Lamb roast with fire, suggests Christ who was subjected to the fires of God's wrath against sin. He cannot be feasted upon except in view of the substitutionary character of His atoning death.

CHAPTER THIRTY-SIX

Contents: Reign and dethronement of Jehoahaz. Final deportation. Captivity of Judah in Babylon.

Characters: God, Jehoahaz, Jehoiachin, Jehoikim, Nebuchadnezzar, Zedekiah, Cyrus, Eliakim, Necho.

Conclusion: God gives sinners both time and inducement to repent and waits to be gracious to them, but if they will profane God's institutions by their sins, it is just with God to suffer them to be profaned by their enemies.

Key Word: Wrath, v. 16.

Strong Verses: 16.

Striking Facts: v. 16. God's methods to reclaim sinners by His Word, by faithful ministers, by providences, by conscience, show His great compassion through Christ and unwillingness that any should perish.

EZRA

Key Thought: Restoration	Number of Chapters: 10	Key Verse: 1:5	Christ seen as: Lord of heaven and earth

Writer of the Book: Ezra	Date: About 536 B.C.	Conclusion of the Book: God's Word should have a place and power in the religious, social and civil life of His people.

SUMMARY

CHAPTER ONE

Contents: Decree of Cyrus for restoration of the temple and preparations for the return of the remnant.

Characters: God, Cyrus, Sheshbazzar, Mithredath.

Conclusion: (v. 1) The hearts of kings are in the hand of the Lord and like the rivulets of water, He turns them whatever way He wills. Therefore whatever good offices are done for the church, God must have the glory.

Key Word: Temple, v. 2.

CHAPTER TWO

Contents: The returning remnant.

Characters: God, Zerubbabel.

Conclusion: Sin debases and diminishes a nation but God always has a faithful remnant who love the ceremonies of His house and give liberally and cheerfully for its upkeep.

Key Word: Remnant's return, v. 1.

Strong Verses: 68, 69.

Striking Facts: Persons from all tribes returned under Zerrubabel, but in the broad sense, the dispersion of Israel still continues and the tribes cannot be identified. Only God knows who they are. At the revelation of Jesus Christ they will be made known.

CHAPTER THREE

Contents: Altar set up and temple foundations relaid. Worship established.

Characters: God, Zerubbabel, Jeshua.

Conclusion: To see any branch of God's work reestablished after long desolations cannot but open fountains of joy and praise in those who love God. We should be thankful for even the beginnings of mercy though we have not yet seen the perfection of it.

Key Word: Established, v 11.

Strong Verses: 11, 13.

Striking Facts: v. 3. If we have enemies, the safest course is to keep on intimate terms with God through His Son Jesus Christ who is typified in the daily Lamb and whose righteousness must be our confidence in all our supplications.

CHAPTER FOUR

Contents: Work hindered by adversaries.

Characters: Zerubbabel, Ahasuerus, Jeshua, Artazerxes, Rehum, Shimshai.

Conclusion: God's work cannot be advanced but Satan will rage and the gates of hell will fight against it. Wonder not at the church's enemies but keep an eye single to God who will ultimately give the victory.

Key Word: Hindered, v. 4.

Strong Verses: 3.

Striking Facts: v. 14. A secret enemy to Christ and His Gospel is often guilded over with a pretended affection to Caesar and his power. The worst enemy is one who claims to be a Christian but is not.

CHAPTER FIVE

Contents: Encouragement of the prophets and the work resumed.
Characters: Zerubbabel, Haggai, Zechariah, Jeshua, Tattenai, Darius, Shethar-bozenai.
Conclusion: It is a sign that God has mercy in store for a people when He raises up men of God among them to encourage and help them in His work. When we cannot do what we would in His service, we should take courage and do all we can.
Key Word: Work resumed, v. 2.
Striking Facts: v. 2. It is the business of Christian ministers to stir up God's people to that which is good, especially to the work of completing the temple of Christ which is being erected out of "living stones."

CHAPTER SIX

Contents: Darius confirms the decree of Cyrus. Temple furnished and worship restored.
Characters: God, Darius, Haggai, Zechariah, Tattenai, Shethar-bozenai, Cyrus.
Conclusion: When God's time has come for the accomplishment of His gracious purposes concerning His church, He will raise up instruments to promote it and from men of whom good service was not expected. The wrath of the enemy may be made to praise God.
Key Word: Finished, v. 14.
Strong Verses: 10, 21, 22.
Striking Facts: v. 10. Let men in authority despise not the prayers of the meanest saints who know how to approach God on the ground of Christ's sacrifice. Let God's people pray for those in authority.

CHAPTER SEVEN

Contents: Ezra's expedition to Jerusalem and his thanksgiving.
Characters: God, Ezra, Artaxerxes.
Conclusion: God is able to do for us exceedingly abundantly above all that we ask or think. When magistrates are moved to encourage the work of the church, we should thank God who put it into their hearts to do so.
Key Word: Decree, v. 13.
Strong Verses: 10, 23.

CHAPTER EIGHT

Contents: List of Ezra's companions and his visit to Jerusalem. Treasure placed in the temple.
Characters: God, Ezra, Sherebeah, Hashabiah, Meremoth, Eleazar, Jozabad, Noadiah.
Conclusion: God's servants have His power engaged for them. Those who trust in God will be ashamed of seeking much to the creature for protection. In carrying out God's commissions, we are safe under the shadow of His wings. (v. 22.)
Key Word: Furthered, v. 36.
Strong Verses: 22.
Striking Facts: v. 23. Even the common dangers of our everyday journeys are such as to oblige us to sanctify our going out with prayer and our return in peace with thanksgiving through Jesus Christ.

CHAPTER NINE

Contents: The remnant loses its separated position. Ezra's prayer and confession.
Characters: God, Ezra.
Conclusion: Let this be the comfort of true penitents, that though their sins have piled up to heaven, God's mercy is in the heavens and if we confess our sins, trusting to the sacrificed One, God is faithful and just to forgive, and to cleanse from all unrighteousness.
Key Word: Confession, v. 6.
Strong Verses: 6, 13, 14.
Striking Facts: v. 5. The evening sacrifice was a type of the propitiation

of the Lamb of God, who, in the evening of the world, took away sin by the sacrifice of Himself. With the eye of faith fixed upon that sacrifice we may confess our sins and hope for full cleansing.

CHAPTER TEN

Contents: Separation restored. Strange wives surrendered.

Characters: God, Ezra, Shecaniah, Jonanan.

Conclusion: There is hope concerning people when they are convinced not only that it is good to part with their sins, but indispensably necessary lest they be undone.

Key Word: Separated, v. 11.

Strong Verses: 1, 11.

Striking Facts: v. 19. The only way of obtaining pardon for sin is to seek it on the ground of Christ's sacrifice, who was our trespass offering, so owning our guilt and His blood as that which washes away the stain and guilt of sin.

NEHEMIAH

Key Thought:	Number of Chapters·	Key Verse:	Christ seen as:
Political	13	2:5	Lord of heaven and earth.

Writer of the Book:	Date:	Conclusion of the Book:
Nehemiah	About 445 to 448 B.C.	Prayer, pains and perseverance are the conditions of successful work for God.

SUMMARY

CHAPTER ONE

Contents: Nehemiah learns of distress in Jerusalem. His prayer.

Characters: God, Nehemiah, Hanani.

Conclusion: The desolation and distresses of the church should deeply concern the Christian and move him to earnest prayer, for there is no other method for bringing relief to God's people, or directions for ourselves as to the way in which we should render help.

Key Word: Fasting and prayer, v. 4.

Strong Verses: 10.

Striking Facts: v. 8. Our best pleas in prayer are those taken from the Word of God on which He has caused us to hope through Jesus Christ. If God were not more mindful of His promises than we are of His precepts, we would be undone.

CHAPTER TWO

Contents: Nehemiah's visit to Jerusalem by permission of Artaxerxes.

Characters: God, Artaxerxes, Nehemiah, Sanballat, Tobiah, Asaph, Geshem.

Conclusion: The Christian should be concerned in the sorrows and desolations of others, having a deep concern for God's honor. When prayer is sincerely offered, it is sure to be seconded with serious endeavors to render aid.

Key Word: Arise, build, v. 20.

Strong Verses: 18, 20.

Striking Facts: v. 4. We are not limited to certain moments in our addresses to the King of Kings but have access to the throne of Grace in every time of need, being emboldened by His invitation, who has, by His blood, made possible our approach into God's holy presence.

CHAPTER THREE

Contents: Wall of Jerusalem built.

Characters: God, Artaxerxes, Nehemiah, Sanballat, Tobiah.

Conclusion: What is to be done for the public good, everyone should have a part in and further to the utmost of his place and power. It is good to be zealously affected in a good cause.

Key Word: Repaired, v. 4.

Striking Facts: v. 10. If everyone would sweep before his own door, the street would be clean. Do your part.

CHAPTER FOUR

Contents: Opposition by ridicule, anger and discouragement.

Characters: God, Nehemiah, Sanballat, Tobiah.

Conclusion: God's people are often a despised people, loaded with contempt, but the reproaches of enemies should rather quicken them to duty than drive them from it. Those who cast contempt on God's people, in reality despise God Himself and prepare for themselves everlasting shame.

Key Word: Opposition, v. 1.

Strong Verses: 6, 9, 20.

Striking Facts: v. 13. Having prayed, they set a watch. **We** cannot secure ourselves by prayer, without watchfulness. Matt. 26:41. Prayer without watchfulness is presumption. Watchfulness without prayer is hypocrisy.

CHAPTER FIVE

Contents: Opposition by greed and heartlessness. Nehemiah's example of unselfishness.

Characters: God, Nehemiah.

Conclusion: Nothing exposes Christianity more to the reproaches of its enemies than the worldliness and hard-heartedness of its professors. Followers of Christ should be careful, lest by these means, they bring a reproach upon their religion.

Key Word: Usury, v. 7.

Strong Verses: 19.

Striking Facts: v. 15. Let us remember the words of the Lord Jesus, how He said, it is more blessed to give than to receive. Acts. 20:35.

CHAPTER SIX

Contents: Opposition by craft. Nehemiah's manly firmness. The wall done.

Characters: God, Nehemiah, Sanballat, Tobiah, Geshem, Gashum, Shemaiah.

Conclusion: Christian fortitude will always be sharpened by opposition. Every temptation to draw us from duty and into a snare, should drive us to God and so quicken us the more to duty.

Key Word: Craftiness, v. 8.

Strong Verses: 3, 11.

Striking Facts: v. 3. Let those who are tempted to waste time from Christ's service by attending idle affairs with vain companions, make use of this answer—"We have work to do and cannot come down."

CHAPTER SEVEN

Contents: Jerusalem put in charge of Hanani and Hananiah. Genealogy of the first remnant.

Characters: God, Nehemiah, Hanani, Hananiah.

Conclusion: Those who fear God will evidence it by being faithful to all men and universally conscientious.

Key Word: Register, v. 5.

Strong Verses: 2.

CHAPTER EIGHT

Contents: The law read and explained. Feast of tabernacles restored.

Characters: God, Ezra, Nehemiah.

Conclusion: Reading the Scripture in religious assemblies is an ordinance of God whereby He is honored and the church edified. It should be delivered distinctly, for it is a requisite that those who hear the **Word** should understand it, else it is to them as an empty sound of words.

Key Word: Bible, v. 8.

Strong Verses: 6, 8.

Striking Facts: v. 14. The feast of tabernacles was a memorial of their dwelling in tents in the wilderness, a representation of our tabernacle state in this world as followers of Christ, and a type of the Gospel church.

CHAPTER NINE

Contents: The people feast and repent. Confession of the priests and Levites.

Characters: God, Jeshua, Bani, Kadmiel, Sherebiah, Shebmah, Bunni, Chenani, Hash-habaliah, Hodijah, Pethahiah.

Conclusion: When we are seeking to God for mercy and relief in time of distress, it is an encouragement to faith to look back upon our own and our fathers' experiences, noticing how all glory belongs to God and all shame to ourselves. When confessing our sins, it is good to reckon up God's many mercies that we may see how ungrateful we have been.

Key Word: Confessed, v. 2.

Strong Verses: 6, 17.

Striking Facts: v. 33. It becomes the Christian when he is under the rebukes of God's providence, no matter how sharp and long they be, to justify God, being assured there is no mistake on God's part.

CHAPTER TEN

Contents: The covenant and the signers.
Characters: God, Nehemiah.
Conclusion: Conversion means a separating of ourselves from the course and custom of this world and devoting ourselves to the conduct of the Word of God.
Key Word: Covenant, v. 29.
Strong Verses: 29.

CHAPTER ELEVEN

Contents: The dwellers at Jerusalem and the cities. •
Characters: Joel, Judah, Zabdrel, Shabbethai, Jozabad, Mathaniah, Uzzi, Pethahiah.
Conclusion: Those who take care of the outward concerns of the church, the common service in connection with it, are as necessary in their place as those who take care of the inward concerns, giving themselves entirely to the ministry of the Word and prayer.
Key Word: Dwellers, v. 1.

CHAPTER TWELVE

Contents: Priests and Levites who went to Jerusalem with Zerubbabel. Dedication of the walls.
Characters: God, Nehemiah, Ezra, Zerubbabel, Jeshua, Seraiah, Jeremiah.
Conclusion: Great mercies call for the most solemn returns of praise in the courts of the Lord's house.
Key Words: Dedication, v. 27.
Strong Verses: 43.
Striking Facts: v. 30. The purifying was a type of the blood of Christ (Num. 19:9) by which our consciences are purged from dead works, making us fit to serve the living God. (Heb. 9:14.)

CHAPTER THIRTEEN

Contents: Cleansing the temple. Nehemiah's second visit to Jerusalem and his further reforms.
Characters: God, Nehemiah, Eliashib, Tobiah.
Conclusion: Nothing grieves a godly man more than to see the ministers of God's house practicing things contrary to God's Word. There is sure to be a general decay of religion and corruption of manners when the people forsake the sanctuary and profane the Sabbath.
Key Word: Cleansed, v. 30.
Striking Facts: v. 8. Those who would expel sin out of their hearts, the living temples, must throw out its household stuff and all the provision made for it, taking away those things which are fuel for lust. Let the blood of Christ be then applied by faith, that it be furnished anew with the grace of God's Spirit.

ESTHER

Key Thought:	Number of Chapters:	Key Verse:	Christ seen as:
Providence	10	4:14	Our Mordecai

Writer of the Book:	Date:	Conclusion of the Book:
Uncertain (Mordecai)	464-434 B. C.	The great God takes a real interest in all our affairs and shapes His providences to work out His glory through them.

SUMMARY

CHAPTER ONE

Contents: Ahasuerus' great feast and the story of Vashti.

Characters: Ahasuerus, Vashti, Memucan, Carshena, Shethar, Admatha, Tarshish, Meres, Marsena.

Conclusion: Better is a dinner of herbs with quietness than the banquet of wine with its tumult and the sin sure to result from it. When wine is in, wit is out.

Key Word: Feast, v. 9.

Striking Facts: v. 12. Whether or not it was the part of wisdom for Vashti to deny obedience to the king, or that the king was ruled by passion, the incident served God's providence making way for Esther to the crown.

CHAPTER TWO

Contents: ' Esther made queen.

Characters: Ahasuerus, Mordecai, Esther, Hegai, Bigthan, Teresh, Shaashgaz.

Conclusion: God sometimes raises up the poor out of the dust to set them among princes. Those who make sure of God's favour usually find favor with man, at least so far as it is good for them.

Key Word: Chosen, v. 17.

Striking Facts: v. 3. To what absurd practices do those come who are destitute of the Word of God and given up to their vile affections. It is the Gospel of Christ alone that can purify men from such lusts of the flesh.

CHAPTER THREE

Contents: Conspiracy of Haman. The king's decree to destroy the Jews.

Characters: Ahasuerus, Haman, Mordecai.

Conclusion: Though religion in no way stands in the way of good manners, but teaches us to render honor to whom honor is due, yet it is the character of a Christian not to hypocritically express respect for one known to be a vile person, merely because he occupies a place of authority. However threatened, it behooves the Christian to be true to conscience, if he is sure his conscience is enlightened by the Holy Spirit.

Key Word: Decree, v. 14.

Strong Verses: 2.

Striking Facts: v. 8. The enemies of the followers of Christ could not give them such bad treatment as they do if they did not first give them a bad name by malicious representations.

CHAPTER FOUR

Contents: Fasting among the Jews. Esther's resolution to defeat the decree.

Characters: Ahasuerus, Esther, Mordecai, Haman, Hatach.

Conclusion: We should consider for what end God has put us in the place where we are and should study to answer that end lest our opportunity slip.

Key Word: Fasting and weeping, v. 3.

Strong Verses: 14, 16.

Striking Facts: v. 11. We should be thankful that nothing need bar us from the court of our King in time of need, for we are welcome in the very holiest through faith in the blood of Jesus.

CHAPTER FIVE

Contents: Esther's courage in proceeding to obtain favor.
Characters: Ahasuerus, Esther, Haman, Mordecai, Zeresh.
Conclusion: If we have had power with God in prayer we shall find favor with men in the time of need, for God can turn the hearts of men which way He pleases.
Key Word: Favor, v. 2.
Striking Facts: v. 9. Those who walk in holy sincerity with Christ may walk in holy security and go on in their work not fearing what man can do to them.

CHAPTER SIX

Contents: Haman compelled to exalt Mordecai.
Characters: Ahasuerus, Esther, Haman, Mordecai, Zeresh.
Conclusion: God's wisdom and grace is seen in the way He times the means of deliverance for His people so as to manifest His own glory. As for God, His way is perfect, and let not enemies think to triumph over those who are in covenant with Him.
Key Word: Honored, v. 11.
Strong Verses: 13.

CHAPTER SEVEN

Contents: Esther's banquet and the hanging of Haman.
Characters: Ahasuerus, Esther, Haman, Harbonah.
Conclusion: Mischief is sure to return upon the person himself who contrives it. The wicked shall be snared in the work of their own hands. Psa. 7:15-16.
Key Word: Hanged, v. 10.
Strong Verses: 9, 10.
Striking Facts: v. 7. The day is coming when those who have persecuted and hated the followers of Christ would gladly be beholden to them, like the rejected virgins (Matt. 25) who cry "give us oil."

CHAPTER EIGHT

Contents: The vengeance order of Ahasuerus.
Characters: Ahasuerus, Esther, Mordecai.
Conclusion: Let the odds be against God's people, they have but to include God in their faith and He will open ways of deliverance and draw conclusions.
The holy joy of those who trust in God is a great ornament to their profession and will encourage others to trust in Him. (v. 16.)
Key Word: Decree, v. 17.
Strong Verses: 16.
Striking Facts: v. 6. Those who are true followers of Christ had rather die in the last ditch than live to see the desolations of the church of God.

CHAPTER NINE

Contents: Vengeance executed; the Jews victorious. Feast of Purim instituted.
Characters: Ahasuerus, Esther, Mordecai.
Conclusion: When we have received signal mercies from God, we should be quick to return our thanks to Him while the impressions are fresh. If the favor has extended to the whole people, steps should be taken to perpetuate the remembrance of it for the honor of God and the encouragement of others to trust in Him.
Key Word: Vengeance, v. 5.
Strong Verses: 22.

Striking Facts: v. 19. Thanksgiving and almsgiving go together. If we have received mercy, the only way to express our gratitude is to show mercy.

CHAPTER TEN

Contents: Mordecai made prime minister.
Characters: Ahasuerus, Mordecai.
Conclusion: Men of virtue and true piety may for a time seem to be kept in obscurity, but often by the hand of God they are suddenly discovered to the world and caused to be preferred.
Key Word: Advanced, v. 2.
Strong Verses: 3.
Striking Facts: The book of Esther testifies to the secret watch-care of Jehovah over His dispersed people, Israel. The name of God nowhere occurs in the book, but in no other book of the Bible is His providence more evident.

JOB

Key Thought:	Number of Chapters:	Key Verse:	Christ seen as:
Testings	42	1:9	Risen Redeemer

Writer of the Book:	Date:	Conclusion of the Book:
Uncertain (Moses, Elihu or Job)	During times of Abraham Oldest Book in Bible	Trial is the school of trust—not always given as chastisement, but sometimes for our education.

SUMMARY

CHAPTER ONE

Contents: Job's family and their piety. Satan's challenge and the calamities that befell Job.

Characters: God, Satan, Job.

Conclusion: God allows Satan power over His saints but it is always limited by the will of God. Nothing shows more accurately what we are than the way in which we stand in the presence of trial and difficulty.

Key Word: Tested, v. 12.

Strong Verses: 8, 21.

Striking Facts: v. 12. The power Satan has over the Christian is bounded by the prayer of the Lord Jesus who "ever liveth to make intercession." No affliction can ever fall upon the believer except by God's permission and when it comes, God has some great purpose in it, which it is our part to ascertain.

CHAPTER TWO

Contents: Job in Satan's seive. Family, property and health gone. His three friends.

Characters: God, Job, Satan, Eliphaz, Bildad, Zophar.

Conclusion: One of the greatest evidences of God's love to those who love Him is to send them affliction, with grace to bear it. If trial makes us complain against God, then the devil laughs and is glad. Trial is the school of trust. (1 Pet. 1:7).

Key Word: Afflicted, v. 7.

Strong Verses: 10.

Striking Facts: v. 4. This verse gives the foundation stone of so-called Christian Science. Body healing is the substitute for soul healing. Men will embrace anything that will relieve pain and distemper of body and hence Satan uses physical ailments to try and draw men from God.

CHAPTER THREE

Contents: Job tells his misery and despair.

Characters: God, Job.

Conclusion: "Pity thyself" is the devil's most popular sermon to one who will listen to him, for he delights to embitter the saint by causing him to misunderstand God's providences. Remember that God's worst is better than the devil's best and if our circumstances find us in God, we shall find God in all our circumstances.

Key Word: Curse, v. 1.

Striking Facts: v. 3. Though many, because of distrust, have cursed the day of their birth, yet no one ever curses the day of their "new birth" nor wishes they had never found Christ as their Saviour.

CHAPTER FOUR

Contents: Eliphaz's theory in regard to Job's suffering.

Characters: God, Eliphaz, Job.

Conclusion: Those who pass rash and uncharitable censures upon their brethren, do Satan's work. We should be careful not to add affliction to saints who are already in grief, unless we are certain we have a God-given message to deliver.

Key Word: Retribution, v. 7

Strong Verses: 8, 9, 17.

Striking Facts: vv. 14, 15. There are certain dogmatists who have to be listened to because they have had some ONE remarkable experience, and everyone else's case is similar to their own. The best and truest comfort is from God's Word. Rom. 15:4.

CHAPTER FIVE

Contents: Eliphaz's discourse continued.

Characters: God, Eliphaz, Job.

Conclusion: Even Satan may be God's servant to make better saints of us, the blow at the outward man proving the greatest blessing to the inward man. We should therefore be more desirous of knowing God's purpose in our trouble than of getting out of it.

Key Word: Chastisement, v. 17.

Strong Verses: 2, 8, 17, 18.

Striking Facts: Fellowship in Christ's sufferings is the qualification for sharing His dignity.

CHAPTER SIX

Contents: Job's answer to Eliphaz. His appeal for pity.

Characters: God, Eliphaz, Job.

Conclusion: No one can judge another justly without much prayer for divine guidance. Affliction does not necessarily prove one to be a hypocrite or a wicked man.

Key Word: Pity, vv. 14, 28.

Strong Verses: 14, 24.

Striking Facts: See 1 Pet. 2:20-23.

CHAPTER SEVEN

Contents: Job's answer to Eliphaz continued.

Characters: God, Job, Eliphaz.

Conclusion: We believe in the sun even when it is hidden behind a cloud, therefore we should not doubt the goodness of God when His face seems for a time to be hidden from us. The Great Physician has never taken down a wrong bottle.

Key Word: Complaint, v. 11.

Strong Verses: 17, 18.

Striking Facts: v. 11. It is better to die praising Jesus and praying than complaining and fretting. The only time our Lord ever asked "why" was when He bore the world's sin and the Father's face was turned away.

CHAPTER EIGHT

Contents: Bildad's theory of Job's affliction.

Characters: God, Bildad, Job.

Conclusion: It is not just or charitable to argue that merely because one is in deep affliction, he is therefore a hypocrite. Let us "judge nothing before the time." A day is coming when the secrets of God's providence will be solved to universal satisfaction.

Key Word: Hypocrisy, v. 13.

Strong Verses: 13, 20, 22.

Striking Facts: Let the afflicted one include the Lord Jesus in his faith and he will eventually be vindicated in the sight of men.

CHAPTER NINE

Contents: Job answers Bildad, denying he is a hypocrite.

Characters: God, Job, Bildad.

Conclusion: Man is an unequal match for his Maker, either in dispute or combat. If God should deal with any of us according to our deserts, we should certainly be undone.

Key Word: Complaint, v. 17.

Strong Verses: 20, 32.

Striking Facts: 2, 3, 33. While it may be possible for us to vindicate our own integrity to friends, we can never plead our integrity for our justification before God. Were it not that the believer stands in Christ's righteousness, he would have no ground whatever before God

CHAPTER TEN

Contents: Job's answer to Bildad continued.
Characters: God, Job, Bildad.
Conclusion: Sometimes, when in affliction, the believer is tempted to think that God's providences and His justice cannot be reconciled. Faith and patience would keep us from being weary of our lives and would show us that when God contends with us, there is always some good purpose in it.
Key Word: Complaint, v. 1.
Strong Verses: 12.
Striking Facts: v. 2. The Christian's comfort is that he is "in Christ" and that although he is afflicted, there is no condemnation. (Rom. 8:1). He is chastised that he might not be condemned with the world. (1. Cor. 11:32).

CHAPTER ELEVEN

Contents: Zophar's theory of Job's condition. He thinks Job a hypocrite and liar.
Characters: God, Zophar, Job.
Conclusion: Those are not always in the right who are most forward to express their judgment and to conclude that if God should speak, He would agree with them. We should seek to put the best possible construction upon the words and actions of our brethren that they will bear, lest we add to their afflictions.
Key Word: Liar, mocker, v. 3.
Strong Verses: 7, 14, 15, 20.
Striking Facts: Zophar is a type of the religious dogmatist who thinks he knows all about God's ways and exactly what God will do in each individual case.

CHAPTER TWELVE

Contents: Job answers his three friends, extolling God's wisdom.
Characters: God, Job, three friends.
Conclusion: There is a wise providence which guides and governs all things by rules with which the wisest men are but imperfectly acquainted. The afflicted one should learn to acquiesce in His disposals and the one who is tempted to criticise and censure should learn not to be over-wise in his expressions of judgment.
Key Word: Hand of God, v. 9.
Strong Verses: 9, 14.
Striking Facts: v. 3. Nothing is more grievous to one who has fallen from prosperity into adversity than to be insulted when he is down. Our Lord Jesus is the wisest and kindest of comforters. To Him let us go in all our troubles.

CHAPTER THIRTEEN

Contents: Job's answer to three friends continued.
Characters: God, Job, three friends.
Conclusion: We should presevere in the way of duty, though it cost us all that is dear to us in this world, rejoicing in God when there is nothing else to rejoice in, knowing that the "sufferings of this present time are not worthy to be compared with the glory which shall be revealed in us."
Key Word: Reasoning, v. 6.
Strong Verses: 15, 16.
Striking Facts: v. 15. Those who walk in unbroken fellowship with Christ, having assurance there is no unconfessed sin in their lives, may cheerfully welcome every event, being in readiness for it.

CHAPTER FOURTEEN

Contents: Job's answer to his friends continued.
Characters: God, Job.
Conclusion: God's providence has the ordering of the period of our lives; our times are in His hand. The consideration of our inability to contend with God, of our sinfulness and weakness, should lead us to throw. ourselves unreservedly into His hands that He might accomplish fully His purposes in us.
Key Word: Trouble, v. 1.
Strong Verses: 14.
Striking Facts: v. 14. Though our friends prove miserable comforters, the believer may rejoice in all circumstances in the comfort that there is a life beyond, victory over even the grave through our Lord Jesus Christ.

CHAPTER FIFTEEN

Contents: Eliphaz's theory about Job, charging him with foolishly justifying himself.
Characters: God, Job, Eliphaz.
Conclusion: Those speeches which do no good, being of no service either to God, our neighbors or ourselves, are better unspoken. If in our troubles we give ourselves to prayer and worship, we will be less apt to drop those expressions which cause others to question our sincerity and constancy in religion.
Key Word: Unprofitable talk, v. 3.
Strong Verses: 15, 31.
Striking Facts: v. 15. Although God uses His saints, He places no confidence in them apart from the ability of the Holy Spirit which He imparts to them for service, and the standing they have in Jesus Christ.

CHAPTER SIXTEEN

Contents: Job charges that Eliphaz is but heaping up words.
Characters: God, Job, three friends.
Conclusion: It is a great comfort to a good man who lies under the censures of brethren who do not understand his case, that there is a God in heaven who knows his integrity and sooner or later will clear it up.
Key Word: Miserable comforters, v. 2.
Strong Verses: 2, 19, 21.
Striking Facts: v. 2. The best friend to plead for us is the Lord Jesus and it is the Holy Spirit through the Word, who comforts effectually.

CHAPTER SEVENTEEN

Contents: Job's answer continued. He longs for death.
Characters: Job.
Conclusion: The believer should recognize that wherever he goes there is but a step between him and the grave and should always be ready. However he should allow no hard providence to deter and discourage him in the service of God, but should be so much the more emboldened to persevere in God's way.
Key Word: Darkness, v. 12.
Strong Verses: 9.
Striking Facts: v. 3. The believer has a surety with God, namely Christ, the heavenly intercessor. He will plead our cause if we look to Him and no one else can lay anything to our charge. (Rom. 8:32, 33).

CHAPTER EIGHTEEN

Contents: Bildad's second discourse on Job's case.
Characters: God, Bildad, Job.
Conclusion: The way of sin is a way of fear and leads to everlasting confusion, of which the present terrors of conscience are but the earnest.
Key Word: The wicked, v. 5.
Strong Verses: 5.
Striking Facts: v. 4. It is not true that all who suffer great distresses in this world should, on that account, be judged wicked when no other proof appears against them. Christ's people are usually a suffering, cross-bearing people.

CHAPTER NINETEEN

Contents: Job's answer to Bildad.   His sublime faith.
Characters: God, Job, friends.
Conclusion: We may easily bear the unjust reproaches of men if we live in expectation of the glorious appearance of the great God, our Saviour, and that we shall be made like Him when we see Him as He is.
Key Word: Hope, v. 27.
Strong Verses: 25, 26, 27.
Striking Facts: Job had very clear beliefs. The brief statement here takes in redemption, assurance, second coming and resurrection.

CHAPTER TWENTY

Contents: Zophar's second discourse on Job's case.
Characters: God, Zophar, Job.
Conclusion: Though wicked men may sometimes prosper, their joy is but for a moment and will quickly end in endless sorrow.
Key Word: Portion of the wicked, v. 29.
Strong Verses: 5.
Striking Facts: v. 2.   Men often mistake the dictates of passion for the dictates of reason and therefore think they are wise for expressing themselves.

CHAPTER TWENTY-ONE

Contents: Job's answer to Zophar in which he denies any secret sin.
Characters: God, Job, three friends.
Conclusion: The providences of God in the government of this world are sometimes hard to be understood.   When we cannot clearly account for the prosperity of the wicked and affliction of the godly, we should silently wait the issue, judging nothing before the time.
Key Word: Prosperity (of wicked), v. 7.
Strong Verses: 22.
Striking Facts: v. 25.   If we have eternal life through Jesus Christ, and spiritual blessings, we have no reason to complain of the little suffering we may be called upon to bear for Christ's sake in this world.

CHAPTER TWENTY-TWO

Contents: Eliphaz's third discourse, accusing Job again of hypocrisy.
Characters: God, Eliphaz, Job.
Conclusion: It is the duty of those especially who are in affliction to keep up a perfect acquaintance with God, accommodating themselves to all the disposals of His providence; thus they shall be possessed of His peace, no matter what the circumstances.
Key Word: Wickedness, v. 5.
Strong Verses: 15, 16, 21.
Striking Facts: v. 5.   Think it not strange, if like the Master, you are misunderstood and blackened, but learn to pass by accusations and commit your cause to Him who judgeth righteously.

CHAPTER TWENTY-THREE

Contents: Job again answers.   He longs for God.
Characters: God, Job, three friends.
Conclusion: Those who keep the way of the Lord may comfort themselves with the thought that they are being tried, that the result will be for their honor and benefit and that when God is through with them they shall come forth as gold (1 Pet. 1:7) pure and precious to the Refiner
Key Word: Tried, v. 10.
Strong Verses: 10.
Striking Facts: v. 10.   Though men do not, can not, or will not understand us, it is a comfort to know that our Lord Jesus, who was tried in all points as we are, does perfectly understand our hearts.

CHAPTER TWENTY-FOUR

Contents: Job's answer continued.   The prosperity of the wicked.
Characters: God, Job, friends.
Conclusion: Though wicked men seem sometimes to be under the special

protection of divine providence, even dying without any disgrace, yet God keeps account of all their wickedness and will some day make it appear that their most secret sins, which they thought no eye saw, were under His eye and will be called over again.

Key Word: Prosperity (of wicked).

Strong Verses: 23.

CHAPTER TWENTY-FIVE

Contents: Bildad's third discourse on Job's case.

Characters: God, Bildad, Job.

Conclusion: Man cannot, in himself, be justified before God for he has no merit of his own to extenuate his guilt.

Key Word: Justification, v. 4.

Striking Facts: v. 4. Since man, by reason of his fallen state and corrupt nature is odious to God's holiness, even in his best righteousness, we have need to be born again, that being justified by faith in Christ, we may have peace with God. Rom. 5:1.

CHAPTER TWENTY-SIX

Contents: Job's answer to Bildad. His faith in God.

Characters: God, Job, friends.

Conclusion: God is infinite and incomprehensible; man's capacities to understand Him and all His ways are weak, therefore the full discovery of God's glory is reserved for the future state. Let us meanwhile be content with His revelations to us.

Key Word: God's power, v. 14.

Strong Verses: 14.

Striking Facts: v. 3. We are often disappointed in the counseling of our friends for they demand what we cannot produce and we need what they cannot give. Our Comforter, the Holy Spirit, never mistakes in His operations or misses in His ends.

CHAPTER TWENTY-SEVEN

Contents: Job's answer to Bildad continued.

Characters: God, Job, friends.

Conclusion: The consideration of the miserable condition of the hypocrite should engage us to be upright.

Key Word: Hypocrites, v. 8.

Strong Verses: 6, 8.

Striking Facts: It is often the lot of upright men to be censured and condemned as hypocrites, but it well becomes them to bear up boldly under such censures, holding fast to Jesus Christ, who will keep from discouragement and eventually vindicate them.

CHAPTER TWENTY-EIGHT

Contents: Job's answer continued. The value of divine wisdom.

Characters: God, Job, friends.

Conclusion: To be truly religious is to be truly wise. If we know God, His wisdom will appear in the practice and observance of our religion and we shall be surely guided in our way.

Key Word: Wisdom, v. 12.

Strong Verses: 28.

Striking Facts: v. 12. There is truer satisfaction in the wisdom which God, through Christ, communicates to the Christian, showing the way to the joys of heaven, than in all the natural philosophies and sciences which only help men to find a way into the earth. (1-11).

CHAPTER TWENTY-NINE

Contents: Job's answer continued. He rehearses the story of his life.

Characters: God, Job, friends.

Conclusion: A gracious soul delights in God's smiles, not the smiles of the world, although virtue and piety challenge respect and usually have it. Those who are not only good, but DO GOOD are worthy of double honor.

Key Word: The past, v. 2.

Strong Verses: 3.

Striking Facts: We can see in this chapter a familiar type of Christ in His power and goodness. Our Lord Jesus is the poor man's Lord, loving righteousness and hating iniquity. Upon Him the blessing of a world ready to perish comes.

CHAPTER THIRTY

Contents: Job's answer continued. He reviews his present condition.
Characters: God, Job, friends.
Conclusion: The best saints often receive the worst of indignities from a spiteful and scornful world, merely because providence appears temporarily to be against them. Our Master Himself was thus abused, therefore we need not deem it strange.
Key Word: Abhored, v. 10.
Strong Verses: 23.
Striking Facts: Those who today cry "Hosannah" may tomorrow cry "Crucify." Job is here a type of Christ who was made the reproach of men and who hid not His face from shame and spitting.

CHAPTER THIRTY-ONE

Contents: Job's answer continued. He insists on his integrity.
Characters: God, Job, friends.
Conclusion: An upright heart does not dread a scrutiny. A good man is willing to know the worst of himself and will be thankful to those who will faithfully tell him of his faults.
Key Word: Integrity, v. 6.
Strong Verses: 4, 14.
Striking Facts: v. 4. The Lord Jesus keeps account of all and will bring every work into judgment. "If our hearts condemn us not, then have we confidence toward God."

CHAPTER THIRTY-TWO

Contents: Elihu's discourse, stating his reasons for interfering.
Characters: God, Job, Elihu, friends.
Conclusion: One who is jealous of the honor of God cannot be grieved when injury is plainly done. It is time to speak when we hear errors advanced and disputed for under pretense of supporting God's cause with them. (1 Tim. 4:12).
Key Word: Opinions, vv. 6, 17.
Strong Verses: 8, 21.
Striking Facts: Elihu shows a deeper spiritual conception than any of Job's three friends, because he has a higher conception of God. Externalists and moralizers, while they see God in His power through His works, know nothing of His grace toward man in Christ Jesus, but look upon Him as being very exacting in all His relations. He who has seen God in the cross of Calvary will have the highest conception of God.

CHAPTER THIRTY-THREE

Contents: Elihu's discourse continued. Affliction is shown to be discipline.
Characters: God, Elihu, Job.
Conclusion: God often afflicts the body in love and with gracious designs of good to the soul. Wherever God finds a submissive heart, He can do great things for the soul.
Key Word: God's working, vv. 29, 30.
Strong Verses: 4, 26.
Striking Facts: v. 14. "Ransom." Jesus Christ is our Ransom, the ransom of God's finding. So great was the injury done by sin, that nothing less could atone for it than the blood of the Son of God.

CHAPTER THIRTY-FOUR

Contents: Elihu's discourse continued. He magnifies God's holiness.
Characters: God, Elihu, Job, friends.
Conclusion: It is absurd and unreasonable to multiply words in complaint against God's ways. His Fatherly corrections are a part of our filial edu-

cation and we should beware of a rebellious heart which only brings added affliction to ourselves and reproach upon God.

Key Word: Rebellious, v. 37.
Strong Verses: 10, 21, 32.

CHAPTER THIRTY-FIVE

Contents: Elihu's discourse continued. Job's rash talk reproved.
Characters: God, Elihu, Job.
Conclusion: It is vain to appeal to God to remove affliction, or to try to acquit ourselves, if we have not studied to know the end for which the affliction was sent. It is equally vain to pray for relief when we do not trust our case in God's hands.

Key Word: Vanity, v. 13.
Strong Verses: 14.

CHAPTER THIRTY-SIX

Contents: Elihu's discourse continued. God's justice defended.
Characters God, Elihu, Job.
Conclusion God does all things well. Though it may seem sometimes that we are neglected and forgotten and that providence has made an oversight, yet the tender eye of the heavenly Father is upon us, and when affliction has accomplished that for which it was sent, we shall be comforted and established.

Key Word: God's discipline, v. 22.
Strong Verses: 11, 22.
Striking Facts: v. 22. Trial is the school of trust. Sore distress is a blessing in disguise if it drives one to Christ and teaches the power of faith and prayer.

CHAPTER THIRTY-SEVEN

Contents: Elihu's discourse continued. God's majesty.
Characters: God, Elihu, Job.
Conclusion: We must all own that our finite understandings cannot comprehend the infinite perfections of God, but we may be sure that because He is infinitely wise, He will do everything for the best. It therefore becomes us, in whatever circumstances, to reverence Him and patiently wait.

Key Word: Majesty, vv. 14, 22.
Strong Verses: 14, 22, 23.

CHAPTER THIRTY-EIGHT

Contents: God's challenge to Job.
Characters: God, Job.
Conclusion: Those who try to call God to account, will be called to account. Seeking to establish one's own character and darkening the counsels of God's wisdom, is an affront and provocation to God. Humble faith can know more of God's secrets than human reasonings.

Key Word: Challenge, v. 3.
Striking Facts: v. 4. Man knows nothing about the making of this world other than what God has revealed in His Word. It is the honor of Jesus Christ that He was present when this was done. (Prov. 8:22; Jno. 1:1, 2).

CHAPTER THIRTY-NINE

Contents: God's challenge to Job continued.
Characters: God, Job.
Conclusion: When we consider God's wonderful works in all nature about us, and see how wonderfully even the brute creatures are fitted for and inclined to the services for which they were designed, we see how unfit we are to dictate to God. Those who see God's hand in everything can best leave everything in His hands.

Key Word: Challenge, v. 1.
Striking Facts: vv. 28-30. The Lord Jesus referred to this instinct of the eagle in Matt. 24:28. See Rev. 19:17-18. Every creature will make toward that which is its proper food.

CHAPTER FORTY

Contents: God's challenge to Job continued. Job's answer.
Characters: God, Job.
Conclusion:: A real vision of God's power and wisdom changes men's opinions of themselves and silences their disputes with God. The valley of humbling is a blessed place, for no one falls there who does not rise to newness of life and service.
Key Word: Challenge, v. 2.
Strong Verses: 4.
Striking Facts: v. 4. God demands a quality no human being is able to present (not even perfect Job) but by His grace, through Jesus Christ, He bestows upon the yielded believer all that He asks.

CHAPTER FORTY-ONE

Contents: God's challenge to Job concluded.
Characters: God, Job.
Conclusion: Man is utterly unable to contend against the Almighty. If the inferior creatures keep man in awe, how wonderful must the majesty of God be, who has sovereign dominion over all.
Key Word: Challenge, v. 1.
Striking Facts: v. 1. "Leviathan." There is a difference of opinion whether a crocodile or whale is meant here. In either case the great power of the Creator is illustrated.

CHAPTER FORTY-TWO

Contents: Job's self-judgment, followed by new prosperity.
Characters: God, Job, Eliphaz, three friends.
Conclusion: Righteousness in a man is excellent but when one becomes too much aware of their own goodness, it reveals deep darkness as to their own real condition before God. If we really know God, we will be humble. If we really know ourselves, we cannot be proud.
Striking Facts: There can be no personal acquaintance with God until we have the sentence of death written upon self, realizing that in ourselves there is no good thing. All we are, we have by God's grace in our Lord Jesus Christ.

The godly suffer that they might come to self-knowledge, 42:3; and self-judgment, 42:6; that they might repent, 42:6; and have greater fruitfulness, 42:7-17; and escape condemnation with the world. 1 Cor. 11:32.

PSALMS

Key Thought·	Number of Chapters:	Key Verse:	Christ seen as:
Praise	150	29:2	Son of God

Writer of the Book:	Date:	Conclusion of the Book:
David, Moses, Asaph	1500 to 1000 B. C.	Worship the Lord in the beauty of holiness and give to Him the glory due His name.
Ethan, Sons of Korah.		

SUMMARY

CHAPTER ONE

Contents: The two ways of man.
Characters: God, righteous man, ungodly man.
Conclusion: Blessed is the man whose footsteps are ordered by the Word of God for he shall find both peace and prosperity. Those who are without God are being hurried to a terrible doom.
Key Word: Godly and ungodly, vv. 1, 4.
Strong Verses: 2, 3.
Striking Facts: Our Lord Jesus was the typical "blessed man" who delighted to do the Father's will.

CHAPTER TWO

Contents: The psalm of the king; rejected, established and finally reigning.
Characters: God, Christ, kings of earth.
Conclusion: The kings of earth are ever setting themselves in array against God and His Annointed King, but in the day when He comes those who will not bend will be broken. Infinitely wise is he who yields his life to Jesus now and dreadful is the folly of those who continue in enmity to Him.
Key Word: God's King, v. 6.
Strong Verses: 8, 12.
Striking Facts: v. 12. The yoke of Christ is intolerable to a graceless neck but to the sinner, saved by His precious blood, it is easy and light. Matt. 11:29.

CHAPTER THREE

Contents: A prayer of David (when he fled from Absalom).
Characters: God, David.
Conclusion: God is a shield for His trusting people. He wards off the fiery darts of Satan and the storms of trouble, at the same time speaking peace to the tempest within the breast.
Key Word: Sustained, v. 5.
Strong Verses: 3, 5, 6.
Striking Facts: In many of the psalms of David, we can see more of David's Lord than of David himself. The agonies of Christ are wonderfully portrayed in this chapter.

CHAPTER FOUR

Contents: David's exhortation to others to serve God.
Characters: God, David.
Conclusion: The godly are chosen, and by distinguished grace set apart and separated from men, all the longings of the soul being satisfied in God. How rash are they, who by rejecting Christ, hate their own mercies merely that they might discover the vanities of sin.
Key Word: Godliness, v. 3.
Strong Verses: 5, 8.
Striking Facts: v. 5. Let the sinner flee to the sacrifice of Calvary and there put his whole trust, for He who died was none other than the Lord Jehovah.

CHAPTER FIVE

Contents: David's prayer in which he extols God's holiness and asks judgment upon the wicked.

Characters: God, David.

Conclusion: Prayer should be both the key of the morning and the bolt of the evening. If we pledge ourselves to Him at the beginning of day, taking sides with Him against the things He abhors, we will be apt to find His way straight before our faces throughout the day.

Key Word: Prayer, v. 2.

Strong Verses: 3, 11, 12.

Striking Facts: v. 7. (Worship toward the temple.) The temple shadowed forth the body of Christ, our Mediator, in whom alone our prayers are accepted with the Father. In our praying the soul should ever look toward Him.

CHAPTER SIX

Contents: David in weakness seeks God's help.

Characters: God, David.

Conclusion: Our way often lies through a vale of tears, but there is One whom we can trust in the greatest straits and difficulties and who can dry our tears and stop our pains. To Him let us betake ourselves waiting upon Him in earnest prayer.

Key Word: Sore vexed, v. 3.

Strong Verses: 9.

Striking Facts: v. 2. In this psalm of sorrow, David is seen as a type of Christ who wept and cried out "My soul is exceeding sorrowful even unto death," but found strength to sustain in the Father above.

CHAPTER SEVEN

Contents: David prays for deliverance from persecutors.

Characters: God, David.

Conclusion: When the believer is slandered he has the court of heaven to fly to and a righteous Judge who is the patron of oppressed innocency. He will be our defense and will return upon the wicked their shame. Self vindication is not judicious or serviceable.

Key Word: Persecutors, v. 1.

Strong Verses: 9' 10, 16.

CHAPTER EIGHT

Contents: Meditation on the majesty of God's works and the insignificance of man.

Characters: God, David.

Conclusion: When we consider the majesty of God's wonderful works in the universe, we cannot but wonder that He should notice such a mean creature as man, yet we may be sure he takes precedence of all the inhabitants of this world, being made but a little lower than angels.

Key Word: Excellence, vv. 1, 9.

Strong Verses: 4, 5, 9.

Striking Facts: The psalm wonderfully foreshadows Christ. He was the revelation of the Father's excellent name; His glory is set above the heavens; He has sovereign dominion and it is He whom God has clothed with glory and honor. For a little time He was made lower than angels, when He took upon Himself the form of a servant. All creatures are under His feet and will eventually own Him to be Lord of all.

CHAPTER NINE

Contents: Praise for victory over enemies.

Characters: God, David.

Conclusion: In the midst of all distresses, we may by faith find a refuge in God and when victory comes, we should not forget that He expects returns of praise.

Key Word: Praise, vv. 1, 11.

Strong Verses: 9, 10, 16, 18.

Striking Facts: v. 18 is one of the sweet promises of the Bible. When pleaded before the throne in the name of the Lord Jesus, who is indeed Himself the great Promise of the Bible, it will be found exceedingly precious.

CHAPTER TEN

Contents: The psalmist meditates on the wicked and desires to see them humbled under God's hand.

Characters: Psalmist, God.

Conclusion: The Christian cannot but lay to heart that which is offensive to God, feeling a tender compassion for those who are oppressed and a zeal for the honor of God. Let us look to God with a firm belief that He will at the proper time give redress to the injured and reckon with the oppressors.

Key Word: Wicked, v. 2.

Strong Verses: 17, 18.

Striking Facts: v. 16. We shall speed well if we carry our complaints to the King of Kings, for at the throne of the Lord Jesus, all wrongs will be redressed. "Come quickly Lord Jesus."

CHAPTER ELEVEN

Contents: The doom of the wicked.

Characters: God, David.

Conclusion: If we get the vision of God on His throne, governing all creatures, rendering to all according to their works, we shall then see no reason to be discouraged by the power of oppressors but will rest in Him.

Key Word: Wicked, v. 2

Strong Verses: 4, 7.

Striking Facts: v. 4. There is One who pleads His precious blood in our behalf in the temple above and an Intercessor at the right hand of the throne who is never deaf to the cries of His trusting people.

CHAPTER TWELVE

Contents: A prayer for help against oppressors.

Characters: God, David.

Conclusion: The believer is commonly tempted to think that because trouble has lasted long, it will last always, but if he will bring his cares and griefs to the throne of grace, he may go away with praise, being assured that all will be well at last.

Key Word: Oppressors, v. 5.

Strong Verses: 3, 6.

Striking Facts: v. 6. Some see in the seven-fold trying of God's Word, an allusion to the seven dispensations of man or to the seven periods of the church, or to that perfection signified in the number seven to which the Scriptures will have been brought at the Revelation of Jesus Christ

CHAPTER THIRTEEN

Contents: Prayer for deliverance from enemies.

Characters: God, David.

Conclusion: The believer's desires often turn to impatience, for days seem long when the soul is cast down, but because God's face is hidden, it does not follow that His heart has forgotten. If we hold to God by faith, we will at the same time be assured that victory is coming and that, after all, God has dealt bountifully with us.

Key Word: Supplication, v. 3.

Strong Verses: 6.

Striking Facts: If, after all our pains, we find Jesus Christ in a new way, it will make full amends for all our long patience.

CHAPTER FOURTEEN

Contents: The corruption and foolishness of man.

Characters: God, David.

Conclusion: Man in his natural state has become odious to God, utterly incapable of answering the ends of his creation, until by God's free grace, a change has been wrought.

Key Word: Corrupt, v. 1.
Strong Verses: 3.
Striking Facts: The only perfect goodness is to be found in Jesus Christ. All have sinned and come short of God's standard; all are therefore concluded under sin, in the same state of damnation, until by God's grace and faith in Christ, they are regenerated.

CHAPTER FIFTEEN
Contents: Those who shall dwell with God.
Characters: God, David.
Conclusion: Those who would find their way to heaven must have some of heaven in them on their way there. The child of God will walk in the ordinances of the Lord, abhoring that which dishonors Him.
Key Word: Who shall abide, v. 1.
Strong Verses: 1, 2.
Striking Facts: v. 1. When we are taught of God, we will see that only our spotless Lord can find acceptance before the Majesty on High. Until we are "in Christ," conformed to His image, there is no abiding place for us in His tabernacle.

CHAPTER SIXTEEN
Contents: Meditation on the goodness of God.
Characters: God, David.
Conclusion: Those who commit themselves to God's care and submit themselves to God's guidance will find a blessed portion in Him. If we have the pleasures of His favor, we should not fail to give Him the praise of it.
Key Word: Goodly heritage, v. 6.
Strong Verses: 8, 10, 11.
Striking Facts: It was the Lord Jesus, who in the fullest sense made the Father His portion, the Father's glory His highest end and the Father's will His delight. He who in soul and body was preeminently God's Holy One was loosed from the pains of death because it was not possible that He should be holden of it. (vv. 8-10.)

CHAPTER SEVENTEEN
Contents: David prays for relief from the pressure of enemies.
Characters: God, David.
Conclusion: If we are abused and misrepresented, we have a righteous God to go to whose judgment is according to the truth and by whose decisions there will be rendered to every man his due. In the prospect of awaking with His likeness, we can cheerfully waive the enjoyments of this life and suffer with patience.
Key Word: Oppressors, v. 9.
Strong Verses: 8, 15.
Striking Facts: v. 15. It is in Christ alone, the first born from the dead, the express image of Jehovah's glory, that the saints will rise immortal, incorruptible, to be eternally satisfied in heaven. We shall see Him as He is and be made like Him.

CHAPTER EIGHTEEN
Contents: Praise for God's marvelous deliverances.
Characters: God, David.
Conclusion: God not only will deliver His trusting people out of their difficulties in due time, but will give them grace to bear up under their trials in the meantime. Give God the glory of all the deliverances and advancements of His Kingdom.
Key Word: Delivered, vv. 17, 50.
Strong Verses: 2, 3, 30, 32.
Striking Facts: David is here a type of Christ who was brought safely through all conflicts with the forces of evil and given to be head over all. Though He sees not yet all things put under Him, yet He knows that He shall reign until all opposing rule is put down and all men acknowledge Him to be both Lord and Christ.

CHAPTER NINETEEN
Contents: God's revelation of Himself in the book of nature, book of the law and the book of human life.
Characters: God, David.
Conclusion: God makes Himself known through three great books, all of which have as their theme the glory and handiwork of God. The book of nature (vv. 1-6) is read by every human being. The book of the law (vv. 7-14) converts the soul and becomes an unfailing guide. The book of human life (vv. 12-14) is a Bible to the unsaved world and must therefore be maintained with unspotted pages.
Key Word: Glory of God, v. 1.
Strong Verses: 1, 7, 14.
Striking Facts: Christ, the Sun of Righteousness, is the Bridegroom who rejoices to reveal Himself to men and like the champion, wins glory to Himself in His union with His Bride, the true church.

CHAPTER TWENTY
Contents: A prayer for God's annointed people.
Characters: God, David.
Conclusion: The children of this world trust in second causes and rise or fall with them but those who have a believing and obedient trust in God have the sure way to preferment and establishment.
Key Word: Saving strength, vv. 1, 6.
Strong Verses: 7.
Striking Facts: vv. 3, 5. In all our conflicts, we are to have an eye to the sacrifice of Jesus, pausing ever at His cross before we march on to battle. Come what may, having trusted in His finished work, we may then rejoice in His saving arm.

CHAPTER TWENTY-ONE
Contents: Praise for blessing and confidence for further victory.
Characters: God, David.
Conclusion: Let praise be the blossom of prayer. Though we cannot sing a note in honor of our own strength, we can always rejoice in our omnipotent God, if we have trusted all to Him.
Key Word: Answered prayer, v. 2.
Strong Verses: 8, 13.
Striking Facts: vv. 2, 5, 6. The psalm looks forward to Jesus, who is God over all blessed forever; once crowned with thorns but now wearing the glory crown. He is the Pleader whose requests are never withheld. Let us make use of this all-prevailing Intercessor.

CHAPTER TWENTY-TWO
Contents: David in great perplexity cries for help.
Characters: God, David.
Conclusion: Trouble and perplexity drive us to earnest prayer and earnest prayer drives away trouble and perplexity. To fall upon the knees is the surest way to whip the enemy.
Key Word: Trouble, v. 11.
Strong Verses: 22, 24, 27.
Striking Facts: The psalm gives a graphic picture of the death of the Lord Jesus and is called "the psalm of the cross."We see both the sufferings of Christ and the glory to follow. Oh for grace to draw near and see this great sight. (Read Matt. 27.)

CHAPTER TWENTY-THREE
Contents: David sees Jehovah as his good shepherd.
Characters: God, David.
Conclusion: Jehovah is with (v. 1) under (v. 2) beside (v. 2) after (v. 6) before (v. 5) and ahead of (v. 6) all His trusting children. They shall not want for food (v. 2) drink (v. 2) strength (v. 3) guidance (v. 3) comfort (v. 4) satisfaction (v. 5) or life (v. 6).
Key Word: Shepherd, v. 1.
Strong Verses: 1, 4.

Striking Facts: The shepherd psalm follows the psalm of the cross.   We must
by experience know the value of the blood shed on Calvary's cross and
see the sword awakened against the Shepherd before we can truly know
the sweetness of the Good Shepherd's care.   Psa. 22 is the Good Shepherd
dying for His sheep.   (Jno. 10:11.)   Psa. 23 is the Great Shepherd caring
for His sheep.   (Heb. 13:20.)   Psa. 24 is the Chief Shepherd coming
again for His sheep.   (1 Pet. 5:4.)

CHAPTER TWENTY-FOUR

Contents: The one who shall stand before Jehovah.
Character: God.
Conclusion: Those who have been made meet for heaven shall be brought
safely into God's presence.   While none may venture to meet God's
standards on the footing of the law, God's grace in Christ can make us
meet.
Key Word: Blessing and righteousness, v. 5.
Strong Verses: 1, 3, 4.
Striking Facts: Christ, the ascended Savior, is here seen as Head and Crown
of the universe, the King of Glory.   He it was who could ascend the hill
of the Lord, meeting perfectly all requirements.   He has entered there as
the forerunner of all who trust Him and shortly is coming out again to
be acknowledged King of Kings and Lord of Lords.

CHAPTER TWENTY-FIVE

Contents: Prayer for guidance, forgiveness, mercy and deliverance.
Characters: God, David.
Conclusion: It is our duty and privilege to trustingly wait upon the Lord in
adoration, supplication and service all the days of our lives.   Those
whose hearts are right with Him, shall not err for want of heavenly
direction in any time of perplexity.
Key Word: Prayer, v. 1.
Strong Verses: 9, 14.
Striking Facts: v. 8.   Good and upright.   God's goodness and uprightness
are in perfect union.   They were perfectly blended in the sacrifice of the
Lord Jesus on Calvary.   Because God Himself has paid the price of the
cross, He can be just and yet justify the ungodly; His goodness and
righteousness are harmonized.   Faith in this sacrifice is the sinner's
only hope of being delivered.

CHAPTER TWENTY-SIX

Contents: David prays for vindication and deliverance and pledges faithful-
ness.
Characters: God, David.
Conclusion: It is a great comfort to those who have a clear conscience toward
God that He is a witness to their sincerity and as the righteous God will
sooner or later vindicate them.
Key Word: Examine, v. 2.
Strong Verses: 6, 7, 11.
Striking Facts: In this chapter is seen a type of Christ who was made a
reproach of men and who forewarned His followers that it would also be
their portion to have all manner of evil spoken against them falsely for
His sake.

CHAPTER TWENTY-SEVEN

Contents: David glories in Jehovah's name and expresses triumphant faith.
Characters: God, David.
Conclusion: God is the believer's light and strength by whom and in whom
he lives.   We should therefore let the heart be fixed in Him and the mind
stayed upon Him, waiting His deliverance in all circumstances.
Key Word: God's goodness, v. 13.
Strong Verses: 1, 3, 5, 10, 14.
Striking Facts: v. 12., We get here a picture of Christ against whom false
witnesses arose, breathing out cruelty, but though He was delivered into
their wicked hands, He was not delivered to their wills, for God exalted
Him far above all principality and power.

CHAPTER TWENTY-EIGHT

Contents: Prayer for deliverance from enemies and testimony as to answered prayer.
Characters: God, David.
Conclusion: The Lord is our strength to support us in either service or suffering, as well as our shield to protect us from the designs of the enemy. The heart that truly believes in Him shall in due time greatly rejoice.
Key Word: Supplication, v. 2.
Strong Verses: 7.
Striking Facts: v. 2. The holy place within the veil was the place where the ark and mercy seat were which foreshadowed the Lord Jesus. If we gain acceptance in prayer, we must ever turn ourselves to the blood-springled mercy seat of His atonement.

CHAPTER TWENTY-NINE

Contents: Adoration of God's mighty power.
Characters: God, David.
Conclusion: Let the crowns, the great ones of earth, acknowledge their dependence upon God and join in worship to the blessed and only Potentate of the universe.
Key Word: Power and majesty, v. 3.
Strong Verses: 2, 11.
Striking Facts: v. 11, Peace. Jesus, the mighty God, is our peace. Having purchased the peace of pardon on the cross, He bequeathed it in His promise to His followers, "Peace I leave with you; my peace I give unto you."

CHAPTER THIRTY

Contents: Thanksgiving for answer to prayer.
Characters: God, David.
Conclusion: We should hem all our blessings with praise lest they unravel. Let us never forget to pray, nor ever doubt the success of prayer.
Key Word: Thanks, v. 12.
Strong Verses: 4, 5.
Striking Facts: v. 7. The Lord Jesus is able to bring substantial consolation to the believer. He Himself was for a time deserted of the Father that those who believe on Him might not be deserted eternally.

CHAPTER THIRTY-ONE

Contents: David implores God's help against enemies and extols God for his preservation.
Characters: God, David.
Conclusion: All our affairs are safe in Jehovah's hands; without reservation therefore, we should yield ourselves to the Father's hand to be sanctified by His grace, devoted to His honor, employed in His service and fitted for His Kingdom.
Key Word: Trouble, v. 9.
Strong Verses: 19, 20, 24.
Striking Facts: v. 5. These living words of David were our Lord's dying words from the cross when He made His soul an offering for sin.

CHAPTER THIRTY-TWO

Contents: The blessedness of those whose sin is forgiven.
Characters: God, David.
Conclusion: The only cover that will hide our sins forever away from God's sight is that provided in the atoning death of His Son. He is blessed indeed who has a Substitute who assumes all accounts to stand for him. If the believer does not humble himself by the confession of his sins to God, God will humble him by chastisements.
Key Word: Forgiven, v. 1.
Strong Verses: 1, 8.
Striking Facts: v. 2. The righteousness of Christ being imputed to the believer, and the believer being made the righteousness of God "in Him" his iniquity is not set to his account. Christ took upon Himself the iniquity of us all and was made sin for us.

CHAPTER THIRTY-THREE

Contents: Praise of God's wisdom and power.
Characters: Psalmist, God.
Conclusion: The righteous who know the goodness of God should never be empty of His praises. Though the residence of God's glory is in the highest heavens, yet His eye is upon every inhabitant of earth and no detail of their lives escapes His observation.
Key Word: Praise, v. 2.
Strong Verses: 4, 10, 12.
Striking Facts: v. 6. The three persons of the Godhead united in the creation of all things. Christ is the Word, (Jno. 1:1) without whom nothing was made. The Holy Spirit is the breath. God made the world, as He rules it and redeems it, by His Son and Spirit.

CHAPTER THIRTY-FOUR

Contents: David thankfully records God's goodness and invites the praise of others.
Characters: God, David.
Conclusion: God's people who share His special favor should concur in His praises and magnify His name together. Upon every fresh occurence of His mercies, let us renew our praises, thus encouraging others to trust Him. The true and only way to happiness is to walk in the love and favor of God.
Key Word: Praise, v 1.
Strong Verses 1, 7, 10, 15, 19.
Striking Facts: v. 20. Although it is strange that we meet with anything of Christ here, this Scripture is said to have been fulfilled in Christ. Jno. 19:36. The passover lamb of which not a bone was broken prefigured Jesus and at the same time the complete keeping of His Body, the Church.

CHAPTER THIRTY-FIVE

Contents: An appeal to heaven for the confusion of enemies.
Characters: God, David.
Conclusion: The most righteous men and the most righteous causes may expect to meet with many mighty and malicious enemies. The safest place to leave a righteous cause is with the righteous God who is able to give judgment upon it in the right way and at the right time. If God is our friend, it does not matter who our enemies are.
Key Word: Persecutors, v. 3.
Strong Verses: 27, 28.
Striking Facts: Herein David was a type of Christ to whom the wicked world was most ungrateful (Jno. 10:32) and who was slandered as no one else ever was (Matt. 26:60). If we are falsely charged, let us remember that so persecuted they the prophets and our Lord Himself.

CHAPTER THIRTY-SIX

Contents: The wicked contrasted with the righteous and the Lord of devout men extolled.
Characters: God, David.
Conclusion: Sinners are self destroyers and when sin is finally made to appear in its true colors to them, they will be made a terror to themselves. But whatever is amiss with the world, we may be sure there is nothing amiss with Jehovah and that those who cleave closely to Him shall be eternally satisfied.
Key Word: Wicked, v. 1 (satisfaction, v. 8).
Strong Verses: 7, 8, 9.
Striking Facts: v. 9. From the Lord Jesus as the self-sufficient spring (Jno. 4:14), proceeds our life and by Him it is sustained. In His light we see light. We cannot see Jesus by the light of self, but we see self in the light of Jesus.

CHAPTER THIRTY-SEVEN

Contents: The riddle of the prosperity of the wicked and the affliction of the righteous.
Characters: God, David.

Conclusion: The believer should never waste a minute fretting about his enemies, but should look forward with the eye of faith, when he will see no reason to envy wicked people their short-lived prosperity. Those who make God their heart's delight will have their heart's desire and will be fully satisfied in Him.

Key Word: Evil doers, v. 1, and righteous, v. 37.

Strong Verses: 1, 3, 4, 5, 7, 16, 23, 24.

Striking Facts: Come what may, the saints are safe in Christ Jesus and because He lives, they shall live also. As heirs with Him, heaven and eternity shall be theirs. Who would not be a Christian on such terms, in spite of all the oppression of the godless?

CHAPTER THIRTY-EIGHT

Contents: David's grief, complaints and confession

Characters: God, David.

Conclusion: God often contends with His children to awaken their consciences and to set their sins in order before them for their humiliation. If we are truly penitent for sin, we will make a particular acknowledgment of what we have done amiss and God will then restore the joy of salvation, with patience to bear our affliction.

Key Word: Bowed down, v. 6.

Strong Verses: 15.

Striking Facts: v. 3. This is the condition of every awakened conscience until given relief through the Lord Jesus. When man sees himself in the light of God's Word applied by the Spirit, he must acknowledge his depravity and helplessness to get deliverance apart from Jesus Christ.

CHAPTER THIRTY-NINE

Contents: The psalmist, bowed down with sorrow and sickness, is burdened with unbelieving thoughts and prays for help.

Characters: God, David.

Conclusion: We should not feed the fire of discontent by poring over our troubles, for we cannot, with all our disquietment, altar the nature of things. Although satisfaction is not to be found at all in the creature, it is always to be found in God, and to Him we should be drawn by our disappointments.

Key Word: Sorrow, v. 2

Strong Verses: 1.

CHAPTER FORTY

Contents: God's salvation extolled and prayer for deliverance.

Characters: God, David.

Conclusion: Those who seek God in all their perplexities shall rejoice and be glad in Him, for He will not only be found of them, but will be their bountiful rewarder, wherefore, they should say continually, "the Lord be magnified."

Key Word: Praise and prayer, vv. 3, 13.

Strong Verses: 2, 16.

Striking Facts: vv. 6-8. The offerings had their worth only as types of the sacrifice of Christ, but when He came, as it was foretold in the volume of the Book, they ceased to be of worth. He alone completely did the will of God. Our expiation from sin is due not to us, but our Substitute's obedience to the will of Jehovah.

CHAPTER FORTY-ONE

Contents: Prayer for relief from sickness and confession of sins.

Characters: God, David.

Conclusion: When we suffer in our reputation, our first concern should be about our integrity and we may then trust our reputation to God. His good will is sufficient to secure us from the ill will of all that hate us.

Key Word: Enemies, v. 5.

Strong Verses: 1.

Striking Facts: v. 9. Betrayal was one of the bitterest drops our Lord Jesus had to take. He applied this passage to Himself (Jno. 18:18, 26) as He gave Judas the sop. The believer need not think it strange if he receives abuses from trusted friends.

CHAPTER FORTY-TWO

Contents: The experiences of a much afflicted saint and his confidence in God.
Characters: God, Psalmist.
Conclusion: God often teaches His saints effectually to know the worth of His mercies by causing them to feel the want of them. A believing confidence in God is the best antidote against disquietude of spirit. The way to forget our miseries is to rest in the God of our mercies.
Key Word: Hope, v. 5.
Strong Verses: 5, 11.
Striking Facts: v. 7. Our Lord Jesus, for our sakes, was overwhelmed with a deluge of grief, like that of the old world, when the fountains of the deep were broken up. He endured all the billows of God's wrath against sin.

CHAPTER FORTY-THREE

Contents: Prayer for God's help and leading.
Characters: God, Psalmist.
Conclusion: We need desire no more to give us satisfaction of heart than the good that flows from God's favor. If we conscientiously follow His light and truth, it will certainly bring us to His holy hill above.
Key Word: Oppression, v. 2.
Strong Verses: 3, 5.
Striking Facts: v. 3. No common light can show us the road to heaven, but only that light sent from heaven, the Holy Spirit, the Spirit of Light and the truth as it is in Jesus, the Light of the world.

CHAPTER FORTY-FOUR

Contents: Complaint of the Lord's apparent forgetfulness and entreaty for His help.
Characters: God, Psalmist.
Conclusion: The tokens of God's displeasure are more grievous to those who have been long accustomed to the tokens of His favor, but the remembrance of His former goodness should be a cause of heart searching and a support to faith.
Key Word: Affliction, v. 24.
Strong Verses: 5, 6.
Striking Facts: v. 22. There is a reference here to those who suffer, even unto death, for the testimony of Christ and to whom it is applied in Rom. 8:36.

CHAPTER FORTY-FIVE

Contents: A psalm of the King, looking to His advent in glory.
Characters: God, Psalmist.
Conclusion: In the eyes of all those enlightened by the Holy Spirit the Lord Jesus, the King of Kings, excells all the children of men in His excellencies. How much more worthy is He of our love.
Key Word: King, v. 1.
Strong Verses: 6, 7.
Striking Facts: In Jesus, the Annointed King, we behold every feature of a perfect character in harmonious proportion. He will never be so beautiful as when He is seen in union with His Bride, the Church.

CHAPTER FORTY-SIX

Contents: A psalm of holy confidence in God.
Characters: God, Psalmist.
Conclusion: God's people may count themselves safe and make themselves strong in Him in whom there is always help sufficient, no matter what is the case and exigence.
Key Word: Refuge, v. 1, 11.
Strong Verses: 1, 10.
Striking Facts: v. 4. God the Father is a river (Jer. 2:13). God the Son is a river, the fountain of salvation (Zech. 13:1, 3). God the Spirit is a river (Jno. 7:38; 4:14). The perfections of the Father, the fullness of Christ, the operations of the Holy Spirit—these make up the great river that makes glad the city of God.

CHAPTER FORTY-SEVEN

Contents: The people exhorted to shout over God's triumphs.
Characters: God, Psalmist.
Conclusion: Let all who know God and own His sceptre sing His praises forever; for while we dwell under the shadow of such a throne there is eternal reason for thanksgiving.
Key Word: Praises, v. 6.
Strong Verses: 8.
Striking Facts: The prospect of the coming universal reign of Christ as Prince of Peace is enough to make the tongue of the dumb sing.

CHAPTER FORTY-EIGHT

Contents: Praise of the beauty and strength of Mount Zion, the city of God.
Characters: God, Psalmist.
Conclusion: There is one city which is the world's star (Jerusalem), the most precious pearl of all lands, because it is God's city on which His eye is ever resting. (Although it has long been in the dust, it will be restored again as the capital of the whole earth (Isa. 62:6-7; Mic. 4:8).
Key Word: Mount Zion, v. 2.
Strong Verses: 1, 14.
Striking Facts: There is a spiritual Zion equally glorious and which shall never be overthrown, the Church, against which the gates of hell shall not prevail. She is putting on her garments to welcome the King when He comes to reestablish the literal Zion and to rule over the whole earth.

CHAPTER FORTY-NINE

Contents: The despicable character of those who trust in their wealth.
Characters: God, Psalmist.
Conclusion: There is no security in the possession and enjoyment of wealth, for money cannot buy the redemption of the soul. God's children, though poor, are truly happy above the most prosperous of this world because they are guarded against the terrors of death and judgment to come.
Key Word: The rich, v. 6.
Strong Verses: 15, 16, 17.
Striking Facts: v. 7. Christ has done that for us which all the wealth of the world cannot do, redeeming us with His precious blood (1 Pet. 1:18-19). The redemption of the soul is precious because of its tremendous cost. Having been once wrought, it ceases forever, never needing to be repeated. (Heb. 9:25-26; 10:12.)

CHAPTER FIFTY

Contents: The arraignment of the ungodly and the greatness of Jehovah.
Characters: God, Asaph.
Conclusion: Every man shall be called to give an account of himself to God. In that great day, He will make those to hear judgment who would not hearken to His calls in Grace. Those only will be gathered to God who have sincerely covenanted with Him through the sacrifice of His Son.
Key Word: Judgment, v. 6
Strong Verses: 15, 23.
Striking Facts: v. 5. It is only by the sacrifice of Christ that sinners can be accepted of God. Those who have so covenanted will be gathered unto Christ at His coming (2 Thes. 2:1) to be assessors with Him in the later judgment of the world (1 Cor. 6:2)

CHAPTER FIFTY-ONE

Contents: The penitential prayer of David.
Characters: God, David.
Conclusion: All the believer's wrong doing comes to a climax at the foot of the throne, being violation of God's law. While the penalty of sin has been blotted out by the blood, the defilement of all subsequent sin remains. Confession brings sin out of its hiding place and enables the sinner to take sides with God against it. See 1 Jno. 1:9.
Key Word: Confession, v. 3.
Strong Verses: 1, 7, 10, 17.

Striking Facts: v. 7. The sinner is purged by blood upon acceptance of Christ (Heb. 1:3; 9:12; 10:14) which takes away the guilt of sin. The washing (v. 2) takes away the defilement of sin in the Christian, being accomplished by the application of the Word by the Spirit. (Eph. 5:25-26.).

CHAPTER FIFTY-TWO

Contents: The triumph of God's people over all oppressors.
Characters: God, David.
Conclusion: Those who think to support themselves in their own power and wealth without God and His Word, are wretchedly deceived, for their houses are built on sand. The ruin of mighty, yet godless men cannot but be universally noticed when that day comes.
Key Word: Triumph, v. 6.
Strong Verses: 8, 9.
Striking Facts: v. 8. Those whose confidence is in God are compared to green olive trees, which are fat as well as flourishing (92:14). The wicked are compared (37:35) to a green bay tree, which has an abundance of large leaves but no useful fruit.

CHAPTER FIFTY-THREE

Contents: The foolishness and iniquity of atheism.
Characters: God.
Conclusion: Bad practices are the fruit of bad principles and bad principles are the natural fruit of denial of God. Atheists, whether in opinion or practice, are the biggest fools of earth. There cannot be right living where there is not right believing.
Key Word: Atheist, v. 1.
Strong Verses: 1.
Striking Facts: v. 6. Those who meet the atheism and sinfulness of men cannot but long for the hastening of the glorious return of the Lord Jesus to earth to bring joy to the Church, His Bride, and restoration to His people Israel.

CHAPTER FIFTY-FOUR

Contents: Prayer for rescue from oppressors.
Characters: God, David.
Conclusion: If we are for God, we may be assured God will be for us and that we will have such care from Him that we need never stand in fear of enemies. Let us make His strength our refuge and confidence.
Key Word: Oppressors, v. 3.
Strong Verses: 7.
Striking Facts: v. 6. In all our perplexities, if we have an eye to the Great Sacrifice of Calvary, we can look up and praise God. Apart from our Substitute, we have no ground for prayer.

CHAPTER FIFTY-FIVE

Contents: Complaint concerning false friends.
Characters: God, David.
Conclusion: The best salve for every sore is prayer. One of the greatest griefs is to find ourselves deceived in some who have made great pretentions to friendship in the name of religion, but if our minds are stayed on Christ, we may ever have peace of heart, for His peace passes understanding (Phil. 4:6-7).
Key Word: Complaint, v. 2.
Strong Verses: 16, 17, 22.
Striking Facts: David's suffering at the hands of false friends is here a type of Christ's sufferings. Ahitiphel, who is undoubtedly referred to, is a type of Judas, for they both hanged themselves.

CHAPTER FIFTY-SIX

Contents: David pours out complaint about enemies.
Characters: God, David.

Conclusion: When we are surrounded on all sides with difficulties and dangers because of enemies, we have but one retreat—the mercy of God. Faith in Him will surely banish fear.

Key Word: Enemies, v. 2.

Strong Verses: 3, 4, 11.

CHAPTER FIFTY-SEVEN

Contents: David in faith pleads God's mercy in his calamities.

Characters: God, David.

Conclusion: God's glory should be nearer our hearts than any interests of our own. Whatever God performs concerning His people, it will finally appear to have been performed for their benefit. By faith and prayer, let us therefore take refuge in Him in every time of pressure.

Key Word: Calamities, v. 1.

Strong Verses. 3.

Striking Facts: The Psalm may be construed of Christ, who in the days of His flesh was assaulted by the tyranny of enemies. Herod and Pilate, with the Gentiles and Jews furiously raged and took counsel together against Him. The chief priests and princes were like lions in readiness to devour Him. In it all, He taught us that if we seek the Father's glory our interests are safe in His hands.

CHAPTER FIFTY-EIGHT

Contents: Prayer for the defeat of ungodly men.

Characters: God, David.

Conclusion: However wicked people may prosper and bid defiance to divine justice, they will eventually learn that there is a God who judges in the earth. Whatever hazard; whatever hardship, the believer may be assured of being an unspeakable gainer in the issue.

Key Word: Wicked, v. 3.

Strong Verses: 11.

CHAPTER FIFTY-NINE

Contents: Complaint of the malice of enemies and comfort and confidence in God.

Characters: God, David.

Conclusion: Those who are for Christ's sake, harmless and innocent may expect to be hated of wicked men. It is their wisdom and duty in times of such difficulties, to wait upon God, for He is their defense, their refuge in whom they shall be safe.

Key Word: Enemies, v. 1.

Strong Verses: 9, 16, 17.

Striking Facts: v. 6. The persecutors of our Lord Jesus are compared to dogs (22:16). They ran Him down with barking, for otherwise they could have found no way to take Him. What they lacked in reason and justice, they made up in noise.

CHAPTER SIXTY

Contents: Prayer for the deliverance of God's people from enemies.

Characters: God, David.

Conclusion: God often gives His own people a hard course in this world that they may not take up their rest in the world but may dwell at ease in Him alone.

Key Word: Prayer, vv. 1, 11.

Strong Verses: 11, 12.

Striking Facts: v. 4. Christ, the Son of David, is given for an ensign of the people (Isa. 11:10), a banner to those who fear God. His love is the banner over them. In His name and power they war against the powers of darkness. Let us unfurl our banners to the breeze in confident joy.

CHAPTER SIXTY-ONE

Contents: Encouraged by experiences and expectation, David calls on God for further deliverance.

Characters: God, David.

Conclusion: Past experiences of the benefit of trusting God implicity should ever engage us to keep close to Him and encourage us to hope for fresh mercies in the time of stress.
Key Word: Prayer, v. 1.
Strong Verses: 3, 4.
Striking Facts: v. 2. The rock is Christ. Those are safe who are in Him, but none can mount this rock except God, by His Spirit, help them to it. The Spirit is able to effect such a leading even in the case of one who is on the border of despair.

CHAPTER SIXTY-TWO

Contents: David professes his confidence in God and encourages himself to wait on God.
Characters: God, David.
Conclusion: Hope in God will always be an anchor to the soul, sure and steadfast. Though enemies be mighty and malicious, if God is for us and we are for God, we need not fear what man can do.
Key Word: Refuge, vv. 7, 8.
Strong Verses: 2, 5, 6, 11.

CHAPTER SIXTY-THREE

Contents: David's desire toward God and joyful dependence upon Him.
Characters: God, David.
Conclusion: The believer need desire nothing more than the favor of God to make him happy and satisfied. The consciousness of communion with God is the sure pledge of deliverance.
Key Word: Longing, v. 1.
Strong Verses: 1, 7.
Striking Facts: v. 11. Those who heartily espouse the cause of Christ who is to be manifested as King of Kings, shall glory in His victory at last.

CHAPTER SIXTY-FOUR

Contents: David prays for deliverance from the malicious designs of enemies.
Characters: God, David.
Conclusion: God will turn the tables on the adversaries of His people and defeat them at their own weapons, therefore the righteous need not worry about the arts of self defense, but may safely leave their avengement in His hands.
Key Word: Preservation, v. 1.
Strong Verses: 10.

CHAPTER SIXTY-FIVE

Contents: David gives to God the glory of His power and goodness.
Characters: God, David.
Conclusion: Praise is due to God from all the world because of His mighty works, but praise especially waits for Him in His church among His people.
Key Word: Praise, v. 1.
Strong Verses: 4.

CHAPTER SIXTY-SIX

Contents: A call to praise God for His sovereign dominion and power in the whole creation.
Characters: God, Psalmist.
Conclusion: God's works are wonderful in themselves and if duly considered, will fill the soul with amazement and praise, for it will ever be discovered that His grace and love lay at the bottom of every testing and that everything works for the benefit of His glorious purposes.
Key Word: Praise, v. 2.
Strong Verses: 16, 18, 20.
Striking Facts: v. 13. Even the thankful heart dares not come to God apart from the Great Sacrifice. Never attempt to pray without Jesus.

CHAPTER SIXTY-SEVEN

Contents: Prayer for the prosperity of God's cause in the world.
Characters: God, Psalmist.

Conclusion: Those who themselves delight in praising God cannot but desire that others may be brought to praise Him, and long for the day when all nations shall bow before Him.

Key Word: Praise, v. 3.

Strong Verses: 1, 2.

Striking Facts: v. 7. Christ is coming to set up His Kingdom on the earth when all the ends of the earth shall end their idolatry and adore Him. Not until the Lord Himself is made King of Kings will God's love, light, life and liberty reach to all peoples.

CHAPTER SIXTY-EIGHT

Contents: Prayer against enemies and for God's people. All called upon to praise God for His greatness and goodness.

Characters: God, David.

Conclusion: The glory of Zion's King is that He is a Savior and benefactor to all His willing people and a consuming fire to all those who are impenitent and enemies of God's work in the world. He continually furnishes His people with occasion for praise, and His praises shall eventually cover the earth.

Key Word: Praise, vv. 4, 32.

Strong Verses: 19, 34.

Striking Facts: v. 18. This may refer to the triumph of bringing the ark into the hill of Zion, but mystically certainly was penned with foresight of Christ who arose from the dead, with triumph ascended into heaven, taking with Him the captive spirits of the just in Paradise and thence sending the Holy Spirit unto His disciples.

CHAPTER SIXTY-NINE

Contents: David complains of great distress and begs God to succor him.

Characters: God, David.

Conclusion: When the waters of affliction rise about us, the only course is to commit the keeping of our souls to God, that we may be neither soured with discontent nor sink with despair. Our prospects are as bright as the promises of God.

Key Word: Deep waters, vv. 2, 15.

Strong Verses: 13, 30.

Striking Facts: This Psalm has been called the psalm of Christ's humiliation and rejection. vv. 14-20 describe His Gethsemane experience (Matt. 26:36-45). v. 21 describes the cross (Matt. 27:34-48). The present blindness of Israel is pictured in vv. 22-28 (Rom. 11:9-10). v. 25 pictures Judas (Acts 1:20) a type of his generation.

CHAPTER SEVENTY

Contents: Prayer for help for the godly and shame for enemies.

Characters: God, David.

Conclusion: God sometimes delays help to His own people that He might excite earnest desires on their part. A heart to love His salvation and to desire His glory before our own is a good earnest of the answer to prayer and of His good will toward us. Rest assured that the enemies of Christ will have wages for their work.

Key Word: Enemies, v. 2.

Strong Verses: 4.

Striking Facts: v. 3. These exclamations of exulting insolence were hurled at our Lord Jesus as He was accompanied to the cross. Our Savior caught in His ears the distant mutter of all the violent exclamations and felt the keen poisoning edge of every insult in His omniscience, as they cried "aha, aha."

CHAPTER SEVENTY-ONE

Contents: Prayer that enemies might be put to shame. Joyful praise of God's goodness.

Characters: God, Psalmist.

Conclusion: Those who live a life of confidence in God and continually resort to Him by faith and prayer, may promise themselves a strong habitation in Him, such as will never fall of itself, nor can ever be broken down by any invading power.

Key Word: Trust, vv. 1, 5, 14.

Strong Verses: 3, 15, 16.

CHAPTER SEVENTY-TWO

Contents: The glories of the reign of the coming King.

Characters: God, David.

Conclusion: A day is coming when all shall sing "All hail the power of Jesus name, let angels prostrate fall; bring forth the royal diadem and crown Him King of All."

Key Word: King, v. 11.

Strong Verses: 17.

Striking Facts: v. 11. Jesus Christ is coming to be acknowledged Imperial Lord and King by all men, no matter how high their state. Every knee shall bow to Him and every tongue confess that He is Lord to the glory of the Father. "Come quickly, Lord Jesus."

CHAPTER SEVENTY-THREE

Contents: The temptation to envy the prosperity of wicked people and how to fortify ones self against it. The awful fate of the ungodly.

Characters: God, Asaph.

Conclusion: Observing that many wicked men prosper in their impiety and that many godly people have to drink deeply of the bitter cup of affliction, often brings one the temptation to think that, after all, all is left to blind providence. But the prosperity of the wicked will be found to be short and uncertain and sure to end in destruction and misery. The righteous man's afflictions end in peace and eternal joy.

Key Word: Prosperity of wicked, v. 3.

Strong Verses: 24, 25, 28.

Striking Facts: v. 25. The truly pious soul longs for the Lord Jesus in all places, objects and events. Heaven would be no heaven at all if He were not there. He is better than all on earth—more excellent than all in heaven.

CHAPTER SEVENTY-FOUR

Contents: The deplorable condition of God's people spread before Him with petition for deliverance.

Characters: God, Asaph.

Conclusion: The desolations of God's house cannot but grieve the believer more than any desolations that might come to his own house. In the time of such distress, he cannot sit still in apathy but will turn to God seeking to know "why?" (v. 1) the desolations have come, looking to Him for deliverance.

Key Word: Desolations, v. 3.

Strong Verses: 12.

Striking Facts: v. 12. The Christian may now plead the ancient work of the Lord Jesus, that which was finished on Calvary, which was the overthrow of Satan, sin, death and hell. He who wrought such a wonderful salvation for us cannot desert the Christian now.

CHAPTER SEVENTY-FIVE

Contents: A rebuke for those who fail to reckon with God.

Characters: God, Asaph.

Conclusion: A word from God soon abases the lofty, and hence failure to reckon on God is madness. Even kings serve His purpose when they rise and when they fall, for He is back of the scenes controling all things.

Key Word: Promotion, v. 6.

Strong Verses: 6, 7.

Striking Facts: v. 3. This verse may well be applied to Christ. The world's inhabitants were being dissolved by sin and destruction was threatened to the whole creation. Christ bore up the pillars and saved the world from utter ruin by saving His people from their sins. "He upholds all things by the word of His power."

CHAPTER SEVENTY-SIX

Contents: The glory of God's power celebrated.
Characters: God, Asaph.
Conclusion: The hardships which God's people suffer by the wrath of their enemies will be made to redound to the glory of God when He rises to make His judgments heard and sets the bounds to the wrath of man. Force is of no avail when leveled against the God of Hosts.
Key Word: Greatness (of God), v. 1.
Strong Verses: 7, 10.
Striking Facts: This psalm expresses the advantages the Christian enjoys in Jesus Christ through whom God is known, in whom God's name is made great. He has spoiled principalities and powers and will make a show of them openly.

CHAPTER SEVENTY-SEVEN

Contents: Sorrowful complaints followed by encouragement by remembrance of God's former mighty deliverances.
Characters: God, Asaph.
Conclusion: The thoughts of unbelief can always be argued down if we but stop to meditate upon God's great deliverances of former days, for He is a God who changes not.
Key Word: Remember, vv. 2, 6, 10.
Strong Verses: 10, 11, 12.
Striking Facts: v. 11. Whatever else may be forgotten, the marvelous works of the Lord Jesus in the days of old must not be suffered to be forgotten, for the memory of the cross is always the handmaid for faith and the foundation of all true prayer.

CHAPTER SEVENTY-EIGHT

Contents: Israel's sins wherewith they had provoked God. The tokens of God's displeasure as the result.
Characters: God, Asaph.
Conclusion: God's people limit Him by forgetfulness of His benefits (v. 11) refusing to walk in His commands (v. 10) and by believing not in His promises (v. 22). Yet He is full of compassion, ever waiting to forgive their iniquity and spare them from being cut off entirely.
Key Word: Longsuffering, v. 38.
Strong Verses: 72.
Striking Facts: v. 72. The psalm describing the varying conditions of the people, ends in peace with the reign of the Lord's annointed, David. When the Lord Jesus, the Chief Shepherd, comes, these desert roamings will be ended and we shall enter into the rest of a peaceful Kingdom.

CHAPTER SEVENTY-NINE

Contents: The deplorable condition of God's people and prayer for relief.
Characters: God, Asaph.
Conclusion: If God's people degenerate through sin from what their father's were, they may expect that God will let a just reproach come upon them that they might be brought to true repentance. Those who desire God to avenge them must themselves be upon praying ground.
Key Word: Reproach, v. 4.
Strong Verses: 8, 9.
Striking Facts: v. 10. The day is coming when God will make bare His everlasting arm on behalf of His people, taking glory to His own name by sending back the Lord Jesus, the King of Kings, by the brightness of whose coming the wicked shall be destroyed and God's name glorified.

CHAPTER EIGHTY

Contents: The tokens of God's favor besought and the former blessings cited as a basis for present deliverance.
Characters: God, Asaph.
Conclusion: There is no obtaining favor with God until we are converted unto Him and there will be no turning unto Him except as we submit to His grace, for it is He who turns us. When we confess that it is our own

sinful ways which have provoked God to hide His face, we are beginning at the right end and are on the road to victory.

Key Word: Turn us again, vv. 3, 7, 14, 19.

Strong Verses: 17.

Striking Facts: v. 17. Their king is called the man of God's right hand, as he was also under-shepherd under Him who was the Great Shepherd of Israel (v. 1) Christ is the Great Shepherd to whom we may commit His sheep in faith.

CHAPTER EIGHTY-ONE

Contents: God chides His people for their ingratitude and pictures their happy state had they but obeyed Him.

Characters: God, Asaph, Joseph, Jacob.

Conclusion: God gives those up to their own heart's lust who are determined to give themselves up to be led by them. Those who will listen to the counsels of His Spirit will find those joys and consolations which always reward the obedient.

Key Word: Abandoned, v. 12.

Strong Verses: 10, 16.

Striking Facts: v. 16. The honey out of the rock speaks to us of Christ, the Rock of our Salvation (1 Cor. 10:4) and the fullness of grace in Him and the blessings of the Gospel. Those who hearken to Christ are filled and satisfied with all that is good.

CHAPTER EIGHTY-TWO

Contents: Instructions for the judges of the earth.

Characters: God, Asaph.

Conclusion: God judges among the mighty of earth. They have their power from Him and are accountable to Him. Magistrates should therefore do good with all their power, remembering that it is their special office and duty to protect and deliver the poor.

Key Word: Judging, v. 2.

Strong Verses: 3.

Striking Facts: v. 8. This may be taken as a prayer for the hastening of the coming of Christ who is the Judge of the earth, the King by right divine who is to inherit all nations. When He comes, all unrighteous potentates will be broken like potter's vessels.

CHAPTER EIGHTY-THREE

Contents: An appeal to God's jealousy for His cause and prayer for defeat of enemies.

Characters: God, Asaph, Sisera, Zeeb, Jabin, Oreb.

Conclusion: We cannot but be zealous against those who federate to strike at God, and should earnestly desire and beg of God that such enemies should be brought to confusion, both that He might be glorified and that they might be brought to repentance. (vv. 15-16.)

Key Word: Enemies, v. 2.

Strong Verses: 17, 18.

Striking Facts: The prophecy reaches to all the enemies of Christ's church. Those who have persistently opposed Christ and His Kingdom, may here read their doom.

CHAPTER EIGHTY-FOUR

Contents: Testimony to God's goodness and the happiness of those who put their confidence in Him.

Characters: God, Psalmist, Jacob.

Conclusion: True subjects love the courts of their King. Favored indeed are those who are constantly engaged in His service (v. 4), who find their strength in Him, and who know Him by the life of real faith. (vv. 5, 12).

Key Word: Blessed, vv. 4, 5, 12.

Strong Verses: 5, 10, 11.

Striking Facts: v. 11. God has given both grace and glory, for the Lord Jesus is the fullness of both. In Him we shall find comfort and protection and in Him no good thing may be withheld, for His grace secures every covenant blessing to the believer.

CHAPTER EIGHTY-FIVE

Contents: Prayer for an afflicted people. Remembrance of former mercies and faith for future good.

Characters: God, Psalmist.

Conclusion: The sense of present affliction should not be allowed to drown the remembrance of former mercies, but should rather cause us to recall them with praise, and encourage us to look for grace and mercy in reference to present distress.

Key Word: Revive us, v. 6.

Strong Verses: 6, 8.

Striking Facts: v. 10. In Christ the attributes of God meet in perfect unity in the salvation of guilty men by a holy and righteous God. By the gift of Calvary, God is as true as if He had fulfilled every letter of His threatenings and as righteous as if He had never spoken peace to a guilty sinner. Christ, our perfect Substitute, has taken the full penalty of our sins.

CHAPTER EIGHTY-SIX

Contents: The malice of enemies deplored. God's goodness pleaded in prayer for mercy.

Characters: God, David.

Conclusion: The best self preservation is to commit ourselves to God's keeping and by faith and prayer to make Him our preserver.

Key Word: Supplication, v. 6.

Strong Verses: 5, 11, 15.

Striking Facts: In this Psalm we may hear the voice of Christ, who was both Son of God and Son of man, one God with the Father and one man with men. He prays for us as our Priest. He prays in us as our Head through His Spirit. He is prayed to by us, as our God.

CHAPTER EIGHTY-SEVEN

Contents: God's favor to Zion and His great love for it

Characters: God, Psalmist.

Conclusion: God has expressed a particular affection for Jerusalem because there He met and conversed with His people and showed them the great tokens of His favor. Because His love is set upon it, His people also should hold it in reverent regard.

Key Word: Zion, v. 2.

Strong Verses: 3.

Striking Facts: v. 3. Zion may be taken as a type of the Gospel church of which even more glorious things are spoken than of Jerusalem. It is the Bride of Christ, a peculiar people, a royal priesthood, and the gates of hell shall not prevail against it. We need never be ashamed of the church, even in its meanest condition.

CHAPTER EIGHTY-EIGHT

Contents: Lamentation over trouble and pleading with God for mercy.

Characters: God, Psalmist.

Conclusion: Sometimes the best of God's saints are severely exercised with the sorest of inward troubles and would be distracted with dismal apprehensions but for the Throne of grace to which they may seek for mercy and strength. Lest there be offenses which prevent the Lord from giving favorable regard to our requests, such times should be times of earnest heart searching.

CHAPTER EIGHTY-NINE

Contents: Joy over and praise of God's greatness. Complaint of the seeming failure of the covenant and prayer for redress.

Characters: God, David, Psalmist.

Conclusion: Though we may find it hard to reconcile some dark providences with the goodness and truth of God, yet we should hold firmly to His promises, knowing that His truth is inviolable, and pleading them in prayer before Him. No matter how serious the situation, there is ever matter for praise and thanksgiving.

Key Word: Covenant, vv. 3, 34.

Strong Verses: 7, 14, 18.

Striking Facts: v. 27. The covenant looks beyond David and Solomon. Isa. 7:13-15; 9:6-7; Mic. 5:2. Jesus has preeminence in all things, having a more glorious name than any other. When He comes, it will be seen what the covenant stores up for the once despised Son of David, but who is to be exalted as King of Kings and Lord of Lords.

CHAPTER NINETY

Contents: The frailty of man and his consequent need of being submitted to God's sentences.

Characters: God, Moses.

Conclusion: Men are dying creatures and all their comforts in the world are likewise passing away with time. They should therefore stand in awe of God, walk in His ways, and with the constant apprehension of the uncertainty of life, lest they fail to be dilligent and doing their best in His service.

Key Word: Frailty, v. 9.

Strong Verses: 8, 12, 17.

Striking Facts: v. 17. The beauty of the Lord is the beauty of holiness and it shall suffice, if in our lives His holiness is reflected by the Spirit and we are transformed into the image of Christ from one stage of glory to another. That beauty of holiness shone with resplendent lustre in the Lord Jesus, and as He lives in us, it may be reflected in every disciple.

CHAPTER NINETY-ONE

Contents: The preservation of those whose confidence is in God.

Characters: God, Psalmist, Moses.

Conclusion: Those who live a life of communion with God are constantly safe under His protecting wing and may preserve a holy security of mind at all times. He will be their rest and refuge forever.

Key Word: Refuge, v. 9.

Strong Verses: 1, 2, 3, 4, 7, 11.

Striking Facts: v. 1. Into the secret place those only come who know the love of God in Christ Jesus and those only dwell there to whom "to live is Christ."

CHAPTER NINETY-TWO

Contents: The ruin of sinners and the joy of saints.

Characters: God, Psalmist.

Conclusion: Let the Christian not fear the pride and power of evil men nor be in the least discouraged by their impotent menaces. The impenitent workers of iniquity are counted and taken as God's enemies and as such they shall perish and be scattered.

Key Word: Wicked, v. 7.

Strong Verses: 4, 12, 13.

CHAPTER NINETY-THREE

Contents: The honor of God's kingdom.

Characters: God, Psalmist.

Conclusion: The majesty of God's Kingdom eclipses all others. He can do everything; with Him nothing is impossible. Let not the Christian therefore fear the power of man which is borrowed, but fear Him who has power omnipotent and eternal.

Key Word: Majesty, v. 1.

Strong Verses: 5.

Striking Facts: The King Immortal and Almighty will stand upon His glorious throne in the person of the Son of Man. That the Lord Jesus already does reign in the hearts of His own should be our praise. That He may come and set up His Kingdom on earth should be our prayer.

CHAPTER NINETY-FOUR

Contents: An appeal to God to appear for His people against His and their enemies.

Characters: God, Psalmist.

Conclusion: There is a God to whom vengeance belongs who will certainly call enemies to account. Those who suffer wrong should be encouraged to bear it as His chastisements, committing themselves to Him who judges righteously and works all things together for the good of those who love Him.

Key Word: Evil doers, v. 16.
Strong Verses: 9, 12, 14, 22, 23.
Striking Facts: v. 14. God's people in Christ may be cast down _but_ they can never be cast off. They cannot be utterly forsaken because they are God's inheritance in Christ. Eph. 1:18.

CHAPTER NINETY-FIVE

Contents: A call to praise God as our gracious benefactor.
Characters: God, Psalmist.
Conclusion: It is due our God and King that we should speak forth and sing forth His praises out of the abundance of a heart filled with love, joy and thankfulness.
Key Word: Thanksgiving, v. 2.
Strong Verses: 1, 2, 7.
Striking Facts: v. 1. Christ is the Rock of our Salvation, therefore we must sing our songs of praise to Him who sits upon the throne, and to the Lamb. We are His under all possible obligations, being the people of His pasture, the sheep of His hand (v. 7). By His hand we are led into green pastures, protected and provided for.

CHAPTER NINETY-SIX

Contents: Call to all people to praise God in view of His glory and greatness.
Characters: God, Psalmist.
Conclusion: In God there is everything that is awful, yet everything that is amiable. Those who have come to know Him should go forth in His strength, enamoured with His beauty and to continually praise Him in song, thanksgiving and in service.
Key Word: Praise, v. 4.
Strong Verses: 4, 10.
Striking Facts: vv. 10-13. Let it be told everywhere that Christ's government will be the happy settlement of all things and that it will be incontestably just and righteous. He is coming to judge and to rule and even now is at the threshhold. "Come quickly, Lord Jesus."

CHAPTER NINETY-SEVEN

Contents: The comfort of God's people, arising from His sovereign dominion.
Characters: God, Psalmist.
Conclusion: It is enough to make us rejoice in and adore Jehovah that His throne is fixed upon the rock of eternal holiness, that righteousness is His immutable attribute and that judgment marks His every act. Though we cannot see or understand all that He does, we may be sure that when the books of divine providence are opened, no eye will discern a word that should be blotted out.
Key Word: Exalted, v. 9.
Strong Verses: 10, 11.
Striking Facts: Those who rejoice in Jesus Christ and His exaltation have fountains of joy treasured up for them. While they may expect tribulation in this world, the day is coming when they shall see all powers recognize the chief power and Christ's Kingdom victorious among the heathen.

CHAPTER NINETY-EIGHT

Contents: Exhortation to praise. The joy of the redeemed because of the setting up of God's Kingdom.
Characters: God, Psalmist.
Conclusion: The setting up of Christ's Kingdom is a matter of joy and praise. He shall be welcomed to the Throne with acclamations of joy and with loud shouts until the earth rings.
Key Word: Victory, v. 1.
Strong Verses: 1, 9.
Striking Facts: Jesus, our King has lived a marvelous life, died a marvelous

death, risen by a divine power, by the energy of the Spirit has wrought marvelous things and is yet to be openly proclaimed the conquering King, monarch over all the nations at His second coming.

CHAPTER NINETY-NINE

Contents: Call to praise God because of the glories of His Kingdom among men.
Characters: God, Moses, Samuel, Aaron, Psalmist.
Conclusion: The holiness of God's name makes it truly great to His friends and will make it terrible to His enemies. Let those who worship Him in all humility, praise His great Name and give Him the glory due unto it.
Key Word: Jehovah exalted, v. 5.
Strong Verses: 9.
Striking Facts: v. 5. Jehovah has revealed Himself in Jesus Christ as our reconciled God who allows us to approach to His Throne. Jesus is the King, the Mercy Seat is the throne, and the sceptre which He sways is holy like Himself. As we exalt Him, let us draw near in all humility and adoration.

CHAPTER ONE HUNDRED

Contents: Call to praise God in consideration of His being and His relation to us.
Characters: God, Psalmist.
Conclusion: True worshippers should be joyful worshippers. If we serve Him in uprightness, realizing all His goodness, we cannot but serve Him with gladness, intermixing praise with all our service.
Key Word: Praise, v. 4.
Strong Verses: 3.
Striking Facts: v. 3. It is the Christian's honor to have been chosen out of the world by the Good Shepherd, to be His own special property, and it is his privilege to be guided by His wisdom, tended by His care and fed by His bounty.

CHAPTER ONE HUNDRED ONE

Contents: David's vow to God when he took upon him the charge of the kingdom.
Characters: God, David.
Conclusion: The believer should resolve to walk by the rules of Christian prudence and in the ways of Christian piety, whether he be abroad in public stations, or before his own family.
Key Word: Mercy and judgment, v. 1.
Strong Verses: 2.
Striking Facts: David is here a type of Christ who has His eyes upon the faithful in the land and will ultimately banish the wicked from His presence. v. 8 will have its larger fulfillment when He comes in judgment.

CHAPTER ONE HUNDRED TWO

Contents: Sorrowful complaint of great afflictions and a believing prospect of deliverance.
Characters: God, Psalmist.
Conclusion: The greatest ease to an afflicted spirit is to unburden itself by a humble representation of its griefs before God, who has invited His children to cast all their burdens upon Him, promising to sustain them.
Key Word: Prayer, vv. 1, 17.
Strong Verses: 17, 25, 26, 27.
Striking Facts: vv. 25, 26. The application of these verses to Christ (Heb. 1:10-12) shows that the Psalm has a reference to the days of the Messiah. The Son of God made the worlds (John 1:1-3; Col. 1:16) yet for our sakes He became a man of sorrows, and acquainted with grief.

CHAPTER ONE HUNDRED THREE

Contents: The psalmist, affected with the goodness of God stirs himself up to praise God.
Characters: God, David.

Conclusion: God is the fountain of all good, whatever may be the channel and to His holy name we should concentrate our praise. He has crowned us with loving kindness and tender mercies; He has removed our transgressions far from us, therefore blessing His name should be the alpha and omega of all our service.

Key Word: Bless the Lord, vv. 1, 20, 21, 22.

Strong Verses: 2, 3, 4, 5, 13.

Striking Facts: v. 4. Redemption will ever constitute one of the sweetest notes in the believer's grateful song. Glory be to our Great Substitute who has delivered us from going down into the pit by giving Himself to be our ransom.

CHAPTER ONE HUNDRED FOUR

Contents: God's greatness, majesty and sovereign dominion celebrated.

Characters: God, Psalmist, David.

Conclusion: It is the joy of the saints that He who is their God is a great God who may be seen in all His mighty works in nature, which proclaim Him to be infinitely wise and good.

Key Word: God's greatness, v. 1.

Strong Verses: 24, 34.

Striking Facts: v. 4. This is quoted by the Apostle (Heb. 1:7) to prove the preeminence of Christ above the angels. Heb. 1:3 shows us that it is Christ who upholds all things by the word of His power.

CHAPTER ONE HUNDRED FIVE

Contents: Jehovah extolled for His deliverances of Israel. The coming forth from Egypt described.

Characters: God, Psalmist, Moses, Aaron, Jacob, Joseph, Abraham.

Conclusion: God's marvelous works will be had in everlasting remembrance by the thoughtful and the grateful, and should be the subject of familiar discourse. We should continually give thanks to Him, for at best we can give but poor returns for such rich receivings.

Key Word: Wondrous works, v. 2.

Strong Verses: 4, 5.

CHAPTER ONE HUNDRED SIX

Contents: The badness of Israel made heinous by the great goodness of God.

Characters: God, Psalmist, Moses, Aaron, Dathan, Abiram, Phinehas.

Conclusion: Man's perverseness arises continually from his stupidity toward God. Our understandings are dull; our memories are treacherous, so that we easily lose sight of God's mercies. In spite of our treatment, He is a gracious God who pities us and is ever making merciful allowances for us, not giving us our full deserts.

Key Word: Long Suffering, vv. 43, 45.

Strong Verses: 3, 5.

CHAPTER ONE HUNDRED SEVEN

Contents: God's wisdom, power and goodness celebrated. Man's deplorable forgetfulness of His mercies.

Characters: God, Psalmist.

Conclusion: Those who have no special matter for praise may furnish themselves with matter enough from God's universal goodness. All receive the mercies of His providence and are therefore called upon to give thanks.

Key Word: Jehovah's goodness, vv. 8, 15, 21, 31.

Strong Verses: 8, 9.

Striking Facts: v. 2. Those who have an interest in the Great Redeemer, being saved by Him from sin and hell, of all people have reason to say that God is good and His mercy everlasting.

CHAPTER ONE HUNDRED EIGHT

Contents: Thanks to God for His mercies and His promises pleaded.

Characters: God, David.

Conclusion: We should praise God publicly as those who are not ashamed of our obligations to Him and our thankful sense of His favors, but desire that others also may be affected with a realization of His goodness and the value of leaning upon His promises.

Key Word: Praise, v. 1.

Strong Verses: 12, 13.

Striking Facts: v. 7. With such assurance, we may speak of the performance of God's promise to the Son of David, who is certainly to have the uttermost parts of the earth for His inheritance. He waits at God's right hand for the hour when He shall come forth to be proclaimed both Lord and King.

CHAPTER ONE HUNDRED NINE

Contents: Complaint of the malice of enemies and appeal to the righteous God for judgment.

Characters: God, David, Satan.

Conclusion: When enemies are spiteful and malicious, it is the unspeakable comfort of the Christian that God is for him and that to Him they may apply, knowing that He will concern Himself for them and will visit overwhelming ruin upon the enemy in His own time and way.

Key Word: Adversaries, v. 20.

Strong Verses: 31.

Striking Facts: David is here a type of Christ who was compassed about with hateful enemies, who persecuted Him, not only without cause, but for His love and His good works. (John 10:32).) Yet He gave Himself to prayer to pray for them. However the imprecations here are not appropriate in the mouth of the Saviour. It is not the spirit of the Gospel, but of Sinai which here speaks out of the mouth of David.

CHAPTER ONE HUNDRED TEN

Contents: The Messiah promised to the fathers and expected by them.

Characters: God, David, Christ.

Conclusion: Christ is the rightful Lord whose title is incontestable. He will certainly come to take, and keep possession of, that Kingdom which the Father has promised, and none can hinder.

Key Word: Messiah, v. 1.

Strong Verses: 1.

Striking Facts: This psalm affirms the deity of Jesus, (v. 1) announces His eternal priesthood, (v. 4) and looks to the time when He will appear as the Rod of Jehovah's strength (Rom. 11:25-27) and as the Judge over all powers (vv. 5, 6).

CHAPTER ONE HUNDRED ELEVEN

Contents: Exhortation to praise God for the greatness and glory of His works.

Characters: God, Psalmist.

Conclusion: All who love God delight to meditate upon His works. They are all praiseworthy, and if considered, cannot but cause us to adore Him and to express His praise to others.

Key Word: Jehovah's works, vv. 2, 4, 6, 7.

Strong Verses: 4, 10.

Striking Facts: v. 9. The Christian can indeed sing of redemption, for it is an accomplished act, wrought out for us by Jesus on Calvary. All who have received Him are indeed the Lord's redeemed.

CHAPTER ONE HUNDRED TWELVE

Contents: The eternal happiness of the saints.

Characters: God.

Conclusion: The truly happy man is he who fears the Lord, for he is given outward prosperity as far as it is good for him, and all spiritual blessings which are true and eternal riches.

Key Word: The upright, v. 2.

Strong Verses: 1, 7.

Striking Facts: Fixedness of heart, the sovereign remedy against all disquieting news is one of the believer's inheritances in Christ, who has proved Himself the victor over Satan. Looking to Jesus, the author and finisher of our faith is the sure way of establishing the heart.

CHAPTER ONE HUNDRED THIRTEEN

Contents: A call to praise God.
Characters: God.
Conclusion: Praise is a duty the believer should much abound in and in which he should be frequently employed, for in every place there appears the manifest proofs of God's wisdom, power and goodness.
Key Word: Praise, v. 1.
Strong Verses: 3, 7.

CHAPTER ONE HUNDRED FOURTEEN

Contents: The deliverance of Israel out of Egypt.
Characters: God, Psalmist.
Conclusion: He who made the hills and the mountains to skip, can when He pleases dissipate the strength and spirit of the proudest of His enemies and make them tremble.
Key Word: Jehovah's presence, v. 7.
Strong Verses: 7.

CHAPTER ONE HUNDRED FIFTEEN

Contents: Indignation against the makers and worshippers of idols and exhortation to trust in God.
Characters: God, house of Aaron, Psalmist.
Conclusion: The creatures of men's vain imaginations and the works of men's hands have no divinity in them and to worship such things is the heighth of absurdity. It is wisdom to trust in the living God who proves Himself the help and shield to all who humbly put their confidence in Him.
Key Word: Idols, v. 4.
Strong Verses: 11, 12.

CHAPTER ONE HUNDRED SIXTEEN

Contents: Thanksgiving for the many gracious deliverances God had wrought.
Characters: God, Psalmist.
Conclusion: The experiences we have had of God's goodness in answer to prayer are great encouragements to us to continue praying and should cause us to praise Him continually.
Key Word: Jehovah's benefits, v. 12.
Strong Verses: 1, 15.
Striking Facts: A psalm of thanksgiving in the person of Christ. He proclaims the mercies He experiences from His Father in the days of His incarnation and the glories He has received in the Kingdom above.

CHAPTER ONE HUNDRED SEVENTEEN

Contents: A solemn call to the nations to praise God.
Characters: God.
Conclusion: The Lord is kind to us as His creatures and merciful to us as sinners, therefore praise is due Him from all peoples.
Key Word, Praise, v. 1.
Strong Verses: 2.
Striking Facts: In Jesus Christ God has shown to the world mercy mixed with kindness to the very highest degree. The tidings of His gospel to all nations should cause them to glorify God.

CHAPTER ONE HUNDRED EIGHTEEN

Contents: Cheerful acknowledgement of God's goodness and dependence upon that goodness for the future.
Characters God.
Conclusion Never failing streams of mercy flow from our God. The more our hearts are impressed with the sense of His goodness, the more we are bound to praise Him and the more our hearts will be enlarged in all manner of obedience.
Key Word: Thanks, vv. 1, 29.
Strong Verses: 6, 8 (middle verse of Bible).
Striking Facts: v. 22. Jesus Christ is the tried stone, elect, precious, which God Himself appointed. While the Jews could not see the excellence in Him that they should build upon Him, in raising Him from the dead God

made Him the headstone of the corner, the foundation of the church. To
the rejector He is now a stumbling stone. At His second coming He is the
stone cut out without hands which is to fall upon and crush the unbelieving nations.

CHAPTEN ONE HUNDRED NINETEEN

Contents: The excellency and usefulness of the divine revelation set forth
and exhortation to all to make it their meditation and to be governed
by it.

Characters: God, Psalmist.

Conclusion: Great blessing belongs to those who read and understand the
Word of God, and more blessed is the man whose life is the practical
transcript of the will of God as revealed in the Scriptures.

Key Word: The Word, v. 11.

Strong Verses: 11, 18, 27, 89, 105, 130, 160, 165.

Striking Facts: v. 99.   The disciples of Christ who sit at His feet and let
Him interpret the Word to them are often better skilled in divine things
than the doctors of divinity. The best way to find "the wondrous things"
is to saturate the study of the Word in prayer (v. 18) which makes it
possible for Christ to speak to us out of the Word, through the Holy
Spirit. John 16:13, 14.

CHAPTER ONE HUNDRED TWENTY

Contents: Prayer for deliverance from the mischief designed by false and
malicious tongues.

Characters: God, Psalmist.

Conclusion: It is often the lot of the innocent that there are those who carry
on malicious designs against them under the color of friendship. In such
distresses we always have recourse to God, who, being the God of Truth,
will certainly be the protection of His people from lying lips and will
baffle the enemy at last.

Key Word: Lying lips, v. 2.

Strong Verses: 1.

Striking Facts: David is herein a type of Christ who was greatly distressed
by lying lips and deceitful tongues, and found sufficient grace to bear in
silence by waiting upon His heavenly Father.

CHAPTER ONE HUNDRED TWENTY-ONE

Contents: The guardian care of the Lord and the peace of His house.

Characters: God, Psalmist.

Conclusion: The Christian may stay himself upon Jehovah as a God of power,
a God all-sufficient for us. Our safety is in putting ourselves under His
protection.

Key Word: Keeper, v. 3.

Strong Verses: 2, 7.

Striking Facts: v. 2. Help cometh (lit) "from before the Lord." This suggests Christ incarnate through whom God has made Himself our help and
who helps us constantly by His intercession at God's right hand.

CHAPTER ONE HUNDRED TWENTY-TWO

Contents: Prayer for the welfare of Jerusalem.

Characters: God, David.

Conclusion: When peace comes to Jerusalem there will be peace for all the
world, therefore the saints should earnestly pray for it.

Key Word: Peace of Jerusalem, v. 6.

Strong Verses: 6.

Striking Facts: v. 5. The thought of God reigning in the Son of David, aveng-
ing the just cause, is cheering for disconsolate hearts. Christ's throne
is set and truth and righteousness shall be manifested on the throne with
the King when He comes.

CHAPTER ONE HUNDRED TWENTY-THREE

Contents: Expectation of mercy from God in the day of contempt.

Characters: God, Psalmist.

Conclusion: When man's eyes are toward God, he will always see God's mercy

coming toward him. He who dwells in heaven beholds all the calamities of His people and thence will send to save all trusting ones.
Key Word: Mercy, v. 3.
Strong Verses: 1.

CHAPTER ONE HUNDRED TWENTY-FOUR

Contents: David gives to God the glory of the deliverances of His people.
Characters: God, Israel.
Conclusion: God sometimes suffers the enemies of His people to prevail very far against them, that His own power may appear the more illustrious in their deliverance. Happy be the people whose God is Jehovah and who commit themselves to His keeping.
Key Word: Our help, v. 8.
Strong Verses: 8.

CHAPTER ONE HUNDRED TWENTY-FIVE

Contents: The security of God's people because of His promises, and the jeopardy of the wicked.
Characters: God, Israel.
Conclusion: There is no gap in the hedge of God's protection which He makes round about His trusting people. The happiness of God's people will be the vexation of those who perish in their wickedness.
Key Word: Security, v. 2.
Strong Verses: 1.

CHAPTER ONE HUNDRED TWENTY-SIX

Contents: Thanksfulness for deliverance from captivity.
Characters: God, Zion.
Conclusion: The long want of mercies greatly sweetens them when they are returned to us. When God appears for His people they should give Him the glory and give notice to all about them what wonders He has wrought for them.
Key Word: Deliverance, v. 3.
Strong Verses: 3, 5. 6.
Striking Facts: The return out of captivity may be taken as typical of the sinner's redemption by Christ. Surely He has done great things for us, whereof we should be glad and should give Him glory continually.

CHAPTER ONE HUNDRED TWENTY-SEVEN

Contents: The vanity of worldly care and the wisdom of dependence on God for all things in the home.
Characters: God.
Conclusion: The best designed home will be a failure unless God crowns it with His favor. He would have us keep our eyes upon Him in all the affairs of the family that we might avoid excessive care. He would have us realize that our children are a trust from Him and will be most our honor and comfort if they are dedicated to Him.
Key Word: Home, v. 1.
Strong Verses: 2, 3.

CHAPTER ONE HUNDRED TWENTY-EIGHT

Contents: The prosperity of those who live in the fear of God and in obedience to Him.
Characters: God, Israel.
Conclusion: Those who are truly holy are truly happy. Those may be assured of a prosperous and happy life who walk in reverence of God and evidence it by constant conformity to His will.
Key Word: Prosperity, v. 2.
Strong Verses: 1.

CHAPTER ONE HUNDRED TWENTY-NINE

Contents: Prayer for destruction of all the enemies of Zion.
Characters: God, Israel.
Conclusion: God has many ways of disabling men to do their mischief against His people and of bringing their counsels to naught. He is righteous in allowing His saints for a time to be afflicted and He is righteous in reckoning with all persecutors in the end.

Key Word: The wicked, v. 4.
Strong Verses: 4.
Striking Facts: v. 3. The sufferings of Christ were a prophecy of what His church would be called upon to endure for His sake. The· true church has ever had fellowship with Him under His cruel flagellations.

CHAPTER ONE HUNDRED THIRTY

Contents: The Psalmist's desire toward God and his repentance before God.
Characters: God, Psalmist.
Conclusion: Those who cry to God out of a sincere heart when they are in the depths of despair will soon sing of His mercy in the heights of His love.
Key Word: Supplication, v. 2.
Strong Verses: 3, 5, 6.
Striking Facts: There is but one solution to the sin question since all our transgressions are recorded. God has provided a sacrifice—Christ, through whom there is redemption for all. Our transgressions will not be acted upon if we are in Christ, since He has borne the penalty for us.

CHAPTER ONE HUNDRED THIRTY-ONE

Contents: The lowliness and humility of a sanctified heart.
Characters: God, David.
Conclusion: The love of God reigning in the heart will subdue all inordinate self love. To know God and our duty toward Him is the highest learning to be had in this world.
Key Word: Humility, v. 1.
Striking Facts: v. 2. The Lord Jesus teaches us humility by this same comparison. Matt. 18:3. We must become, not childish, but as little children, childlike in our confidence toward God.

CHAPTER ONE HUNDRED THIRTY-TWO

Contents: A pleading of the divine covenant and its promises.
Characters: God, David, Christ.
Conclusion: Those who have the immutable promises of God for their foundation stand upon a sure rock. God has given us His promises that our faith might have strong confidence at all times, and that we might know that His Annointed will sit upon the throne of earth to reign eternally.
Key Word: Remember David, vv. 1, 10.
Striking Facts: v. 11. Peter applies this to Christ and tells us that David himself so understood it. Acts 2:30. Christ fulfilled all the conditions and the Father has given Him the throne of his father David. Luke 1:32. He is now at the right hand of His Father's throne and when the fullness of the Gentiles is gathered in, the promise of the Davidic throne will be made good, and He will come to reign over all. The saints shall sit with Him upon this eternal throne. Rev. 3:21.

CHAPTER ONE HUNDRED THIRTY-THREE

Contents: The happiness of brotherly love.
Characters: God, Aaron.
Conclusion: To live together in peace, love, concord and mutual agreement, not only in occasional meetings, but all through the course of our lives, is indeed a great blessing and is very pleasing to our heavenly Father.
Key Word: Unity, v. 1.
Strong Verses: 1.
Striking Facts: The finest unity is that which the saints have in Christ. John 17:21. If we are in tune with Christ, we will be in tune with all His. While there may not always be oneness of view, there can always be oneness of spirit and object in Christ.

CHAPTER ONE HUNDRED THIRTY-FOUR

Contents: Exhortation to, and prayer for, those who are constantly ministering before the Lord.
Characters: God, night watchers.
Conclusion: Even by night, God's servants are under His eye and have access to Him. Let them therefore bless the Lord, that spiritual blessings out of Zion· might come upon them.

CHAPTER ONE HUNDRED THIRTY-FIVE

Key Word: Bless the Lord, v. 1.
Contents: A call to the servants of God to praise Him for His mighty works.
Characters: God, Pharaoh, Sihon, Og, house of Aaron, house of Levi.
Conclusion: Jehovah is great indeed, who knows no limits of time or place, who works in all the universe as He pleases. His name should endure forever in the constant and everlasting praises of His people.
Key Word: Jehovah's greatness, v. 5.
Strong Verses: 6 13.

CHAPTER ONE HUNDRED THIRTY-SIX

Contents: Call to praise God as the great Benefactor of the whole creation.
Characters: God.
Conclusion: We should give thanks to God, not only for the mercies which are handed out to us here on earth, but for that which endures forever in the glories and joys of heaven to follow this life.
Key Word: Everlasting mercy, v. 1.
Strong Verses: 26.
Striking Facts: vv. 23-24. In our lost estate, God has extended His great mercy toward us in the gift of His Son to redeem us from sin, death and hell and save us from all spiritual enemies.

CHAPTER ONE HUNDRED THIRTY-SEVEN

Contents: Lamentation over the sad condition of God's people in captivity.
Characters: God.
Conclusion: Those who are glad at the calamities that sometimes in God's providence come to His people, shall not go unpunished, for those who mock their grief shall endure eternal grief.
Key Word: Captivity, v. 3.
Strong Verses: 4.

CHAPTER ONE HUNDRED THIRTY-EIGHT

Contents: Thankfulness for the experience of God's goodness.
Characters: God, David.
Concluson: Praising God is work of which the greatest of men need not be ashamed. A debt of gratitude is due Him for the wonders of His grace, the revelation of His Word, and the confidence derived from the promises that there is no experience that can overwhelm us if we look toward Him.
Key Word: Jehovah's loving kindness, v. 2.
Strong Verses: 2, 6, 7, 8.
Striking Facts: v. 2. Christ is the essential Word, John 1:1. He and His gospel are magnified above all the discoveries God had made of Himself to the fathers.

CHAPTER ONE HUNDRED THIRTY-NINE

Contents: Meditation upon the doctrines of God's omniscience and omnipresence.
Characters: God, David.
Conclusion: The God with whom we have to do has a perfect knowledge of us and all the motions and actions, both of our outward and inward man. We should therefore desire of Him that when He sees sin in our hearts, He might discover it to us that we might walk in the perfect enjoyment of His presence.
Key Word: Omnipresence, v. 7.
Strong Verses: 17, 23, 24.
Striking Facts: v. 7. No one can escape the all-pervading Being and observation of the Holy Spirit. We are, whether we will it or not, as near to God as our soul is to our body, for the Holy Spirit dwells within the Christian (1 Cor. 6:19). This makes it dreadful work to sin, for it is insulting God to His face.

CHAPTER ONE HUNDRED FORTY

Contents: The malice of enemies and prayer for preservation.
Characters: God, David.

Conclusion: Those are safe whom God preserves. In Him believers may count upon security against all real enemies.

Key Word: Preservation, vv. 1, 4.

Strong Verses: 7, 12.

Striking Facts: David is here a type of Christ in that he suffered before his reign and was humbled before he was exalted. As there were many who valued Him, so there were many who hated Him, and those who could not agree in anything else joined themselves faithfully together to persecute Christ.

CHAPTER ONE HUNDRED FORTY-ONE

Contents: Prayer for God's favorable acceptance and powerful assistance.

Characters: God, David.

Conclusion: Though the snares be placed by the enemy with ever so much subtlety, God can, and will, secure His praying people from being taken in them.

Key Word: Keeping, v. 9.

Strong Verses: 3, 8.

Striking Facts: v. 2. Christ in the evening of the world, offered up Himself a sacrifice that a way of approach might be made for the believer into the Holy of Holies. It was the fire under the incense that brought out its sweetness—it is the Holy Spirit who offers fragrant prayer to God. Rom. 8:26-27. The fire, however, was from the blood-sprinkled altar, and apart from Christ's atonement, no acceptable prayer can be offered. Heb. 10:19-20.

CHAPTER ONE HUNDRED FORTY-TWO

Contents: The malice of enemies and expectation of God's deliverance.

Characters: God, David.

Conclusion: There is no cave so deep or dark but that out of it we may send up our souls in prayer to God, with expectation of being brought out of all our perplexities.

Key Word: Trouble, v. 2.

Strong Verses: 5.

Striking Facts: v. 4. David is here a type of Christ, who in His suffering for us was forsaken of all men and trod the winepress alone.

CHAPTER ONE HUNDRED FORTY-THREE

Contents: Complaint of great distresses and dangers and prayer that persecutors might be reckoned with.

Characters: God, David.

Conclusion: If we look with earnest desire toward God, we need not let our heart be troubled, no matter what troubles we are in. John 14:1.

Key Word: Overwhelmed, v. 4.

Strong Verses: 8, 10.

CHAPTER ONE HUNDRED FORTY-FOUR

Contents: Acknowledgment of the great goodness of God and prayer for the prosperity of the kingdom.

Characters: God, David.

Conclusion: Happy is the people whose God is the Lord, for even when they are weak, they may be made strong in the Lord and in the power of His might.

Key Word: Our strength, v. 1.

Strong Verses: 3, 15.

Striking Facts: vv. 12-14. David as king is here a type of Christ who provides effectually for the good of His chosen and who will remove every hurtful thing from earth when He comes to reign.

CHAPTER ONE HUNDRED FORTY-FIVE

Contents: David engages himself and others to praise God.

Characters: God, David.

Conclusion: Praising God should be our daily work, for God is every day blessing us. His greatness and goodness cannot be comprehended, and when we have said what we can in praising Him, there is more to be said.

Key Word: Great goodness, v. 7.

Strong Verses: 3, 8, 14, 16, 18, 19.

CHAPTER ONE HUNDRED FORTY-SIX

Contents: The psalmist engages himself to praise God and exhorts others to trust and praise Him.

Characters: God, Psalmist.

Conclusion: There should be no exemption from the service of praising God. So long as He lets us breathe, we should bless Him for His goodness and mercy.

Key Word: Praise, v. 1.

Strong Verses: 5, 9.

Striking Facts: The psalm is very applicable to Christ, by whom God made the world; who caused the blind to receive their sight and the lame to walk; He will subvert all the counsels of hell and earth that militate against His church and will exercise full judgment at His coming again.

CHAPTER ONE HUNDRED FORTY-SEVEN

Contents: A call to praise God. The greatness and condescending goodness of the Lord celebrated.

Characters: God.

Conclusion: Praise is comely—it becomes us as reasonable creatures on account of God's manifest greatness and goodness in all nature and much more as a people in special covenant relations with Him.

Key Word: Jehovah's greatness, v. 5.

Strong Verses: 5, 11.

CHAPTER ONE HUNDRED FORTY-EIGHT

Contents: A call to all living things to praise God.

Characters: God.

Conclusion: No place is too high for the praises of the Most High. All creatures on earth should also speak the Lord's praise, for He is Creator and Preserver; Maker and Ruler

Key Word: Praise, v 1.

Strong Verses: 13.

Striking Facts: v. 14. The blessing of nearness to God has now, through Christ, come upon the Gentiles. Those who were afar off are now made nigh by His blood. Eph. 2:13.

CHAPTER ONE HUNDRED FORTY-NINE

Contents: Triumph in the God of Israel.

Characters: God.

Conclusion: Our praises of God should flow from a heart filled with delight and triumph in His attributes and our relation to Him

Key Word: Praise, v. 1.

Strong Verses: 4.

Striking Facts: vv. 7-10. Our Lord Jesus is coming as King to overthrow all evil, to display His justice against evil-doers, and with Him, the saints shall judge the world.

CHAPTER ONE HUNDRED FIFTY

Contents: The psalmist would fill all the world with God's praises.

Characters: God.

Conclusion: What have we our breath for but to spend it in praising God and how can we spend it better? Since we must shortly breathe our last, while we have breath, let us praise the Lord.

Key Word: Praise, v. 1.

Strong Verses: 6.

Striking Facts: The first psalm began with "blessed" and ended with "blessed." The fruit of the blessedness of meditating on God's Word, is now shown in the last psalm which begins and ends (lit.) with "Hallelujah."

PROVERBS

Key Thought:	Number of Chapters	Key Verse:	Christ seen as:
Wisdom	31	9:10	Wisdom

Writer of the Book:	Date:	Conclusion of the Book:
Solomon	990 to 995 B. C.	The most intensely practical thing in the world is godliness.

SUMMARY

CHAPTER ONE

Contents: Wisdom's reasoning with the children of men and the certain ruin of those who turn a deaf ear to Wisdom's call.

Characters: God, Solomon, his son, Wisdom, (Christ).

Conclusion: Of all things to be known, the most important is that God is to be reverenced and served, and those know little who do not know this. All true knowledge takes rise from reverence of God and tends to it as its perfection and center.

Key Word: Wisdom, v. 2.

Strong Verses: 7, 33.

Striking Facts: v. 20. It is Christ who pleads with sinners and passes sentence on them. He calls Himself Wisdom, Luke 7:35. In Him are hid all the treasures of wisdom and knowledge. He is the center of all divine revelation—the eternal Word by whom God speaks to men.

CHAPTER TWO

Contents: How wisdom is to be obtained and used. The unspeakable advantage of true wisdom.

Characters: God, Solomon, his son.

Conclusion: God has provided that those who are sincerely disposed to do His will shall have that knowledge and understanding necessary for them. His wisdom will preserve us from men of corrupt principles whose business it is to debauch lives, and from women of corrupt practices.

Key Word: Wisdom, v. 7.

Strong Verses: 6, 7, 21, 22.

Striking Facts: v. 7. Wisdom is laid up for the righteous, in Christ, who is made unto the believer, wisdom and knowledge.

CHAPTER THREE

Contents: The power of true wisdom to make men both blessed and a blessing.

Characters: God, Solomon, his son.

Conclusion: Those who have a continual regard to God's precepts and put themselves under divine guidance by acknowledging God and praying in faith to Him, shall find health of soul, good habits of body and true success in life.

Key Word: Favor, vv. 4, 33.

Strong Verses: 5, 6, 11, 26.

Striking Facts: vv. 13-14. In all the wealth of the world is not to be found a taste of that transcendant happiness which is gained in Christ, in whom are stored the treasures of wisdom, which consist in the knowledge and love of God.

CHAPTER FOUR

Contents: Earnest exhortation to the study of true wisdom.

Characters: God, Solomon, his son.

Conclusion: True wisdom from God is the principle thing. It is that which recommends us to God, which beautifies the soul, which enables us to answer the ends of our creation, to live to some good purpose in the world and which makes our path brighter and brighter until we get to heaven at last.

Key Word: Wisdom v. 5.
Strong Verses: 18, 23.
Striking Facts: v. 18. The Christian walks in a way of light. Christ is their way and Christ is the light. They are guided by the Bible which is a light to their feet.

CHAPTER FIVE

Contents: Caution against the sin of whoredom.
Characters: God, Solomon, his son.
Conclusion: We ought industriously to avoid everything that might be an occasion of the sin of adultery or a step towards it, for it is destructive of all the seeds of virtue of the soul and those who are entangled in it have but a step between them and hell.
Key Word: Strange woman, v. 3.
Strong Verses: 21, 22.
Striking Facts: v. 21. Those who practice adultery promise themselves secrecy (Job 24:15). All the workings of the heart and all the outgoings of the life are wide open to God, Christ and the Holy Spirit. Every action will be brought into judgment when Jesus comes.

CHAPTER SIX

Contents: Caution against rash suretiship, slothfulness, forwardness, and whoredom.
Characters: God, Solomon, his son.
Conclusion: Suretiship is to be avoided, because by it poverty and ruin are often brought into families. Poverty and want will certainly come upon those who are slothful. The froward man who devises mischief will surely fall into mischief. Adultery is to be looked upon with utmost dread and detestation as a sin that impoverishes men, debauches their consciences, threatens death and brings infamy upon the reputation.
Key Word: Warnings (5:1).
Strong Verses: 6, 23, 32.

CHAPTER SEVEN

Contents: Warning against all approaches to the sin of adultery.
Characters: Solomon, his son.
Conclusion: The Word of God, if used for a defense and armor, will keep one from the strange woman and the destroying sin of adultery. Let the Word therefore discover to us the fallacies of this sin and suggest to us the answers to all its flatteries.
Key Word: Strange woman, v. 5.
Strong Verses: 2.

CHAPTER EIGHT

Contents Praise of divine wisdom. Christ, the Wisdom of God, speaks to men.
Characters: God, Wisdom (Christ).
Conclusion: Right knowledge of the divine will concerning us is to be preferred above all the wealth of this world, for it brings favor with God, and eternal life.
Key Word: Wisdom, v. 1.
Strong Verses: 35, 36.
Striking Facts: v. 22. Wisdom here is certainly more than the personification of an attribute of God, or the will of God, but is a distinct representation of Christ. John 1:1-3; Col. 1:17.

CHAPTER NINE

Contents: Wisdom (Chr'st) and sin, as rivals for the soul of man.
Characters: God, Wisdom.
Conclusion: Christ and sin are both seeking to have the uppermost place in the soul of man. We are therefore concerned to put a value upon our own souls and to sit down at the rich feast provided at Wisdom's table. There is no true wisdom but in the way of Christ and there is no true life but in the end of His way.
Key Word: Wisdom.
Strong Verses: 10.

Striking Facts: vv. 1-5. Heaven is the place where **Wisdom** (Christ) has prepared many mansions. Christ Himself is the sacrifice which has been killed and it is His flesh that is meat indeed. His disciples have gone forth with the invitation to the Gospel feast, even the simple being freely invited.

CHAPTER TEN

Contents: The blessedness of the ways of righteousness and the folly of the ways of wickedness.
Characters: God Solomon.
Conclusion: The head of the just man will be crowned with the blessings both of God and man, and they shall leave behind them blessed memories. The wicked man's ways will turn out to be his shame and when his body is in the grave, his name will be spoken only with contempt.
Key Word: Wickedness and righteousness, v. 2.
Strong Verses: 7, 9, 19, 22, 28.

CHAPTER ELEVEN

Contents: Proverbs contrasting good and evil.
Characters: God.
Conclusion: The ways of righteousness are plain and safe and in them we may enjoy a holy security. The ways of wickedness are dangerous and those who indulge themselves in sin are fitting themselves for destruction.
Key Word: Righteousness and wickedness, v. 5.
Strong Verses: 24, 25, 30.

CHAPTER TWELVE

Contents: Proverbs contrasting good and evil.
Characters: God.
Conclusion: In the life of the righteous, there is all true comfort and satisfaction and at the end of life there is eternal joy. The man who devises wickedness is under condemnation and all his triumphing on earth is but for a moment.
Key Word: Goodness and wickedness, v. 2.
Strong Verses: 21 28.

CHAPTER THIRTEEN

Contents: Proverbs contrasting good and evil.
Characters: God.
Conclusion: The destruction of sinners is unavoidable, for God's wrath pursues them, and whom God pursues is sure to be overtaken. The happiness of the saints is indefeatable, for God has promised that they shall be abundautly recompensed for all the good they have done and the ill they have suffered.
Key Word: Righteousness and wickedness, v. 5.
Strong Verses: 7, 13.

CHAPTER FOURTEEN

Contents: Proverbs contrasting good and evil.
Characters: God.
Conclusion: The house of the wicked, though built ever so strong and high, shall be brought to disgrace and at length made extinct. The tabernacle of the upright, though moveable and despicable shall, at all events have grace and comfort, and shall be eternally established.
Key Word: Righteousness and wickedness, v. 2.
Strong Verses: 11, 12, 16, 26, 27.

CHAPTER FIFTEEN

Contents: Proverbs contrasting good and evil.
Characters: God.
Conclusion: The course of the wicked man is an abomination to God, neither is there any offering he can make to God that can be accepted, as long as the heart is resolved to go on in sin. The upright man is regarded as the friend of God, whose prayer is God's delight, and to whom He is very near.
Key Word: Righteousness and wickedness, v. 6.
Strong Verses: 3, 8, 9, 16, 33.

CHAPTER SIXTEEN

Contents: Proverbs contrasting good and evil.
Characters: God.
Conclusion: The safest way in which to travel is the way of the upright, a way which God makes plain to those who desire to walk in it:— We should take heed of deceiving ourselves by resting in that which seems right, but is not really so.
Key Word: Righteousness and wickedness.
Strong Verses: 3, 7, 8, 18, 25, 31, 32.
Striking Facts: v. 4. God makes no man wicked, but He made those whom He foreknew would be wicked of their own choice, because He knew how to get glory to Himself and honor upon them (Rom. 9:22) by the display of His grace in Christ Jesus.

CHAPTER SEVENTEEN

Contents: Proverbs contrasting good and evil.
Characters: God.
Conclusion: About the most satisfactory substitute for wisdom is silence. Discretion of speech is better than fluency of speech.
Key Word: Wicked and unjust, v. 15.
Strong Verses: 3, 13.

CHAPTER EIGHTEEN

Contents: Proverbs contrasting good and evil.
Characters: God.
Conclusion: The only zone of safety is the name of the Lord which is the strong tower in which one may find rest and be fortified against the evil one, if they will but come into it by faith in God's Word.
Key Word: Wicked and righteous, v. 5.
Strong Verses: 10, 24.
Striking Facts: v. 24. Christ is the true friend to all believers, who sticks closer than a brother. To Him therefore let us show ourselves friends.

CHAPTER NINETEEN

Contents: Proverbs contrasting good and evil.
Characters: God.
Conclusion: If we keep God's Word, God's Word will keep us from all things that are really hurtful. Those who despise the ways of His Word are on the high road to ruin.
Key Word: Goodness and wickedness, vv. 16, 28.
Strong Verses: 16, 17, 23.
Striking Facts: v. 17. What is given to the poor out of love for Christ, God places to our account as lent to Him. Jesus said "Inasmuch as ye have done it unto one of the least of these, my brethren, ye have done it unto me."

CHAPTER TWENTY

Contents: Warnings and instructions regarding the ways of folly.
Characters: God.
Conclusion: Here in this imperfect state, no person can claim to be sinless, but the just man, walking by the rule of God's Word may have the comfort of a good conscience, and his children will fare the better for his sake.
Key Word: Counsel, v 5.
Strong Verses: 1, 7, 9, 22.
Striking Facts: v. 9. This is a challenge to any man in the world to prove himself sinless. Only saints in heaven, who "have seen Him as He is" , and been made like Him, can say it. Though the believer, through the work of the Spirit, is pure from the sins of many others, yet each one still has sins that easily beset him—sins of omission and sins of commission which they have to continually confess in order to maintain unbroken fellowship with Christ.

CHAPTER TWENTY-ONE

Contents: Warnings and instructions.
Characters: God.

Conclusion: Those who follow after righteousness, shall find righteousness, honor and life.

Key Word: Counsel (20:5).

Strong Verses: 3, 13, 21, 30.

Striking Facts: v. 3. The sacrifice which typified the great sacrifice of Christ, was a divine institution. Religious ceremonies based upon Christ's sacrifice are pleasing to God when offered in faith and repentance, but when not backed by true devotion, are an abomination.

CHAPTER TWENTY-TWO

Contents: Warnings and instructions.

Characters: God, Solomon.

Conclusion: Those who walk humbly with God in obedience to the commands of His Word and in submission to the disposals of His providence, shall find true riches, honor, comfort and long life in this world, and eternal life at last.

Key Word: Counsel (20:5).

Strong Verses: 1, 4.

CHAPTER TWENTY-THREE

Contents: Warnings and instructions.

Characters: God, Solomon, his son.

Conclusion: The indulgence of the appetites is a sin that easily besets us. We should apprehend ourselves to be in danger when in the presence of luxury, gluttony and sensuality, and should restrain ourselves from such gratifications, lest our hearts be overcharged with surfeiting and that day come upon us unawares.

Key Word: Instruction, v. 12.

Strong Verses: 17, 23.

CHAPTER TWENTY-FOUR

Contents: Warnings and instructions.

Characters: God, Solomon, his son.

Conclusion: If wicked people prosper, we should not be inclined to do as they do, nor complain of what God does in His providence. They have no real happiness of heart, their prosperity is only for the present and there is no good for them in the world to come. Let us therefore honor and reverence God and be dutiful to the government God has set over us.

Key Word: Counsel, v. 6.

Strong Verses: 16, 19, 20, 24.

CHAPTER TWENTY-FIVE

Contents: Warnings and instructions.

Characters: God, Solomon, Hezekiah.

Conclusion: (Principal lesson, vv. 21, 22.) The way to turn an enemy into a friend is to act friendly towards him. If it does not gain him it will aggravate his sin and punishment, and will heap the coals of God's wrath upon his head.

Key Word: Proverbs, v. 1.

Strong Verses: 21, 22

Striking Facts: v. 1. Herein Christ is greater than Solomon for John 21:25 tells us that if we had on record all the good things that Christ said the world could not contain the books.

CHAPTER TWENTY-SIX

Contents: Warnings and instructions.

Characters: God.

Conclusion: (Principal lesson, vv. 20-25.) God gives us two ears and two eyes, but only one tongue. We should therefore see and hear more than we speak, for we cannot recover our words.

Key Word: Proverbs, v. 1 (25:1).

Strong Verses: 12, 20, 27.

CHAPTER TWENTY-SEVEN

Contents: Warnings and instructions.

Characters: Solomon, his son.

Conclusion: (Principal lesson.) Use the present time with diligence and wisdom and presume not upon tomorrow. We should speak of the morrow as those who are submitted to the will of God, knowing the uncertainty of one moment, except as God allows it to us.
Key Word: Proverbs (25:1)
Strong Verses: 1, 6.

CHAPTER TWENTY-EIGHT
Contents: Warnings and instructions.
Characters: God.
Conclusion: True religion is true wisdom, making men wise in every relation. Those who make conscience of God's law will find a security in the worst of times and will always be found vigorously opposing sin.
Key Word: Proverbs (25:1).
Strong Verses: 4, 6, 9, 13, 26.

CHAPTER TWENTY-NINE
Contents: Warnings and instructions.
Characters: God.
Conclusion: Those who never regard the Word of God are an easy prey to the enemy of souls. A confidence in God and His Word enables one to look with gracious contempt upon the most formidable designs of the devil, and will keep one in the way of duty, and above the fear of man.
Key Word: Righteous and wicked, v. 2.
Strong Verses: 1, 18, 25.

CHAPTER THIRTY
Contents: The words of Agur.
Characters: God, Agur, Ithiel, Ucal.
Conclusion: God's Word is sure and pure, and venturing our souls upon it, we shall find it a shield against temptations, a safe protection in the midst of greatest dangers. God will certainly reckon with any who presume to add to His Word, or advance anything in competition with it.
Key Word: Proverbs, v. 1.
Strong Verses: 5, 6.
Striking Facts: v. 4. It is God who has gathered the winds in His fists and His name is "I am that I am" (Ex. 3:14), a name to be adored, not to be understood. He has a Son, Jesus Christ, whose name was to be called "Wonderful, Counsellor, the Mighty God, Prince of Peace." By Him, God made all that was made, and by Him He controls all things.

CHAPTER THIRTY-ONE
Contents: Words of King Lemuel on the dangers of intemperance and the worth of a godly woman.
Characters: God, Lemuel, his mother.
Conclusion: A virtuous woman who has command of her own spirit, who is pious and industrious, who is firm for the principles of God's Word, is a rare prize. Such a one is of unspeakable worth, and he who has such a wife, should show to her great kindness and respect, and to God, thankfulness of heart.
Key Word: Virtuous woman, v. 10.
Strong Verses: 10, 30.
Striking Facts: The scope of all the various proverbs of this book is one and the same—to direct our manner of life aright and to point us to the Lord Jesus Christ, who is "made unto us Wisdom and Righteousness."

ECCLESIASTES

10

Key Thought:	Number of Chapters:	Key Verse:	Christ seen as:
Vanity	12	2:11	Above the Sun

Writer of the Book:	Date:	Conclusion of the Book:
Solomon	980 to 985 B. C.	Apart from God, life is full of weariness and disappointment.

SUMMARY

CHAPTER ONE

Contents: The doctrine of the vanity. of the creature, and the impossibility of finding satisfaction without God.

Characters: God, Solomon.

Conclusion: All things, considered as abstract from God, and apart from Him, all worldly employments and enjoyments, are vanity of vanities, and if there were no supernatural method of giving peace to.the heart and another life to follow, were indeed made in vain.

Key Word: Vanity, v. 2.

Strong Verses: 8.

Striking Facts: All is indeed vanity if Christ is not in the heart and if there be no hope of eternal life through acceptance of Him. The things of earth are passing away and hence are vanity if they be trusted in. There is a kingdom coming in which believers shall inherit substance and where there is no vanity. Matt. 11:28-29; 1 Cor. 15:19.

CHAPTER TWO

Contents: Solomon shows that there is no true happiness and satisfaction to be had in mirth, pleasure and the delights of sense.

Characters: God, Solomon.

Conclusion: True and lasting happiness and satisfaction consist not in mirth, the gratifying of appetites, the spending of money or the getting of wisdom. Only he who sets God always before him and employs himself for God may find heart rest in this world and that joy which He alone can give.

Key Word: Vanity, v. 1.

Strong Verses: 26.

CHAPTER THREE

Contents: The mutability of all human affairs and the unchangeableness and unsearchableness of the divine counsels.

Characters: God, Solomon.

Conclusion: We live in a world of changes. The events of time and the conditions of human life are continually passing and repassing, yet every change is determined by the supreme power and we should therefore accommodate ourselves to His purposes. The only true pleasure of life is in making good use of the things God has given us, making ourselves serviceable to those about us.

Key Word: Man's portion, v. 22.

Strong Verses: 12, 14, 17.

Striking Facts: v. 17. In the midst of all the inequalities of human affairs it is a great comfort to know that the eye of faith can see that Jesus Christ, the Judge, stands before the door and that when He comes, He will reward the righteous and punish the pride and cruelty of oppressors. Though the day of affliction may seem long, we may patiently wait His coming, when there will be an examination into every purpose and every work done under the sun.

CHAPTER FOUR

Contents: Discontent and impatience because of the oppressions and iniquities of life.

Characters: Solomon.
Conclusion: The world is full of trouble. By reason of man's perversity, he is ever disturbed and perplexed by social conditions around him. If Christ and the hope of heaven were not taken into account, to die as soon as possible would be desirable.
Key Word: Vanity, v. 7.
Strong Verses: 6, 13.
Striking Facts: v. 4. For every right work, the Christian is remembered by the Lord Jesus, and at His coming will be rewarded. Though he be hated by a neighbor for a right work, the Christian will always be abounding in the work of the Lord knowing his labor will not be in vain in the Lord.

CHAPTER FIVE

Contents: Warnings against a vain religion. The vanity and vexation attending the possession of wealth.
Characters: God, Solomon.
Conclusion: We should address ourselves to the worship of God with all possible seriousness and care, for religious exercises if not rightly directed, may become empty ceremony, and we will miss our end in coming into His presence.
Key Word: Vanity, v. 10.
Strong Verses: 1, 2, 12.
Striking Facts: Those who labor only for the world, to fill their hands with that which they cannot take away, will not only die an uncomfortable death, but will miss the only satisfaction of life.
(v. 12.) The sleep of the diligent Christian is sweet, for having spent his strength and time in Christ's service, he can cheerfully return to Him and repose in Him who gives rest. Matt. 11:28-29

CHAPTER SIX

Contents: The vanity of worldly wealth as pertaining only to the body.
Characters: God, Solomon.
Conclusion: Man deprives himself of the good he might have had of his worldly possessions by not consecrating them to God. If one does not have the will to serve God with what he has, God may deny him the power to even serve himself with it.
Key Word: Vanity, v. 2.
Strong Verses: 2.
Striking Facts: v. 7. Those who have ever so much, yet do not know Christ, are ever craving. Wealth to a worldling is like drink to one who has dropsy, which only increases the thirst. Christ is the true Bread which satisfies; the Water of life which quenches all thirst of the soul.

CHAPTER SEVEN

Contents: Prudence recommended as a means of avoiding much of the vanity and vexation of the world.
Characters: God, Solomon.
Conclusion: The best way to save ourselves from the vexation which the vanity of the world creates, is to make use of wisdom, maintaining strict government of the passions. Wisdom is a defense (v. 12)
Key Word: Wisdom, vv. 11, 19.
Strong Verses: 9, 29.

CHAPTER EIGHT

Contents: Wisdom recommended as an antidote against the temptations and vexations arising from the vanity of the world.
Characters: God, Solomon.
Conclusion: Heavenly wisdom makes a man a good man, emboldening him against his adversaries, their attempts and their scorn. It teaches him that sentence is passed by a righteous Judge against all evil works, even though the execution of sentence is long delayed, and that it shall be well in the end with those who fear God.
Key Word: Wisdom, v. 1.
Strong Verses: 11, 12.

CHAPTER NINE

Contents: The universality of death and the need of minding the business of life and using wisdom.

Characters: God, Solomon.

Conclusion: While there is life there is opportunity of preparing for death, and since death is certain, it is our wisdom to make the best possible use of life while it lasts, cheerfully taking our share of life's enjoyments, applying ourselves diligently to life's business, and being governed by divine wisdom in all its affairs.

Key Word: Vanity, v. 9.

Strong Verses: 10, 16.

Striking Facts: v. 1.   Regardless of how the outward condition of men may seem to us, let it be remembered that all men's affairs are in God's hand and that prosperity is not necessarily a sign of God's love or affliction of His hatred.   If a man has Christ as His Savior, he may be happy though the world frowns upon him, and if he is without Christ, he may be miserable, though the world smiles upon him.

CHAPTER TEN

Contents: Proverbs recommending wisdom as of great use for the right ordering of our lives.

Characters: Solomon.

Conclusion: Fools are apt, at every turn, to proclaim their folly, for if one is lacking in true wisdom, it cannot be concealed.   True wisdom is true honor and will gain a man a reputation which is very valuable.

Key Word: Wisdom and folly, vv. 6, 10.

Strong Verses: 8, 10.

Striking Facts: v. 1.   Those who profess to be followers of Christ, who is said to be "made unto us wisdom," have need to walk very circumspectly lest they be guilty of any instance of folly, for many eyes are upon them.

CHAPTER ELEVEN

Contents: Exhortation to works of charity and right living.

Characters: God, Solomon.

Conclusion: Since we have death and judgment to prepare for, we should do good to others and abound in liberality to the poor, which will (if we are in Christ) abound to our account.

Key Word: Give, v. 2.

Strong Verses: 1, 9.

CHAPTER TWELVE

Contents: Exhortation to the young to be religious.   The vanity of the world.

Characters: God, Solomon.

Conclusion: The great antidote against the diseases of youth, the love of mirth, the indulgence of sensual pleasures, and the vanities to which youth is subject, is the reverence of God reigning in the heart and a respect to His commandments.   To reverence God is the summary of religion.

Key Word: Fear God, v. 13.

Strong Verses: 1, 13, 14.

Striking Facts: v. 13.   This is on the ground of law, not grace.   To fear God and keep the commandments is the best that man, apart from redemption, can do.   The Christian, under the Gospel, has Christ living in Him (Gal. 2:20) and his body is a shrine of the Holy Ghost (1 Cor. 6:19).

SONG OF SOLOMON

Key Thought:	Number of Chapters:	Key Verse:	Christ seen as:
Love	8	6:3	Altogether Lovely One

Writer of the Book:	Date:	Conclusion of the Book:
Solomon	980-985 B. C.	Christ covets the full communion of His people and blessedness comes to all who walk in His fellowship.

SUMMARY

CHAPTER ONE

Contents: The Bride and Bridegroom in joyful communion.
Characters: Solomon, Bride (Christ, Church).
Conclusion: Those who are full of Christ earnestly desire the manifestations of His love to their souls, with humble professions of love to Him and complacency in Him above all.
Key Word: Love, v. 2.
Strong Verses: 4.
Striking Facts: The spiritual and larger interpretation of this book is of Christ, the Son and His heavenly Bride, the Church (2 Cor. 11:1-4). The Church is beautiful to Christ as Christ is beautiful to the Church.

CHAPTER TWO

Contents: The Bridegroom speaks concerning himself and his Bride. The Bride speaks remembering her satisfaction in her beloved.
Characters: Solomon, Bride (Christ, Church).
Conclusion: Humble souls see the most beauty in the Bridegroom. To them He is the rose and He is the lily, and all excellency is in Him in the highest degree. Those are made like Him in whose hearts His love is shed abroad.
Key Word: Beloved, v. 8.
Strong Verses: 4, 16.
Striking Facts: Those whose hearts are filled with love to Christ and the hope of heaven, know best the meaning of this chapter—the rejoicing in Him and the longing to see Him.

CHAPTER THREE

Contents: The Bride seeking the favor of the Bridegroom. She calls upon all to admire Him.
Characters: Solomon, Bride (Christ, Church).
Conclusion: Those who are truly of the Bride, will evince the sincerity of their love to Christ by continual and solicitous enquiries after Him and will not be satisfied until Christ Himself is apprehended by faith.
Key Word: My beloved, v. 1.
Strong Verses: 2.
Striking Facts: Under the figure of Solomon, his bed and his guards about it the Church here admires Christ, the true Bridegroom. Solomon is used as an illustrious type of Christ because of his wisdom and wealth and the fact that he built the temple.

CHAPTER FOUR

Contents: The Bridegroom commends the beauty of the Bride and delights in her affection.
Characters: Solomon, Bride (Christ, Church).
Conclusion: Whatever others think of the Bride of Christ, she is amiable and

beautiful in His eyes because of the comliness of grace which He has put upon her. All the beauty of saints is derived from Him.

Key Word: My love, v. 1.

Strong Verses: 7 (See Eph. 5:27).

Striking Facts: The representations here made of the beauty of the Church, do not represent external beauty but the beauty of holiness, the hidden man of the heart as seen by heaven through the blood of Christ.

CHAPTER FIVE

Contents: The distress of the Bride because of the temporary withdrawal of the groom, due to the Bride's neglect.

Characters: Solomon, Bride (Christ, Church).

Conclusion: The slights which careless souls put upon Christ are grievous to Him and He suspends the communication of His comfort to those who are remiss and drowsy in His service. The loss of the sense of His presence is a matter of great grief to the believer.

Key Word: Beloved withdrawn, v. 6.

Strong Verses: 10.

Striking Facts: v. 6. Rev. 3:20 describes the state of the Church in coldness toward Christ. He has knocked for entrance, but in their drowsiness and coldness, they have not responded. They find themselves at last deserted by Him.

CHAPTER SIX

Contents: The Bridegroom applauds the beauty of the Bride, preferring her before all others.

Characters: Solomon, Bride (Christ, Church).

Conclusion: Christ takes delight in His redeemed and in the workings of His own grace in them, notwithstanding their weaknesses, and though He often has to hide His face temporarily, yet He gathers them back to His heart when they return to their duty, and He always prefers His own to the best of the unsaved of the world.

Key Word: My love, v. 4.

Strong Verses: 3.

Striking Facts: v. 3. Though Christ may have justly hid His face from His Bride for a time, yet His covenant continues firm, and true believers may always say, "I am His and He is mine."

CHAPTER SEVEN

Contents: Further description of the beauties of the Bride.

Characters: Solomon, Bride (Christ, Church).

Conclusion: The Bride of Christ bears the image of the King of Kings and in the beauty of holiness, is beyond anything nature can reach. In answer to the expressions of Christ's regard for His own, the believer should triumph in his relation to Him and rejoice in the hold He has of him.

Key Word: Beauty, v. 1.

Strong Verses: 10.

Striking Facts: v. 11. Those who love Christ will go forth from the amusements of the world, contriving to attend upon' Him without distraction. If we keep our eyes upon Christ, we may have the realization of His presence with us wherever we go (I walk with the King, hallelujah!).

CHAPTER EIGHT

Contents: The affections between the Bridegroom and His Bride.

Characters: Solomon, Bride (Christ, Church).

Conclusion: Those who are espoused to the Lord Jesus, should desire constant intimacy and freedom with Him. Let us be ready to own our relation to Him and affection for Him, never fearing being despised by the world for it.

Key Word: Love, v. 7.

Strong Verses: 7.

Striking Facts: v. 14. "Even so come, Lord Jesus: come quickly." Only those who can in sincerity call Christ their beloved, can desire Him to hasten His second coming. Let believers long for it, pray for it and work for it.

ISAIAH

Key Thought: Salvation	Number of Chapters: 66	Key Verse: 53:5	Christ seen as: Suffering and glori- fied prophet.

Writer of the Book: Isaiah	Date: 766 to 679 B. C.	Conclusion of the Book: Salvation is by the grace of God and through the vicarious suffering of Christ.

• SUMMARY

CHAPTER ONE

Contents: Charge against Israel for their ingratitude and degeneration. Call to repentance and reformation.

Characters: God, Isaiah.

Conclusion: The backslidings of those who have professed relations to God are very provoking to Him and all departures from Him and opposition to Him are aggravated by the constant manifestation of His goodness and mercy toward the backslider. Those who will break off their allegiance with sin are always welcome to come back to fellowship with Him.

Key Word: Sinsick, v. 5.

Strong Verses: 18.

Striking Facts: v. 11. The costly devotions of those who have not apprehended Christ, He of whom the sacrifices were but a faint shadowing, are an abomination to God. The ceremonial observances were all done away by the death of Christ.

CHAPTER TWO

Contents: The coming glory of Jerusalem and Israel. The humbling of the haughty and the shame of sinners in that day.

Characters: God, Isaiah.

Conclusion: In view of the terribleness of that day when Christ shall come to shake the earth and to judge among men, we should shun the ways of sin. In view of the privilege the righteous have of sharing in His universal Kingdom, we should seek to walk in the light of the Lord all our days.

Key Word: Last days, v. 2.

Strong Verses: 11, 22.

Striking Facts: vv. 19-21. Rev. 6:12-17 shows that the reference here is to the time of Christ's return to judge in terrible majesty. Those who do not flee to Christ before that day will flee from Him then. The prophecy of this chapter relates entirely to Christ's kingdom, still future, when once more the laws of God shall go forth out of Zion.

CHAPTER THREE

Contents: The coming desolations of Jerusalem because of sin and the judgment of sinners.

Characters: God, Isaiah.

Conclusion: Whatever evil befalls sinners, it is of their own procuring. Those who provoke God make Him their enemy and bring sure misery upon themselves. The greatest of men cannot secure themselves from the sentence of the judgment day.

Key Word: Judgment, v. 13.

Strong Verses: 10, 11.

Striking Facts: v. 10. Whatever becomes of an unrighteous nation, those who are "in Christ" will be "safe by the blood of the Crucified One."

CHAPTER FOUR

Contents: The coming restoration of Jerusalem's peace and purity.

Characters: God, Isaiah.

Conclusion: The issue of all the troubles of this present dispensation is to be in happy days for the righteous, when Christ's kingdom will be set up universally, and He will be exalted as its beauty, glory and joy in the esteem of all the living.
Key Word: That day, v. 1.
Strong Verses: 2.
Striking Facts: v. 2. "Branch" is a name used of Christ, because He was planted by God's power and flourishes to His praise.

CHAPTER FIVE

Contents: Parable of Jehovah's vineyard and the six woes upon Israel.
Characters: God.
Conclusion: God expects vineyard fruit from those who enjoy vineyard privileges, not the mere leaves of profession, or the wild grapes of hypocritical performances in religion. God will deny His grace to those who have long received it in vain. The curse of barrenness is the punishment of the sin of barrenness.
Key Word: Woe, v. 8.
Strong Verses: 20, 21.
Striking Facts: v. 4. Some believe Christ thought these words when He beheld Jerusalem and wept over it (Luke 19:41), and had reference to it in the parable of the vineyard. Matt. 21:33

CHAPTER SIX

Contents: Isaiah's transforming vision and his new commission.
Characters: God, Isaiah.
Conclusion: Those who are to teach others the knowledge of God must themselves have the vision of God. Those are fittest to be employed for Him who, having heard His voice, have been humbled before Him in the sense of their own vileness and are made deeply sensible of their own weakness.
Key Word: Vision, v. 5.
Strong Verses: 8.
Striking Facts: vv. 9-10. These verses are referred to six times in the N. T. It pictures the attitude of the Jews especially toward Christ, a condition which still remains with them, and with all who wilfully reject Him.

CHAPTER SEVEN

Contents: Evil confederacy of Rezin and Jekah. The sign of the Virgin's Son. Prediction of impending invasion of Judah.
Characters: God, Christ, Ahaz, Rezin, Pekah, Isaiah, Shear-jashub.
Conclusion: The sin of a land is sure to bring foreign invasion and all kinds of trouble, but to those who will trust Him, God sends seasonable comforts, and the strongest consolations in times of trouble are those which come from expectation of and from Christ.
Key Word: Sign, v. 11.
Strong Verses: 14.
Striking Facts: v. 14. The Virgin's Son, Immanuel, God with us, was fulfilled in Jesus. Matt. 1:21-25. If He had not been Immanuel, God with us, He could not have been Jesus (A Savior).

CHAPTER EIGHT

Contents: Predictions of the Syrian invasion and of the desolations of Judah and Israel.
Characters: God, Israel, Uriah, Zechariah, Maher, Shalal-hash-baz, Rezin, sons of Remaliah.
Conclusion: If a nation insists on rejecting God's counsels, it is just with God to apply the scourge. However in the deluge of trouble that may come to a nation, God will keep the heads of His trusting people above water, if they will make His statutes, rather than those having familiar spirits, their counsellors.
Key Word: Trouble and darkness, v. 22.
Strong Verses: 9, 10, 19, 20.

Striking Facts: v. 14. When Israel rejected Christ, He became to them a stone of stumbling. This passage is quoted in application to all those who persist in their unbelief of the Gospel (1 Pet. 2:8). Being disobedient to God's Word, men stumble at it.

CHAPTER NINE

Contents: A divine child, the only hope of Israel. Vision of the outstretched hand. The unavailing chastisement.

Characters: God, Christ, Isaiah, Rezin.

Conclusion: In the worst of times, God's people have a "nevertheless" to comfort them (v. 1) and balance their troubles. As the saints then comforted themselves with the hope of Christ's first coming, so now His second coming is the great hope of every dark day.

Key Word: Great light, v. 2.

Strong Verses: 6, 7.

Striking Facts: vv. 6-7. Christ was Wonderful in His earthly ministry (Luke 24:19); is Counsellor in His priestly service (1 John 2:1); will be Mighty God in His coming manifestation (Psa. 45:36); Everlasting Father in His ultimate relation (Prov. 8:23); Prince of Peace in His kingdom (Acts 10:36).

CHAPTER TEN

Contents: The commission to invade Judah and its execution. Threatening of the invaders ruin after serving God's purpose. New encouragement given to God's people.

Characters: God.

Conclusion: God sometimes makes an idolatrous nation that serves Him not at all, a scourge to a hypocritical nation that serves Him not in sincerity and truth. Yet when God has done His work through the idolatrous nation, He will certainly do His work upon them and their day will come to fall because they have not had God in all their thoughts.

Key Word: Indignation, v. 25.

Strong Verses: 33.

CHAPTER ELEVEN

Contents: Prophecy of the Davidic Kingdom and restoration of Israel.

Characters: Christ, Holy Spirit.

Conclusion: The great comfort in days of distress is the hope of the coming universal kingdom of righteousness and peace, when Christ, who is in every way qualified to be King of earth, shall take the throne. Then God's people shall be delivered, not only from evil, but from the fear of it forever.

Key Word: Kingdom.

Strong Verses: 4, 5, 9.

Striking Facts: Nothing of this chapter occurred at Christ's first coming. Israel was then dispersed and Christ was killed. The Messiah-King was then rejected, but His earth-kingdom will be set up when He returns in glory. Luke 1:31-32; Acts 13:15-16.

CHAPTER TWELVE

Contents: The worship of the coming Kingdom.

Characters: God.

Conclusion: When Jesus comes to set up His Kingdom, God's regathered people Israel and all the redeemed, shall as one man, with one mind and mouth, praise Him, who is One and His name one.

Key Word: Joy, v. 3.

Strong Verses: 2, 3.

Striking Facts: The Christian does not have to wait until the Kingdom is set up to joy in His praises, for by Jesus Christ, the root of Jesse, God's anger has been turned away, and the believer can say "He is my peace."

CHAPTER THIRTEEN

Contents: Prophecy concerning last days, when punishment will be visited upon the nations, and Israel shall pass through the Great Tribulation.

Characters: God, Isaiah.

Conclusion: Men have their day now, and many think to carry the day, but

God's day is coming, and His day of reckoning will be cruel with wrath and fierce anger.

Key Word: Day of the Lord (vv. 6, 9) (fierce anger, v. 13).

Strong Verses: 9, 11.

Striking Facts: The chapter looks forward to the apocalyptic judgments. (Rev. 6 to 13) Babylon has never yet been destroyed in the way here foretold, and many believe Babylon will in the last day be rebuilt, and the everlasting destruction here predicted will then fall upon it.

CHAPTER FOURTEEN

Contents: Christ's Kingdom set up on earth with Israel restored, the Beast of hell. Satan's fall and doom. Babylon's final judgment.

Characters: God.

Conclusion: It is the comfort of God's people that God has purposed through the exaltation of His Son to set up a righteous and eternal Kingdom on earth, when Israel shall have rest from their wanderings and the days of affliction of all His people shall have an end forever. The rod of the wicked shall be broken, and Satan and all his followers shall be cast into hell.

Key Word: Rest, v. 7.

Strong Verses: 7, 27.

Striking Facts: vv. 12-14. This is a reference to Satan, the real, though unseen ruler of successive world powers. This tells the story of the beginning of sin in the universe. The universal catastrophe here predicted has never occurred and has to do with the close of the times of the Gentiles and the setting up of Christ's Kingdom.

CHAPTER FIFTEEN

Contents: The burden of Moab. Prophecy of great desolations upon the earth.

Characters: God, Isaiah.

Conclusion: Great and dismal changes may in the providence of God be made within a very short time. Let us therefore live as those who know not what an hour may bring forth.

Key Word: Desolation, v. 6.

CHAPTER SIXTEEN

Contents: Women of Moab anticipate the Davidic Kingdom and lament the pride of Moab.

Characters: God.

Conclusion: Those who will not yield to the fear of God, will be made to yield to the fear of everything else.

Key Word: Stricken, v. 7.

Strong Verses: 5.

Striking Facts: v. 5. Though the thrones of earth be overturned, the throne of David will surely be established in mercy and Christ will sit upon it and will be a protector to all who have been a shelter to the people of God. (Especially Israel.)

CHAPTER SEVENTEEN

Contents: The burden of Damascus, foretelling destruction of cities of Syria and Israel.

Characters: God

Conclusion: The God of our salvation is the rock of our strength. It is our forgetfulness of Him that is at the bottom of all sin, and brings great calamities upon us.

Key Word: Woe, v. 12.

Strong Verses: 7, 8, 12, 13.

CHAPTER EIGHTEEN

Contents: Woe of the land beyond the rivers of Ethiopia, in the day of Israel's regathering.

Characters: God.

Conclusion: Though God's covenant people are trampled on as a nation, scattered and abused, no nation, however formidable, will be able to swallow them up. Though they are cast down, they are not utterly forgotten of God.

Key Word: Woe, v. 1.

CHAPTER NINETEEN

Contents: Burden of Egypt, looking forward, through desolations, to Kingdom blessing with Israel.

Characters: God.

Conclusion: The barbarous usage which the enemies of God have given His people, even of long ago, will be remembered against them and they will be paid in their own coin. Let not the bold be secure, for God can easily cut off their spirit and bring their land to nothing.

Key Word: Egypt, v. 1.

Strong Verses: 20.

Striking Facts: v. 20. Jesus Christ is the Savior and the Great One here spoken of, who will eventually bring about the conversion of such perverse nations as Egypt. At His coming, they will receive the light and submit themselves to His rule.

CHAPTER TWENTY

Contents: Prophecy of the wasting of Egypt and Ethiopia by Assyria.

Characters: God, Isaiah, Tartan, Sargon.

Conclusion: Those who make the creature their expectation and glory and so put it in the place of God, will sooner or later be brought to shame for it and will be utterly disappointed in creature confidences.

Key Word: Shame, v. 5.

Striking Facts: v. 2. This would be a great hardship upon God's servant, exposing him to ridicule and endangering his health. When we are doing as God commands, however foolish it may seem, we may trust Him with our credit and safety.

CHAPTER TWENTY-ONE

Contents: Four burdens anticipating Sennacherib's invasion.

Characters: God, Isaiah.

Conclusion: Neither the skill of archers nor the courage of mighty men can protect a people from the judgments of God.

Key Word: Grievous vision, v. 2.

CHAPTER TWENTY-TWO

Contents: The burden of the valley of vision, telling of coming grievous distress.

Characters: God, Isaiah, Elam, Kir, Shebna, Eliakim.

Conclusion: When God threatens His people with judgment, He expects and requires that they will humble themselves under His mighty hand, and if they do not do so, His judgments will follow them to the grave.

Key Word: Treading down, v. 5.

Strong Verses: 22.

Striking Facts: vv. 22-23. Jesus Christ describes His own power as Mediator by allusion to this. (Rev. 3:7) He has the key of David. He opens and no man shuts. He shuts and no man opens. He is also a nail in a sure place. His Kingdom cannot be shaken, and He Himself is "the same yesterday, today and forever."

CHAPTER TWENTY-THREE

Contents: Burden of Tyre. Desolations preceding the final deliverance of Israel.

Characters: God.

Conclusion: The proud boasts of worldly nations, who bid defiance to their neighbors, will surely be silenced by the judgments of God in due time. Pomp and splendor are no guarantee against Him judgments.

Key Word: Contempt, v. 9.

Strong Verses: 9.

CHAPTER TWENTY-FOUR

Contents: Looking through national troubles to the Kingdom age. The coming tribulation for the Jews, destruction of Gentile powers and opening of the Kingdom.
Characters: God.
Conclusion: Earth, polluted by the sins of men, will at last be made utterly desolate and empty by the judgments of God. Satanic hosts and anti-Christian world powers will be cast into the pit. Then it shall appear that Jehovah is King above all and He shall reign gloriously in the earth.
Key Word: Dissolved, v. 19.
Strong Verses: 4, 21, 23.
Striking Facts: v. 23. The Lord Jesus Christ will appear as King and Judge in that day and the earth shall shine forth in His glory. Rev. 21:2, 3.

CHAPTER TWENTY-FIVE

Contents: Triumphs of the coming Kingdom age.
Characters: God, Isaiah.
Conclusion: God should be exalted by His people for the wonderful things He has done, and is to do, according to His promises, for these are proofs of His power beyond what any creature could perform, and of His goodness, beyond what such sinful creatures could expect.
Key Word: Wonderful things, v. 1.
Strong Verses: 1, 4, 8.
Striking Facts: This chapter looks forward to the coming glorious Kingdom of Christ when all evil shall be put down, death shall be swallowed up in victory and all tears wiped away. Then indeed, His saints will exalt Him for His wonderful works and for fulfilling all His counsels.

CHAPTER TWENTY-SIX

Contents: Worship and testimony of restored and converted Israel in the Kingdom age.
Characters: God.
Conclusion: God's people Israel, banished and driven out by the iniquity of the former times will yet be restored as a nation to God's favor. When the Deliverer comes out of Zion, they will join in the song of all the redeemed, rejoicing that the days of distress are over and that God has ordained peace on earth forever.
Strong Verses: 3, 4, 12, 21.
Striking Facts: v. 21. The Father has given to Jesus Christ authority to execute judgment because He is the Son of Man. John 5:27. At His coming, at the close of the Great Tribulation, the blood of thousands of martyrs will be brought to light and to account.

CHAPTER TWENTY-SEVEN

Contents: Punishment of the proud enemy of God's people. Israel restored and fruitful.
Characters: God, serpent, dragon.
Conclusion: When the Lord comes to punish the inhabitants of the earth, He will first of all punish the serpent, and his proud oppressing tyrants. In that day the sins of Israel will be purged and they will again bring forth fruit to God. Jerusalem will again be a great center of worship, when out of all countries Israel shall be led forth by God's hand.
Key Word: Gathered, v. 12.
Strong Verses: 6.

CHAPTER TWENTY-EIGHT

Contents: Woe of Ephriam due to drunkenness. Prediction of Assyrian captivity of Ephriam. Ephriam's fate a warning to Judah.
Characters: God.
Conclusion: The glorious beauty and the plenty of the land is but a fading flower to those who indulge themselves in sensuality and drunkenness. God will throw it to the ground to be broken in pieces with a hand they are powerless to oppose and will not suffer either His providences or His ordinances to be brought into utter contempt.
Key Word: Woe, v. 1.

Strong Verses: 5, 16.
Striking Facts: v. 16. This is expressly applied to Christ in the N. T., 1 Pet. 2:6-8. He is that stone which has become the head of the corner.

CHAPTER TWENTY-NINE

Contents: Warnings to Judah and Jerusalem of impending discipline. The blessing after the final deliverance.
Characters: God, David, Abraham.
Conclusion: Those who are formal and hypocritical in their exercises of devotion, without spiritual vision, thinking to hide their counsels from the Lord, do but invite His judgments upon themselves.
Key Word: Woe, v. 1.
Strong Verses: 15, 18, 19, 24.
Striking Facts: vv. 18, 19. This portion of the chapter looks forward to the happy settlement of the affairs of Jerusalem and Judah after the second coming of Christ. Then those who understood not the prophecies shall see God's hand in all events, and will rejoice in Him.

CHAPTER THIRTY

Contents: Warnings against alliance with Egypt against Sennacherib and exhortation to turn to the Lord for help.
Characters: God, Pharoah.
Conclusion: When sin has brought men into distress, it is their wisdom, in repentance, to turn to God for deliverance, but those who think to prosper in their sin, by the help of man, add sin to sin and invite worse disaster upon themselves. If we would be saved from the evil of every calamity and secured from the curse of it, we should turn to Jehovah and repose in Him.
Key Word: Shame and confusion, v. 3.
Strong Verses: 15, 18.

CHAPTER THIRTY-ONE

Contents: Judah again warned against the Egyptian alliance. Jehovah's defense of Jerusalem.
Characters: God.
Conclusion: It is gross absurdity to forsake the Rock of Ages for broken reeds. If men will not court God's wisdom and power to act for them in the time of danger, they will find it to act against them, though they have the strongest of men to aid them. Make not man your confidence, for man can do nothing without God.
Key Word: Trust in man, v. 1.
Strong Verses: 1

CHAPTER THIRTY-TWO

Contents: Promise of coming Kingdom. Warning of great tribulation. The King Deliverer.
Characters: God.
Conclusion: Wasting and desolating judgment upon the land and people of Israel was pronounced because they lived in pleasure and wanton, ignoring God's commands, and all who set their hearts upon the world will meet like wretched disappointment. It is the comfort of the faithful few that blessed times of righteousness and eternal rest are promised when the Prince of Peace shall come forth to reign.
Key Word: Tribulation and kingdom, vv. 10-15.
Strong Verses: ' 1, 17, 18.
Striking Facts: v. 1. This Scripture certainly looks forward to the Day of the Lord (2:10-22; Rev. 19:11-21) and the Kingdom blessing to follow when Christ shall return to reign.

CHAPTER THIRTY-THREE

Contents: The distress of Judah and Jerusalem because of coming woes.
Characters: God.
Conclusion: The righteous God pays sinners in their own coin. When they have filled up the measure of their iniquity, God will begin, for the sinner's day is sure to come. The godly man's comfort is that he shall,

in any event, have communion with God in this life, and afterward look upon the King in His beauty.

Key Word: Judgment, v. 5

Strong Verses: 6, 15, 16, 17, 22.

Striking Facts: v. 17. Those who walk uprightly shall not only be preserved through the judgments that visit mankind upon the earth, but shall with the eye of faith, ever see the King in His beauty, and shall at last stand in His presence, when His beauty shall be upon them. 1 John 3:2.

CHAPTER THIRTY-FOUR

Contents: Prophecy of the Day of the Lord and Armaggedon.

Characters: God.

Conclusion: There is a day fixed in the divine counsels for the deliverance of God's people and cause in the earth and the destruction of all enemies —a year of recompense for the controversy of Zion. Those who make the Book of the Lord their meditation and rule of life, will have complete deliverance from the coming judgment of nations (v. 16).

Key Word: Day of vengeance, v. 8.

Strong Verses: 16, 17.

Striking Facts: v. 5. It is Christ who will come in the clouds of heaven to execute judgment, and out of whose mouth goes a sharp sword, as He judges and makes war upon the nations. Rev. 19:11, 15

CHAPTER THIRTY-FIVE

Contents: The coming Kingdom blessing and regathering of Israel.

Characters: God.

Conclusion: The precious promises of peace in the Gospel will shortly culminate in the endless joys and rest of the coming Kingdom when the saints shall reign with Christ. Vengeance will then be taken on the powers of darkness and recompense will be made to the saints for all injuries and losses. All the earth shall break forth in beauty and great wonders will be wrought among men.

Key Word: Everlasting joy, vv. 1, 10.

Strong Verses: 1, 4, 5, 6, 10.

Striking Facts: It is Christ who is coming in the fullness of time in flaming fire, to spoil and make an open show of all evil powers and to set up the millennial Kingdom, to which all the prophets bear witness.

CHAPTER THIRTY-SIX

Contents: Sennacherib's invasion and Jehovah's deliverance. The threats of Rabshakeh.

Characters: God, Sennacherib, Rabskakeh, Hezekiah, Eliakim, Shebnab, Joab, Pharaoh.

Conclusion: The enemies of God's people are ever trying to frighten them from their confidence in God. That we may keep our ground against the enemies of our souls, it concerns us to keep a firm hope in God that we may not lose spirit in the day of trial.

Key Word: Confidence unshaken, vv. 4, 21.

Strong Verses: 21.

CHAPTER THIRTY-SEVEN

Contents: Jehovah's message to the people by Isaiah. Sennacherib's message to Hezekiah. Hezekiah's prayer and Jehovah's answer. Destruction of Assyrians.

Characters: God, Hezekiah, Eliakim, Shebna, Isaiah, Rabshakeh, Tirhakah, Abrammelech, Sharezer.

Conclusion: The best way to baffle the malicious designs of the enemy of our souls, is to be driven by them to God in prayer. When dangers are most pressing, it is fitting that prayer should be most lively, for God will be a defense to those who truly look to Him.

Key Word: Jehovah a defense, v. 35.

Strong Verses: 31, 35.

CHAPTER THIRTY-EIGHT

Contents: Hezekiah's sickness and recovery in answer to prayer.

Characters: God, Isaiah, Hezekiah.

Conclusion: Neither men's greatness nor goodness will exempt them from the arrests of sickness. If one is sick, let him pray (Jas. 5:13) for God's love is sufficient to bring one from the very pit of corruption, if it be His will. Those whose life is as from the dead are in a special manner obliged to praise God all their days.

Key Word: Healing, v. 9.

Strong Verses: 17, 19.

Striking Facts: Some think that in turning his face toward the wall, he was turning, as was customary, toward the temple, which was a type of Christ. To Him we must look, by faith, in every prayer.

CHAPTER THIRTY-NINE

Contents: Hezekiah's folly. Babylonian captivity of Judah foretold.

Characters: Isaiah, Merodach-baladan, Hezekiah.

Conclusion: It is folly for one whom God has dignified to be overproud of the respect paid him by unbelieving princes. We have need to watch our own spirits when showing another what we have done and what we have gotten, as if our own merit had secured it. God will take that from us on which we build a carnal confidence.

Key Word: Impending captivity v. 6.

Strong Verses: 8.

CHAPTER FORTY

Contents: Joyful prospect given to the people of God of the happiness of coming redemption. Reproof for their despondencies.

Characters: God, Holy Spirit, Isaiah.

Conclusion: Nothing can be spoken more comforting to those who realize themselves undone, than the coming of the Redeemer as the Lamb of God and as the Good Shepherd. Those who are ready to acknowledge they have no might, may wait upon Him, for He will be their help if they will humbly depend on Him.

Key Word: Comfort, v. 1.

Strong Verses: 5, 8, 11, 26, 28, 29, 31.

Striking Facts: v. 11. Christ is the Good Shepherd. John 10:11. He has a special care for the lambs that are weak and cannot help themselves, gathering them into the arms of His power and carrying them in the bosom of His love.

CHAPTER FORTY-ONE

Contents: Greatness of God and weakness of man. Admonition to shun idols and encouragement to trust in God.

Characters: God, Christ, Jacob.

Conclusion: Jehovah is infinite, eternal and unchangeable. He has governed the world from the beginning and will until the end of time. Let the believer therefore depend upon Him as the God sufficient for him in the worst of times. He would not have His people to be a timorous people, o His grace can silence fears, even when there is the greatest cause for them.

Key Word: Fear not, vv. 10, 13, 14.

Strong Verses: 10, 13, 17.

Striking Facts: v. 14. Christ is the Redeemer and the Holy One of Israel, engaged by promise of God's people. In Him is help found, therefore let Him be worshiped in the beauty of holiness.

CHAPTER FORTY-TWO

Contents: Christ, servant of Jehovah. Chastening of Israel and the final restoration.

Characters: God, Christ.

Conclusion: A day is coming when all who have contradicted and blasphemed the Gospel of Christ shall be put to silence and shame, and when all the oppositions of the powers of darkness shall be thrown down. Let the believer therefore delight in Christ, rely upon Him and rejoice in Him, for all who are "in Him" will be well-pleasing to God.

Key Word: Judgment, vv. 1, 4.

Strong Verses: 1, 4.

Striking Facts: vv. 1-7. Fulfilled in Christ (Matt. 12:17-21). Note the two-fold account of the coming servant. 1. As weak, despised, rejected and slain. 2. As mighty conqueror taking vengeance. The former class of passages were fulfilled in the first advent. The second await His return for fulfillment.

CHAPTER FORTY-THREE

Contents: The chosen nation redeemed and restored.

Characters: God, Christ.

Conclusion: Israel is God's peculiar people, distinguished from all others, and having the promise that they shall never be absorbed and that nations • shall be sacrificed to their welfare. They will be finally gathered from all the earth to their own land, and when Christ shall appear as King of Kings, their sins will be blotted out, and they shall be restored to full favor.

Key Word: Gathered, v. 5.

Strong Verses: 2, 10, 11, 25.

Striking Facts: Christ, the Great Redeemer, will appear for Israel (Rom. 11:25). At His coming, the spiritual seed of Israel (through the Gospel of grace) will be gathered to heaven as their home and given glorified bodies. Believers under the Gospel are the Bride of Christ who will "reign with Him" in His coming Kingdom on earth.

CHAPTER FORTY-FOUR

Contents: The promise of the Spirit and the coming restoration. The folly of idolatry.

Characters: God, Holy Spirit, Cyrus.

Conclusion: There is no God besides Jehovah. He is infinite and therefore there can be no other. He is sufficient, and therefore no other is needed. It is foolishness to expect any good from gods of man's own making and only the blind and ignorant can look to graven images.

Key Word: Ashamed, restored (vv. 11, 22, 26).

Strong Verses: 6, 8, 22.

Striking Facts: vv. 23-27. When Christ returns and is received by Israel, their idolatry and sin will be remembered no more, and recognizing Him whom they pierced, they will be restored to a place of great fruitfulness. (Rom. 11:25.)

CHAPTER FORTY-FIVE

Contents: Promises to Cyrus for Israel's sake. Proof of God's eternal power and sovereignty. Encouragement to believing Jews. Doom of idol worshippers.

Characters: God, Christ, Cyrus.

Conclusion: Beside Jehovah there is no God. He alone is self-existent, self-sufficient, being infinite and eternal. Those are in woeful condition who strive with their Maker and give honor to images which cannot give good. Those who trust in God will never be made ashamed of their confidence in Him.

Key Word: Jehovah omnipotent.

Strong Verses: 9, 18, 22, 24.

Striking Facts: v. 22. This verse has a further reference to the conversion of the Gentiles that live in the ends of the earth through the lifting up of Christ on Calvary's Cross. As the stung Israelites looked to the brazen serpent, so all were invited to look to Christ and be saved.

CHAPTER FORTY-SIX

Contents: Israel exhorted to remember the power of God and powerlessness of idols.

Characters: God.

Conclusion: False gods will certainly fail the worshippers when they have most need of them. It is absurd to think of making any creature equal with the Creator, who is infinitely above all He has created. Let all remember that they have been the constant care of His kind providence and are absolutely dependent upon Him.

Key Word: Remember, vv. 8-9.

Strong Verses: 8, 9, 10.
Striking Facts: vv. 12-13. This may be applied to the Jews in their rejection of Christ, for they thought to establish their own righteousness, and would not accept the righteousness of God in Christ, by faith.

CHAPTER FORTY-SEVEN

Contents: Judgment pronounced upon Babylon.
Characters: God.
Conclusion: Those who abuse their honor or power provoke God to deprive them of it utterly and to make them sit in dust. While God often makes use of evil men for the correction of His people, He always breaks the rod of His wrath because of their boastfulness and cruelty.
Key Word Vengeance, v. 3.
Strong Verses: 4.
Striking Facts: v. 4. Christ is the Great Redeemer, who as the Holy One of Israel saves His people, and as Lord of Hosts will take vengeance upon the wicked.

CHAPTER FORTY-EIGHT

Contents: The dullness of Israel. Restoration under the Servant of Jehovah. Israel reminded of the promises.
Characters: God, Christ, Holy Spirit.
Conclusion: God often finds His people obstinate and perverse, but for all that He makes it redound to the honor of His mercy to spare and reprieve them, refining them in the furnace of affliction, rather than cutting them off. O, that men would own Him as the true and only God, receiving His promises and looking to His Redeemer.
Key Word: Anger deferred, v. 9.
Strong Verses: 12, 17, 22.
Striking Facts: vv. 16-17. The Spirit of God is here spoken of as a person distinct from Father and Son, as that which is said to the same purpose with this (61:1) is applied to Christ (Luke 4:21), so may this be. Christ the Redeemer was sent by the Father and He had the Spirit without measure.

CHAPTER FORTY-NINE

Contents: Israel's coming Redeemer. Preservation and restoration of Israel and judgment on oppressors.
Characters: God, Christ.
Conclusion: God, of old, promised a Redeemer to His people who would also become a Light to the Gentiles. Through Him, the souls of those looking to Him were to be set free from the bondage of guilt and corruption; His own should be wonderfully provided for, and through Him, at length, Israel would be restored and the earth established in righteousness, peace and joy.
Key Word: Redeemer, v. 7.
Strong Verses: 6.
Striking Facts: v. 7. Christ was the Redeemer who was despised and rejected of men, and abhorred by nations, who cried "crucify Him." But God promised Him exaltation in the depths of His humiliation, and at His return He will be acknowledged King of Kings and Lord of Lords.

CHAPTER FIFTY

Contents: The humiliation of the Holy One of Israel.
Characters: God, Christ.
Conclusion: The Lord Jesus, our Redeemer, was to be wise above all men, able to speak the word of comfort to every heart; He was to have the ear of the learned to receive instruction in all things from His Father. In spite of this, He was to be smitten and insulted by men, yet unshaken in constancy and resolution, suffering all patiently and voluntarily for the salvation of the world. Let all who fear God, build their hopes upon Christ who has proven Himself the Savior of mankind.
Key Word: Smitten Redeemer, v. 6.
Strong Verses: 7, 10.

Striking Facts: v. 3. Here we see Jesus in Creative power; v. 4 as the dependent teacher; v. 5 as the faithful servant; v. 6 as the patient sufferer; v. 8 as the justified Redeemer.   I

CHAPTER FIFTY-ONE

Contents: Final redemption of Israel and punishment of oppressors.
Characters: God, Christ.
Conclusion: Although God's people are called upon to suffer much upon earth, they have an eternal cause to rejoice, in that all who trust in His salvation have the approbation of the living God and may therefore despise the censures of dying men who will shortly be punished.
Key Word: Zion's comfort, vv. 3, 11.
Strong Verses: 5, 7, 12, 13.
Striking Facts: v. 5. Christ brought an everlasting righteousness and salvation. Those whose happiness is bound up in His righteousness, will have the comfort of it eternally.

CHAPTER FIFTY-TWO

Contents: Vision of Jerusalem in the Kingdom age. Jehovah's servant marred and afterward exalted.
Characters: God, Christ.
Conclusion: Let God's people prepare for eternal joy, for His Word shall without fail have its accomplishment in due season. Jerusalem shall be made a praise and all the earth shall break forth in joy when He who was rejected and despised of men shall come forth as Lord and King.
Key Word: Jerusalem redeemed, v. 9.
Strong Verses: 7, 11, 14.
Striking Facts: vv. 7, 14. v. 7 has an application to the preaching of the Gospel, a message indeed of good news and victory over spiritual enemies (Rom. 10:15). v. 14 points plainly at Jesus (Acts 8:34-35). Never was man so barbarously treated as was the Son of God. When He returns in glory the kings of the earth shall shut their mouths at Him, and the Jews will look with mourning upon Him whom they pierced.

CHAPTER FIFTY-THREE

Contents: The vicarious sacrifice of Christ, the servant of Jehovah.
Characters: God, Christ.
Conclusion: The whole race of mankind lies under the stain of original corruption, all gone astray from God. God, in love sent His only begotten Son into the world, who voluntarily made Himself an offering for sin. He submitted Himself to the disgraces and afflictions due to the worst of men, that those who should believe on Him, might have the joy and glory due to Him as the one perfect man.
Key Word: Man of sorrows, v. 3.
Strong Verses: 3, 4, 5, 6, 7, 10, 11.
Striking Facts: Christ rose in the world as a tender plant. The greater part of those among whom He lived saw none of His beauty. Because He announced Himself as the Savior of the world, He was abandoned and abhorred. Nevertheless God highly exalted Him, and He appears in heaven to make intercession for all who accept His sacrifice.

CHAPTER FIFTY-FOUR

Contents: Israel as the restored wife of Jehovah in the Kingdom age.
Characters: God, Christ.
Conclusion: We may with greatest assurance depend upon God for the keeping of His covenant with His people (especially Israel) for He will not keep His anger against them forever, but will gather them out of their dispersions that they may return in a body to their land, where He will again be a husband to them.
Key Word: Restored Israel, v. 7.
Strong Verses: 4, 17.
Striking Facts: As Israel is spoken of as the wife of Jehovah, so the church of the present dispensation is called "the bride of Christ" (the Lamb). However this chapter has wholly to do with the fulfillment of God's covenant with Israel.

CHAPTER FIFTY-FIVE

Contents: Jehovah's everlasting salvation.
Characters: God, Christ.
Conclusion: All are invited to partake of God's salvation provided through Christ. All the world's wealth and pleasure cannot satisfy the soul, but God's eternal salvation brings true life and peace. It is man's wisdom, therefore, to seek Christ while He may be found, forsaking sin and dislodging all preconceived notions contrary to God's truth, for God will then abundantly pardon.
Key Word: Come, vv. 1, 3, 6.
Strong Verses: 1, 6, 7, 8, 9, 11.
Striking Facts: vv. 4, 5. Christ was given to the world for a witness of God's love and mercy (John 3:16). He is the true leader and commander to show man what to do and enable him to do it. Through Him the door was opened to the Gentile nations to enter into God's eternal salvation.

CHAPTER FIFTY-SIX

Contents: Solemn instruction given to all to make conscience of duty. Charge against the careless and unfaithful.
Characters: God.
Conclusion: The more assurance God gives us of the performance of His promises, the stronger obligations He lays us under to obedience to His commands. Righteousness and justice on our part, are required to evidence the security of our faith and repentance, and to open the way of mercy.
Key Word: Justice and righteousness, vv. 1, 2.
Strong Verses: 7
Striking Facts: v. 1. The great salvation announced and wrought out by Christ was preceded by the call to repentance and faith. In Christ, the righteousness of God was revealed (Rom. 1:17) and he is "made righteousness" unto all who receive Him.

CHAPTER FIFTY-SEVEN

Contents: Further ethical instructions. Sins of the people denounced.
Characters: God.
Conclusion: God is justly displeased when the voice of His rod is not heard, much more, when sin and idolatry are knowingly rejoiced in. Sinners shall find no quietness or satisfaction in their own hearts and will be made to feel the full force of His anger if sin is not repented of and forsaken.
Key Word: Wicked, v. 21.
Strong Verses: 15, 21.

CHAPTER FIFTY-EIGHT

Contents: Hypocritical professions of religion. Instructions how to keep fasts aright.
Characters: God.
Conclusion: It is common for unhumbled hearts, while they perform the external services of religion, to promise themselves acceptance with God, which He has promised only to the sincere. God will not be cheated by hypocritical fasts and ceremonies. Those who fast and pray, yet go on in sin, mock God and cheat themselves.
Key Word: Hypocritical fasts, v. 4.
Strong Verses: 6, 7, 10, 11.

CHAPTER FIFTY-NINE

Contents: Sins which prevented the bestowal of God's blessing and caused chastisements to fall upon Israel.
Characters: God, Christ, Holy Spirit
Conclusion: If prayers are not answered and the salvation we wait for is not wrought for us, it is not evidence that God is weary of hearing prayer, but that, for some reason, He cannot answer. Sin hides His face from us, provokes Him to withdraw His gracious presence and suspend the tokens of His favor.
Key Word: Iniquities, v. 2.
Strong Verses: 1, 2.

Striking Facts: v. 20. Christ was the kinsman Redeemer who came to His own and was rejected. (John 1:11-12.) He is coming a second time to receive His own and to give full deliverance to Israel. (Rom. 11:25-26.)

CHAPTER SIXTY

Contents: The Deliverer out of Zion and the peace and joy of His coming.
Characters: God, Christ.
Conclusion: When the Redeemer shall appear in glory to be received as the Light of Israel, the knowledge of Him shall fill the whole earth and all the Gentile nations will honor them and flock to them. Wasting and destruction shall be no more and all will be filled with praise to God.
Key Word: Israel's light, vv. 1, 3, 19.
Strong Verses: 19.
Striking Facts: v. 1. This had a near fulfillment in the first advent of Christ, who came as the Light of the world. However, He was rejected and the Church came in as a parenthesis. Christ is coming again, first for His Church as "the bright and morning star," and then to Israel and all the world, as the "sun of righteousness."

CHAPTER SIXTY-ONE

Contents: Two advents of Christ in one view. Kingdom blessing after the day of vengeance. Israel's restoration.
Characters: God, Christ, Holy Spirit.
Conclusion: After the day of Christ's vengeance, comfort will be given to restored Israel. The setting up of the Kingdom in the earth will mean the repairing of all the waste places and all the ends of the earth shall see God's great salvation.
Key Word: Universal righteousness, v. 11.
Strong Verses: 10, 11.
Striking Facts: v. 2. See Luke 4:16-21 and note that Jesus suspended the reading of this passage at the comma, after the word "Lord." The first advent opened the day of grace "the acceptable year of Jehovah," but does not fulfill the day of vengeance. When He returns this will be fulfilled being followed by the Kingdom of righteousness (4, 11)

CHAPTER SIXTY-TWO

Contents: Restoration of Israel to God's favor, and honor with the nations.
Characters: God, Christ.
Conclusion: Israel's full salvation is sure to come when they are regathered and their Redeemer recognized. In that day their land will no longer be called "desolate" but "Beulah land," and Jerusalem will be a praise in the earth. All the ends of the earth will know that God has pleaded Israel's cause and fulfilled His prophecies concerning them.
Key Word: Israel's salvation, v. 11.
Strong Verses: 11.
Striking Facts: This prophecy was not fulfilled in the first advent and the preaching of the Gospel of grace. God has made definite promises to Israel, before whom Christ will yet appear again, to be recognized. We have no right to put the church in Israel's place in the promises.

CHAPTER SIXTY-THREE

Contents: Day of vengeance, and the fear and hope of the remnant of Israel.
Characters: God, Christ, Holy Spirit, Moses, Abraham.
Conclusion: Christ is coming to tread the winepress of the wrath of God (Rev. 19:14-15) to take fierce vengeance on all sinners. In that day the remnant of Israel will remember their days of rebellion and will see how God has nourished them through the ages.
Key Word: Day of vengeance, v. 4.
Strong Verses: 1.
Striking Facts: v. 1. Rev. 19:11-21 describes this same day of vengeance, when Christ shall come forth in power, wearing vesture dipped in blood, crowned with many crowns and revealing Himself as King of Kings.

CHAPTER SIXTY-FOUR

Contents: Fear and hope of remnant of Israel in day of vengeance.
Characters: God, Christ.
Conclusion: The remnant of Israel in the day of Christ's vengeance will bewail their sins, thereby justifying God in all their afflictions, owning themselves unworthy of His mercy and thereby preparing for the deliverance He has promised them.
Key Word: Mercy implored, vv. 9, 12.
Strong Verses: 4, 6.
Striking Facts: v. 4. This is likewise, true of those saved under the Gospel of grace (1 Cor. 2:9) to whom is revealed by the Spirit the deep things of God as the result of their acceptance of the crucified and risen Savior.

CHAPTER SIXTY-FIVE

Contents: Answer of Jehovah to remnant of Israel. Eternal blessing in the renovated earth.
Characters: God.
Conclusion: Although Jehovah has long stretched forth His hand to a disobedient and gainsaying people, Israel, yet He will spare the remnant at Christ's return, purging them from their sins, establishing them in a purified earth.
Key Word: Israel's hope, v. 8
Strong Verses: 17, 24.
Striking Facts: Chap. 21 and 22 of Rev. look also to this same time of restoration of all things. The church appears then with Christ, as His Bride, to rule with Him, not as subjects of the earthly kingdom. Israel's glory in the prophecies is always an earthly glory.

CHAPTER SIXTY-SIX

Contents: Blessings of the coming universal Kingdom.
Characters: God, Christ.
Conclusion: Following the day of Christ's vengeance the sorrows of Israel will be turned into abundant joys. All the Gentiles spared shall rejoice in her salvation. All nations will look upon the glory of God as it shines in the face of Christ, the King, and worship will be carefully and constantly attended upon by all the peoples of the earth.
Key Word: Universal kingdom, v. 23.
Strong Verses: 15, 16, 23.
Striking Facts: The Christian watches with great interest the providences of God towards the Jews, knowing that their return to their land is a preparation for the fulfillment of much prophecy, a sign of the approach of the close of the age and Christ's coming. "Come, Lord Jesus."

JEREMIAH

Key Thought:	Number of Chapters:	Key Verse:	Christ seen as:
Warning	52	7:28; 46:1	Lord of Righteousness.

Writer of the Book:	Date:	Conclusion of the Book:
Jeremiah	About 580 to 600 B. C.	Judgment is the certain result of sin. God is longsuffering, not willing that any should perish.

SUMMARY

CHAPTER ONE

Contents: Jeremiah's call and enduement.   The sign of the almond rod and seething pot.

Characters: God, Holy Spirit, Jeremiah, Josiah, Jehoiakim.

Conclusion: God, by His special counsel and foreknowledge designs certain men for certain work for Himself, and whom He calls He fits for their work.   Those having His message to deliver, while they should feel their own insufficiency, should not be afraid of the face of man, for God has pledged Himself to be with them.

Key Word: Called of God, v. 5.

Strong Verses: 1, 19.

CHAPTER TWO

Contents: First message to backslidden Judah concerning their ingratitude to God and wickedness against Him.

Characters: God, Jeremiah.

Conclusion: It is a great affront to God to neglect Him and forget Him, failing to acknowledge His kindnesses, withholding the tributes of love and praise due Him, and worst of all, to turn to idols which cannot possibly do them any good.   Such backslidings are invariably followed with severe corrections that the backslider might read his sin in the punishment.

Key Word: Jehovah forgotten, v. 32.

Strong Verses: 13, 32.

CHAPTER THREE

Contents: Jeremiah's message concerning the impenitence of Judah.   Encouragement to backsliders to return and repent.

Characters: God, Jeremiah.

Conclusion: Those will justly be divorced from God that join themselves to such as are rivals with Him, but God is ever ready to pardon sin and receive those who will return to Him humbly confessing their sins and acknowledging their dependence upon Him for salvation.

Key Word: Backsliding Israel, v. 11.

Strong Verses: 4, 23.

CHAPTER FOUR

Contents: Jeremiah's second message, continued.   Warning of the consequences of sin and exhortation to return to God.

Characters: God, Jeremiah.

Conclusion: It is the evil of men's doings that kindles the fires of God's wrath against them and brings destruction upon the land.   That which is to be before He moves, which makes a way of escape for those who will sincerely turn to Him and receive His mercy.

dreaded above everything else is the wrath of God, but God always warns

Key Word: Desolations, v. 7.

Strong Verses: 22.

CHAPTER FIVE

Contents: Jeremiah's second message, continued. God's charges against them and the judgments threatened.
Characters: God, Jeremiah.
Conclusion: Sinners have reason to expect punishment on account of God's holiness to which sin is highly offensive. Sin will not go unpunished, else the honor of God's government cannot be maintained, and sinners will be tempted to think Him altogether such a one as themselves.
Key Word: Vengeance, vv. 9, 29.
Strong Verses: 22.

CHAPTER SIX

Contents: Jeremiah's second message, continued. The terrors that should come because of sin.
Characters: God, Jeremiah.
Conclusion: The God of mercy is loath to depart even from a provoking people, and earnestly entreats them by true repentance to prevent the necessity of His fierce judgments. Those who perish in their sin will be utterly forsaken of Him, and whom He forsakes is certainly undone
Key Word: Desolations, v. 8.
Strong Verses: 16.

CHAPTER SEVEN

Contents: The message in the gate of the Lord's house. Coming desolations because of sin.
Characters: God, Jeremiah.
Conclusion: It is common for those who are furthest from God to boast themselves most of being in the Church, but God is holy and will not be the pattern of sin even though it be covered up in a form of godliness. When His anger breaks upon them, such sinners have only themselves to thank.
Key Word: Abominations, v. 30.
Strong Verses: 9, 10, 11, 23.

CHAPTER EIGHT

Contents: Message in the temple gate, continued. Terrible judgments impending.
Characters: God, Jeremiah.
Conclusion: Impenitence brings certain ruin. All the boasted wisdom of man cannot serve to keep him from the consuming judgments pronounced upon those who mock at God's Word and take their own course.
Key Word: Consuming judgment, v. 12.
Strong Verses: 7, 9.
Striking Facts: v. 22. The blood of Christ is a balm from Gilead for the healing of the sin-sick heart, and He is the great Physician who is all-sufficient for any case however difficult.

CHAPTER NINE

Contents: Message in the temple gate, continued. Detestation of the sins of the people. The vanity of trusting in anything but God.
Characters: God, Jeremiah.
Conclusion: Those who will not know God as their law giver will be made to know Him as their Judge. If the furnace of affliction will not purify them from their dross, He will cut them off with terrible desolations.
Key Word: Vengeance, v. 9.
Strong Verses: 23, 24.

CHAPTER TEN

Contents: Message in the temple gate, concluded. Greatness of the true God. Coming distresses in the land because of sin.
Characters: God, Jeremiah.
Conclusion: Jehovah is the one only living and true God, and to set up any other in competition with Him is the greatest affront. Those who will not believe His Word nor recognize His power will be made to feel His judgments to their ruin.
Key Word: Distress, v. 18.
Strong Verses: 6, 7, 10, 12, 23, 24.

CHAPTER ELEVEN

Contents: Jeremiah's message on the broken covenant.
Characters: God, Jeremiah.
Conclusion: Those who enter into solemn covenant with God must expect on their part to fulfill the conditions, else He cannot on His part fulfill the promise. If we do not by obedience meet our end of the contract, we will by disobedience bring ourselves under its curses, and it is just with God to inflict heavy penalty.
Key Word: Broken covenant, 8.

CHAPTER TWELVE

Contents: Message on the broken covenant, concluded. Jeremiah's complaint to God and God's rebuke.
Characters: God, Jeremiah.
Conclusion: When we find it hard to understand God's providences toward wicked men, we should remember His sure Word that "what a man soweth that shall he also reap." God often lets wicked men have a time of prosperity that by their pride and luxury they might fill up the measure of their iniquity, and so be ripening for a terrible destruction.
Key Word: Prosperity of wicked, v. 1.
Strong Verses: 1, 13.

CHAPTER THIRTEEN

Contents: Sign of the linen girdle and sign of the bottles filled with wine.
Characters: God, Jeremiah.
Conclusion: Those who persist in sin, ignoring God's Word, make themselves vessels of wrath fitted to destruction. If one judgment does not do the work, God will send one upon another until they are utterly brought to ruin.
Key Word: Punishment, v. 21.
Strong Verses: 16, 23.

CHAPTER FOURTEEN

Contents: Message on the drought.
Characters: God, Jeremiah.
Conclusion: Man's sins bring those judgments upon the earth which make even the inferior creatures to groan. There will come a time when the sinners' expectation from God will utterly fail them. We should dread nothing more than God's departure from us.
Key Word: Drought, v. 1.
Strong Verses: 22.

CHAPTER FIFTEEN

Contents: Message on the drought, concluded. The people abandoned to ruin. Jeremiah complains of his hardships.
Characters: God, Jeremiah, Moses, Samuel.
Conclusion: Miserable is the case of those who have sinned so long against God's mercy that at length they have sinned it away. There is no mercy for those who persist in apostasy.
Key Word: Destruction, v. 6.
Strong Verses: 16, 21.

CHAPTER SIXTEEN

Contents: Sign of the unmarried prophet, forecasting coming calamities.
Characters: God, Jeremiah.
Conclusion: God often makes men's sins their punishment and fills the backslider in heart with his own ways. Those have cut themselves off from all true peace who have thrown away the favor of God by persisting in wilful sin and idolatry.
Key Word: v. 10.
Strong Verses: 17.

CHAPTER SEVENTEEN

Contents: Sign of the unmarried prophet, concluded. Message in the gates concerning the Sabbath.
Characters: God, Jeremiah.

Conclusion: The heart of man, out of communion with God, is wicked and deceitful above all things. Those who have wedded themselves to sin invite God's judgments upon their own heads. There is only disappointment and vexation for those who depend upon the arm of flesh instead of God, but those who by faith derive strength and grace from God will be enabled to do that which will redound to God's glory, the benefit of others and their own account

Key Word: v. 1.

Strong Verses: 5, 7, 9, 10.

Striking Facts: v. 5. Those who trust to their own righteousness and strength, thinking to get salvation without the merit and grace of Christ, thus make flesh their arm and fail of God's salvation.

CHAPTER EIGHTEEN

Contents: Sign of the potter's house. Declaration of God's ways of dealing with nations. Jeremiah's complaint.

Characters: God, Jeremiah.

Conclusion: Jehovah has incontestable and irresistible ability to form (frame) and fashion nations as He pleases. If they do not turn from evil ways, He will turn His hand against them. Sin ruins the comforts of nations, prolongs their grievances, and at length brings total ruin upon them

Key Word: Potter and clay, vv. 6, 7.

Strong Verses: 6, 7, 8.

CHAPTER NINETEEN

Contents: Sign of potter's house, concluded. Coming calamities

Characters: Jeremiah, Kings of Judah.

Conclusion: Let men great and small know that the Lord of Hosts is able to do what He threatens, and will therefore sorely punish those who have persisted in wickedness in spite of all His entreaties. They will be abandoned to utter ruin.

Key Word: Broken, v. 11.

CHAPTER TWENTY

Contents: Jeremiah's first persecution. His complaint to God and encouragement in God.

Characters: God, Pashur, Jeremiah, Nebuchadnezzar.

Conclusion: Those who declare the whole counsel of God may expect to be plotted against, ridiculed and represented as dangerous to the government, which presents a strong temptation to stop preaching or tone down the message. However, the faithful preacher can successfully set all enemies at defiance, for Jehovah has promised to take his part, and to make the Word preached answer the end of its designs.

Key Word: Persecution, v. 11.

Strong Verses: 9, 11.

Striking Facts: vv. 7, 8. Thus our Lord Jesus on the cross was reviled by priests and people for nothing but His faithful witness to God's Word.

CHAPTER TWENTY-ONE

Contents: Message to King Zedekiah. Babylonian captivity foretold.

Characters: God, Jeremiah, Zedekiah, Pashur, Zephaniah, Nebuchadnezzar.

Conclusion: If God be for us, none can be against us, but if He be against us, who can be for us to stand us in any stead? Our God is a consuming fire, and when once He is angry because of men's sins, no one can stand in His sight.

Key Word: Jehovah's fury.

Strong Verses: 8.

CHAPTER TWENTY-TWO

Contents: Message to Zedekiah, concluded. The King exhorted to execute judgment.

Characters: God, Zedekiah, Shallum, Jeremiah, Jehoiakim, Coniah, Nebuchadnezzar.

Conclusion: God never casts one off until they cast Him off, but when men ʙ revolt from their allegiance to Him and trample under foot their covenants with Him, He gives them up to destruction, and who can contend with the destroyers of His preparing?

Key Word: Desolations, v. 5.

Strong Verses: 13, 29.

Striking Facts: vv. 28, 30. Coniah was of David's line through Solomon, and the throne rights were cut off with Coniah. Joseph, the husband of Mary, was of this line. Had Jesus been born in the natural way, He would have had no title to the Davidic throne. However, Mary was of David's line through Nathan, the first born of David, and Jesus being conceived of the Holy Ghost, holds the royal title to the throne, which He will possess • at His return

CHAPTER TWENTY-THREE

Contents: Future restoration and conversion of Israel. Message against the faithless shepherds.

Characters: God, Christ.

Conclusion: Woe be to those who are commanded to feed God's people and pretend to do it, but instead drag them from God, speaking messages that are the product of their own invention, and slighting the authority of His Word. God disowns all prophets who soothe people in their sins.

Key Word: Lying prophets, v. 25.

Strong Verses: 5, 24, 29, 32.

Striking Facts: vv. 5, 6. Jesus Christ is spoken of as the branch from David, small in His beginnings, but growing to be great and loaded with divine fruits. He is the Lord our righteousness (especially to be manifested before the Jews at His coming again). He is the Lord (Jehovah), denoting eternity and self-existence. As Mediator, He is our righteousness.

CHAPTER TWENTY-FOUR

Contents: Sign of the figs. Judah's restoration, but not those of the second deportation.

Characters: Jeremiah, Nebuchadnezzar, Jeconiah, Zedekiah.

Conclusion: The same providence which to some is a savour of death unto death may by God's grace be made to others a savour of life unto life. God knows all who are His, and will protect and deliver them whatever may come.

Key Word: Good and evil figs, v. 3.

CHAPTER TWENTY-FIVE

Contents: Prophecy of seventy years' captivity. Sign of the wine cup of fury.

Characters: Jeremiah, Jehoiakim, Nebuchadnezzar, Pharaoh.

Conclusion: Men would never receive from God the desolating punishments did they not provoke Him by the evil of their persistent sin. That which is provocation to God will prove in the end at least the utter ruin of man, for the day of His fierce wrath is coming upon all the earth.

Key Word: Desolations, v. 11.

Strong Verses: v. 31.

Striking Facts: vv. 29, 33. This prophecy leaps to the end of the age, the day of the Lord when Christ will return to execute God's wrath. Rev. 19:11-21; 14:14.

CHAPTER TWENTY-SIX

Contents: Message in the temple court. Spiteful treatment of Jeremiah and his brave stand. Martyrdom of Urijah.

Characters: Jehoiakim, Jeremiah, Micah, Hezekiah, Urijah, Elnathan, Ahikam.

Conclusion: God's ambassador must keep close to divine instructions, not compromising to please men or to save himself. If he speaks what God appointed him to speak, he will be under God's protection, and whatever affront the people offer to the ambassador, it will be resented by God Himself.

Key Word: Faithful prophet, vv. 14, 15.

Strong Verses: 13.

CHAPTER TWENTY-SEVEN

Contents: Sign of the yokes, to surrounding Gentile kings. Warning of great calamity.

Characters: God, Jehoiakim, Nebuchadnezzar, Zedekiah, Jeconiah.

Conclusion: Those who refuse to serve the God who made them may be justly made by God to serve their enemies who sought to ruin them. God has an indisputable right to dispose of kingdoms as He pleases.

Key Word: Yoke of Babylon, v. 11.

Strong Verses: 5.

CHAPTER TWENTY-EIGHT

Contents: Sign of the yokes, continued. False prophecy and death of Hananiah.

Characters: Zedekiah, Hananiah, Jeremiah, Nebuchadnezzar, Jeconiah.

Conclusion: Those have a great deal to answer for who tell sinners that they shall have peace in spite of their contempt of the admonitions of God's Word and the exhortations of His true prophets. It is no new thing for lying prophets to father their message upon the God of truth, but they will surely be brought to shame.

Key Word: False teachers, v. 16.

Strong Verses: 9.

CHAPTER TWENTY-NINE

Contents: Message to the Jews of the first captivity. Action against false prophets. Destruction foretold.

Characters: Jeremiah, Nebuchadnezzar, Jeconiah, Elasah, Gemariah, Ahab, Zedekiah, Shemaiah, Zephaniah, Jehoiada.

Conclusion: As long as we have God's sure Word before us, it is our own fault if we be deceived, for by it we may be undeceived. If vengeance shall be taken on those who rebel against God's Word, much more on those who teach rebellion by their destructive doctrines.

Key Word: True and false prophecies, vv. 20, 21.

Strong Verses: 11, 12, 13.

CHAPTER THIRTY

Contents: Jeremiah's first writing. Summary of Israel in the coming great tribulation.

Characters: God, Jeremiah.

Conclusion: Israel, after many years of wandering among all nations, is to be finally purified in a season of tribulation such as the world has never known nor ever shall know thereafter. The purposes of God's wrath will all be fulfilled, and then Israel shall be gloriously restored as a nation.

Key Word: Jacob's trouble, v. 7.

Strong Verses: 24.

Striking Facts: The time of Jacob's trouble is a period of seven years coming at the close of the present dispensation, followed immediately by the return of Christ in glory to set up His kingdom. See Christ's own Word: Matt. 24:15-31.

CHAPTER THIRTY-ONE

Contents: Israel in the last days.

Characters: God.

Conclusion: God will again at the end of the age take Israel into new covenant relation with Himself, from which they have for hundreds of years been cut off because of rebellion against His Word. At that time, all shall come to the knowledge of God, and the earth shall be filled with songs of joy.

Key Word: New covenant, v. 31.

Strong Verses: 3, 33, 34.

Striking Facts: vv. 33, 34. This can be applied in the Gospel dispensation to those who have accepted Jesus Christ, those who are yielded to the Holy Spirit to have God's will revealed to them, and have the assurance that their sins through Christ are remembered no more.

CHAPTER THIRTY-TWO

Contents: Sign of the field of Hanameel. Jeremiah's second persecution, his prayer and Jehovah's answer.

Characters: God, Jeremiah, Zedekiah, Nebuchadnezzar, Hanameel, Baruch.

Conclusion: When we are perplexed about the methods of God's providence, it is good to go to Him in prayer, by which we shall be taught that not one word of all His counsel shall fail. Though we cannot reconcile one word with another, we may be sure both words are true and both will be made good.

Key Word: Chastisement and promises, v. 42.

Strong Verses: 17, 19, 27.

Striking Facts: v. 2. God, who has been faithful to His threatenings against＊ Israel throughout the centuries, will just as certainly fulfill His promise to the remnant of them in His own good time when Christ returns. They will surely be re-gathered as a nation and made fruitful unto God (v. 42).

CHAPTER THIRTY-THREE

Contents: Prophecy concering the Davidic kingdom.

Characters: God, Christ, Jeremiah.

Conclusion: The Davidic covenant will in God's own time be literally fulfilled, to the great joy of the remnant of Israel when Christ shall come to execute judgment in righteousness in the earth. Their sins will be purged away, their nation will be honored by all nations, and to crown all their blessings, they will recognize Christ as their righteousness and worship Him as their King and Lord.

Key Word: Israel's joy, v. 11.

Strong Verses: 3.

Striking Facts: v. 15. Christ is the Branch of righteousness, born of David's line and holding legal title to the promised throne. While under the gospel He is made "righteousness unto all true believers," at His return He will be acknowledged by Israel who rejected Him as their righteousness.

CHAPTER THIRTY-FOUR

Contents: Message to Zedekiah concerning the coming captivity. Zedekiah's ineffectual decree.

Characters: God, Jeremiah, Nebuchadnezzar, Zedekiah.

Conclusion: God's compassion toward us should engage our compassion toward our fellow-men, and in any case the plain statement of His Word should be obeyed. Those who will not be in subjection to God's law put themselves under His wrath and curse.

Key Word: Desolations, v. 22.

CHAPTER THIRTY-FIVE

Contents: Obedience of the Rechabites in the reign of Jehoiakim.

Characters: God, Jeremiah, Jehoiakim, Jaazaniah, sons of Hanan, Jonadab, Nebuchadnezzar.

Conclusion: The obedience of many unsaved people to the moral laws laid down by wise men of the world should put to shame many professing Christians who are disobedient to an infinite God and utterly forget His precepts.

Key Word: Obedience, v. 8.

CHAPTER THIRTY-SIX

Contents: Jeremiah's writing in the days of Jehoiakim. Reading on the fast day. Burning of the roll and orders to persecute Jeremiah.

Characters: God, Jeremiah, Jehoiakim, Josiah, Baruch, Gemariah, Michaiah. Elishama, Delaiah, Elnathan, Zedekiah, Jehudi, Jerahmeel, Seraiah, Shelemiah.

Conclusion: Though the attempts of those who despise the Word of God are very daring, yet not one tittle of it shall fail. Though many a Bible be burned, this cannot abolish it nor deter the accomplishment of its prophecies.

Key Word: Book burned, vv. 2, 23.

CHAPTER THIRTY-SEVEN

Contents: Jeremiah's imprisonment in the days of Zedekiah.

Characters: Zedekiah, Coniah, Nebuchadnezzar, Jeremiah, Jehucal, Zephaniah, Jonathan, Irijah.

Conclusion: It is no new thing for those who have faithfully declared the Word of God and are the best friends of the Lord, to be represented as enemies, imprisoned and persecuted. When God's servants are accused, they may boldly deny the charge, commit their cause to Him who judges righteously, and continue to contend for the faith.

Key Word: Imprisonment, v. 15.

CHAPTER THIRTY-EIGHT

Contents: Jeremiah's imprisonment, continued. His private conference with the king.

Characters: Shephatiah, Gedaliah, Jucal, Pashur, Jeremiah, Zedekiah, Malchiah, Ebed-melech, Jonathan.

Conclusion: God's faithful ministers, who show men what enemies they are to themselves, are often looked upon as enemies of the country, and are wickedly abused. They may, however, commit the keeping of their spirits to God, their Rewarder, who can even raise up friends for them in their distress (vv. 8, 9), if it be for His glory.

Key Word: Persecuted, v. 6

Strong Verses: 20.

CHAPTER THIRTY-NINE

Contents: Final captivity of Judah in accordance with the prophets.

Characters: Zedekiah, Nebuchadnezzar, Nergal-sharezer, Samgar-nebo, Sarsechim, Rab-saris, Rab-mag, Nebuzaradan, Jeremiah, Nebushasban, Gedaliah, Ebed-melech.

Conclusion: Truly there is a God who judges in the earth in this world as well as in the next. When sin has provoked Him to withdraw His protection, the greatest city is helpless (the false prophets fell by those judgments which they said would never come. The true prophet Jeremiah escaped those judgments which he maintained would come).

Key Word: Broken up, v. 2.

Strong Verses: 17, 18.

CHAPTER FORTY

Contents: Jeremiah discharged. The Jews under Gedeliah as Governor. Ishmael's design against Gedeliah.

Characters: God, Jeremiah, Nebuzaradan, Gedeliah, Ishmael, Johanan, Seraiah, Jezaniah, Baalis.

Conclusion: Sooner or later God's true prophets will be justified before the persecutors, and they will be made sensible that their sin is the cause of all their misery. (God in His wrath still remembers mercy and admits a remnant upon a further trial of their obedience.)

Key Word: Jeremiah loosed, v. 4. Remnant of Judah, v. 11.

CHAPTER FORTY-ONE

Contents: Gedeliah slain, and many Jewish captives released by Johanan

Characters: Ishmael, Gedeliah, Asa, Nebuzaraden, Johanan.

Conclusion: God sometimes permits bloody work to be done for the completing of the ruin of an unhumbled people and the filling up of the measure of their judgments. Murderous work should inspire us with awe of God's judgments, as well as with indignation at the wickedness of men.

Key Word: Murder, v. 2.

CHAPTER FORTY-TWO

Contents: God's answer to the inquiry of the people and Jeremiah concerning the calamities recently befallen. God's charge to the people in the land.

Characters: God, Johanan, Jezaniah, Jeremiah.

Conclusion: In very difficult circumstances, our eyes must be upon God for direction, and our hearts much be intent on obeying His voice. It is folly to quit the place where God has put us merely because we have met with trouble in it. The difficulty we think to escape by disobeying God's voice we will inevitably run ourselves into

Key Word: Admonished, v. 11.

Strong Verses: 6.

CHAPTER FORTY-THREE

Contents: Jeremiah carried to Tahpanhes in Egypt. Sign of the hidden stones.

Characters: God, Azariah, Johanan, Baruch, Nebuzaradan, Gedeliah, Nebuchadnezzar.

Conclusion: It is common for unhumbled men who persist in sin to represent those who speak God's word as grafters having designs for themselves. However, this does not change the Word of God, and those who think to better themselves by going contrary to the Scriptures will come to ruin.

Key Word: Disobedience, v. 4.

CHAPTER FORTY-FOUR

Contents: Message to the Jews in Egypt. Further judgments threatened. Contempt of the people for the admonitions.

Characters: God, Jeremiah, Pharaoh-hophra, Zedekiah, Nebuchadnezzar.

Conclusion: God's past dealings with sinful people should be a warning to us of the danger of sin and the fatal consequences of it. To those who are impenitent sinners God will be found an implacable Judge. In a contest between God's Word and man's word, God's Word will be sure to stand.

Key Word: Jehovah provoked, v. 8.

Strong Verses: 28 (b).

CHAPTER FORTY-FIVE

Contents: Message of Baruch in the days of Jehoiakim.

Characters: God, Jeremiah, Baruch.

Conclusion: God takes notice of the frets and discontents of His people and is displeased with them. To seek great things for ourselves when the public is in danger is unbecoming. We should count even the preservation of our lives in such times a great mercy, and continue faithful to our service.

Key Word: Impending evil, v. 5.

CHAPTER FORTY-SIX

Contents: Prophecies against Egypt.

Characters: God, Jeremiah, Pharaoh-Necho, Nebuchadrezzar.

Conclusion: When men think to magnify themselves by pushing on unrighteous enterprises, let them expect that God will sooner or later glorify Himself by blasting them and making an end of them, for He has numberless hosts at His command.

Key Word: Day of vengeance, v. 10.

Strong Verses: 28.

Striking Facts: vv. 27, 28, certainly look forward to the judgments of the nations at the coming of Christ (Matt. 25:42) after Armageddon, (Rev. 16:14), and the deliverance of Israel.

CHAPTER FORTY-SEVEN

Contents: Prophecies against Philistia and Tyre and Sidon.

Characters: God, Jeremiah.

Conclusion: The sword of the Word, as it is charged from the Lord of Hosts to punish the crimes of nations, cannot be sheathed until it has accomplished that for which He has sent it.

Key Word: Cut off, v. 4.

Strong Verses: 6, 7.

CHAPTER FORTY-EIGHT

Contents: Prophecy against Moab.

Characters: God, Jeremiah.

Conclusion: Jehovah has all armies at His command. He will in His own time plead the cause of His people against a people that have always been

vexatious to them and rebellious toward Him, and will punish them until there is nothing left of them.
Key Word: Spoiling and destruction, v. 3.
Strong Verses: 10.

CHAPTER FORTY-NINE

Contents: Prophecies against the Ammonites, Edom, Damascus, Kedar, kingdoms of. Hazor, Elam.
Characters: God, Jeremiah, Nebuchadrezzar, Zedekiah.
Conclusion: Nations that despise and persecute God's people may make a mighty figure for a time, but their pride shall deceive them, for God will surely visit them with desolations, and they themselves shall be despised among men.
Key Word: Desolations, v. 2.
Strong Verses: 16 (a)

CHAPTER FIFTY

Contents: Prophecies against Babylon and Chaldea.
Characters: God, Jeremiah, King of Assyria, Nebuchadrezzar.
Conclusion: The pride of men's hearts sets God against them and ripens them in due time for utter ruin. Whatever wrong is done against God's people will certainly be reckoned, for though God may have used their persecutions for the good of His people, God has a variety of instruments at command in the earth, and when He opens His armories, all enemies will find themselves overmatched.
Key Word: Vengeance, v. 28.
Strong Verses: 6, 25.
Striking Facts: v. 34. It is the comfort of Christians in distress that they have a Redeemer, Jesus Christ, who is strong, and will thoroughly plead their cause and give them rest

CHAPTER FIFTY-ONE

Contents: Prophecies against Babylon, continued.
Characters: God, Jeremiah, Nebuchadrezzar, Seraiah.
Conclusion: Let no nation think it will exempt them from God's judgment that they have been executing God's judgments on others. Those who have proudly carried everything before them will at length meet with their match, and their day will come to pass.
Key Word: Judgment, v. 9.
Strong Verses: 5, 15.

CHAPTER FIFTY-TWO

Contents: A retrospect: overthrow and capture of Judah. The latter days of Jehoiachin.
Characters: Zedekiah, Jeremiah, Jehoiachin, Jehoiakim, Nebuchadrezzar, Seraiah, Zephaniah, Evil-merodach.
Conclusion: Iniquity leads to the certain ruin of those who follow it, and if it be not forsaken will certainly end by the sinner being cast out of God's presence. The unbelief of man shall not make God's threatenings of no effect, but events will fully answer the predictions of His Word.
Key Word: Behold His anger, v. 3.

LAMENTATIONS

Key Thought:	Number of Chapters:	Key Verse:	Christ seen as:
Chastening	5	2:11	Man of Sorrows

Writer of the Book:	Date:	Conclusion of the Book:
Jeremiah	About 588 B. C.	Sin brings misery. The compassion of Jehovah for the subjects of His wrath, is marvelous.

SUMMARY

CHAPTER ONE

Contents: Jeremiah's first complaint of the calamities of Judah. Appeal to God for deliverance.

Characters: God, Jeremiah.

Conclusion: Whatever our troubles are which God is pleased to inflict upon us, we must own that therein He is righteous and we are sinful. Our fetters are usually of our own making, and it is with our own rod that we are beaten. Those who are without God's presence are without all true comfort.

Key Word: Comforters, vv. 2, 17, 21.

Strong Verses: 18 (b).

CHAPTER TWO

Contents: Lamentation on the effect of the calamities of Judah. God's passionate consideration appealed to.

Characters: God, Jeremiah.

Conclusion: The wormwood and gall in affliction is the thought that God has become one's enemy in His hot displeasure at sin. In all sore providences, it is well to reflect that God has fulfilled His Word, for there will be found to be a perfect agreement between the judgments of God's hand and those threatened by His Word upon the unrepentant.

Key Word: Swallowed up, v. 5.

Strong Verses: 17 (a).

CHAPTER THREE

Contents: Complaint of God's displeasure and comfort to God's people. Appeal to God's justice against persecutors.

Characters: God, Jeremiah.

Conclusion: Bad as things may be, it is owing to the mercy of God that they are not worse, for if we had been dealt with according to our sins, we should have been consumed long ago. Since we are dealt with according to God's mercy, we should acknowledge it to His praise.

Key Word: Bitterness, v. 15.

Strong Verses: 22, 23, 24, 25, 26, 31, 32, 33.

CHAPTER FOUR

Contents: Lamentation on the direful effects of calamities of Judah. Sins of the leaders acknowledged.

Characters: God, Jeremiah.

Conclusion: Nothing ripens a people more for ruin, nor fills the measure faster than the sins of the priests and prophets (v. 13), by which they are led blindly away from God and into His judgments.

Key Word: Devoured, v. 11.

Strong Verses: 9.

CHAPTER FIVE

Contents: Lamentation of the state of Judah in captivity. Supplications for the return of mercy.

Characters: God, Jeremiah.
Conclusion: All our woes are owing to our own sin and folly, and God is
    therefore righteous in it. Though we may not quarrel with God, we may
    yet plead with Him and hope for mercy even when He seems to have
    utterly forsaken.
Key Word: No rest, vv. 7, 15.
Strong Verses: 7, 19.

EZEKIEL

Key Thought:	Number of Chapters:	Key Verse:	Christ seen as:
Visions	48	1:1	High Priest of God

Writer of the Book:	Date:	Conclusion of the Book:
Ezekiel	About 570-590 B. C.	God is marvelously good to those who show a desire to walk with Him, and terribly severe upon those who persistently rebel against Him.

SUMMARY

CHAPTER ONE

Contents: Vision of the glory.

Characters: God, Holy Spirit, Christ, Ezekiel, Jehoiachin, (v. 26).

Conclusion: While no man has seen God at any time, many have had visions of Him, displays of divine glory, which prostrated man before Him in humbled sense of his own unworthiness, and of the infinite distance between man and God.   The more God is pleased to make known to us of His glory, the more humble we should be before Him.

Key Word: Visions of God, v. 1.

Striking Facts: v. 26.   We have here a glimpse of the glory and dignity of Christ at His incarnation, a hint of what His condescension was in taking upon Himself the form of a servant and giving Himself to the death of the cross.

CHAPTER TWO

Contents: Ezekiel filled with the Spirit, and his divine command.

Characters: God, Christ, Holy Spirit, Ezekiel.

Conclusion: If we stand ready to be used of God, we may expect that He will give us a commission.   He is pleased to work that in us which He requires of us.   Those who will do anything to purpose in His service must not be afraid of the voice of man, but faithfully deliver the message regardless of its reception.

Key Word: Called, v. 3.

Strong Verses: 6.

Striking Facts: v. 1.   It is Christ's prerogative to call ministers, enjoin them in their work, and fill them with the Spirit for it (John 15:16).

CHAPTER THREE

Contents: Ezekiel's commission, continued.   Again filled with the Spirit. His dumbness.

Characters: God, Ezekiel.

Conclusion: Ministers are God's mouth to the children of men, but must not undertake to preach the things of God until the Word of God has become part of themselves.   Those who keep close to Him need not fear the proud looks of men.   If the minister is not faithful to his trust, a loss of souls will be charged upon him in the day of account.   Though ministers do not faithfully warn the wicked, it shall not be admitted as an excuse for sin—the wicked will die in their iniquity.

Key Word: Watchman, v. 17.

Strong Verses: 8, 9, 18, 19, 27.

CHAPTER FOUR

Contents: The sign of the tile.   Typical representations.

Characters: God, Ezekiel.

Conclusion: If men will not serve God with cheerfulness in the abundance of all things, God will make them serve their enemies in the want of all things.   In times of public distress, God's ministers must be willing to v endure hardness that they may evidence the sincerity of their faith and serve the glory of God.

Key Word: Israel's iniquity, **v. 5.**

CHAPTER FIVE

Contents: Sign of the sharp knife. Famine, pestilence and the sword impending.

Characters: God, Ezekiel.

Conclusion: When nations (or persons) are made great, it is with design that they may do good, and that they may be as a light to other nations. Contempt of God's Word opens the door to all manner of iniquity, and brings judgments that utterly destroy. Those who refuse God's terms of prosperity cannot expect the continuance of His favor.

Key Word: Judgments, v. 8.

Strong Verses: 7, 8.

CHAPTER SIX

Contents: Message against the mountains of Israel. Remnant to be spared. Desolations upon the land.

Characters: God, Ezekiel.

Conclusion: If men do not, as they ought, destroy idolatry, God will first or last find a way to do it, for idolatry is spiritual whoredom, and therefore a great wrong to God's honor.

Key Word: Desolations, v. 4.

Strong Verses: 10.

CHAPTER SEVEN

Contents: Miserable end of Judah because of sin.

Characters: God, Ezekiel.

Conclusion: The ruin of sinners comes slowly but surely, but when it comes, it will be total. In the heaviest judgments God inflicts, He does but recompense to sinners their own ways. They are beaten with a rod of their own making.

Key Word: Day of trouble, v. 7.

Strong Verses: 4, 19.

CHAPTER EIGHT

Contents: Third vision of the glory. The former profanation of the temple and God's anger because of sin.

Characters: God, Ezekiel, Jaazaniah.

Conclusion: Those are ripe indeed for ruin who have given themselves over to idols, turning their backs upon God and His Word. When their punishment comes, God will be as deaf to their cries as their own idols, to which they vainly cried before.

Key Word: Abominations, v. 6.

CHAPTER NINE

Contents: Visions of the slaying in Jerusalem.

Characters: God, Ezekiel, Christ.

Conclusion: Those who live in sin and hate to be reformed, despising God's Word, will perish in sin, and deserve not to be pitied, for they could have prevented their ruin, but would not. None of those, however, shall be lost whom God has marked for life and salvation.

Key Word: Day of recompense, v. 10.

Strong Verses: 10.

Striking Facts: v. 2. The man clothed in fine linen certainly represents Christ as Mediator, saving those who are His from the flaming sword of vengeance coming upon the earth. This He will do at the end of the age.

CHAPTER TEN

Contents: Visions of the altar fire scattered over Jerusalem. Description of the cherubim.

Characters: God, Christ, Ezekiel.

Conclusion: God's glory and government infinitely transcend all the brightest ideas our minds can receive concerning them. The wheels of his providence move with steadiness and regularity, and all His disposals may be looked upon with wonder, for whatever He pleases He does.

Key Word: Glory, v. 4.

Striking Facts: v. 2. The man in fine linen (same as Chap. 9). The same Jesus who is the Saviour and Protector of those who believe, as all judgment is committed to Him, will come in flaming fire to take vengeance upon sinners.

CHAPTER ELEVEN

Contents: Vision of wrath against lying princes. Promise to spare the remnant. Israel's coming restoration and conversou. Departure of the glory from Jerusalem.

Characters: God, Holy Spirit, Ezekiel, Jaazaniah, Pelatiah.

Conclusion: The fear of the wicked shall come upon him, and there is no fence against the judgment of God. Woe to those entrusted with God's message, who have hidden from the people the things belonging to their peace, for in the day of recompense God will lay at their door the guilt of souls perishing on their account.

Key Word: Judgment, v. 10. (Remnant, v. 13.)

Strong Verses: 19, 20, 21.

Striking Facts: vv. 17, 21. At the Second Coming of Christ, the Jews will be given a new heart, not divided as it has been through the ages among many gods, a new spirit agreeable to Christ, whom they hated. They will look upon Him whom they pierced and will mourn.

CHAPTER TWELVE

Contents: Vision of the prophet as a sign. Full captivity near at hand.

Characters: God, Ezekiel.

Conclusion: Sinners often try to think their works are not evil because sentence upon them is not executed speedily. Putting the evil day far off only provokes God to bring it sooner, and to make it so much the sorer, and so much more a surprise and terror.

Key Word: Captivity (vv. 7, 11) at hand (v. 23).

Strong Verses: 25(a).

CHAPTER THIRTEEN

Contents: Message against lying prophets.

Characters: God, Ezekiel.

Conclusion: Since the devil is the father of lies, those put the highest affront upon God who, claiming to be his prophets, tell lies and father them upon God. A thousand woes upon those who have thus deceived the people and made God their enemy. Though they had claimed to be favorites of heaven, they will in the last day be shown to be the favorites of the devil.

Key Word: False prophets, v. 3.

Strong Verses: 3, 9.

Striking Facts: Matt. 7:22-23. It is Christ who will say to the false preachers in that day, "I never knew you."

CHAPTER FOURTEEN

Contents: Vision of the elders of Israel. Jerusalem on no account to be spared.

Characters: God, Ezekiel, Noah, Job, Daniel.

Conclusion: Many who have no idols in their sanctuary have idols in their hearts, which is no less a usurpation of God's throne. Those who have made gods of money and sensual pleasure cannot expect an answer of peace from God, but on the contrary are ripening for utter ruin.

Key Word: Heart idols, v. 3. (Sore judgments, v. 21.)

Strong Verses: 3.

CHAPTER FIFTEEN

Contents: Vision of the burning vine.

Characters: God, Ezekiel.

Conclusion: Those who set their faces against God to contradict His Word and defeat His purposes will find His face set against them to their ruin.

Though they may come out of one trouble with little hurt, they will soon fall into another and another until they are entirely devoured by the fires of His wrath.

Key Word: Devour, v. 7

CHAPTER SIXTEEN

Contents: The harlotry of Jerusalem, and threatening of destroying–judgments. Promises of future blessing under the new covenant.

Characters: God, Ezekiel.

Conclusion: Let not men flatter themselves with a conceit that because God has hitherto continued His favors to them, notwithstanding their provocations, He will continue to do so, for ultimately as they have forsaken God, they will be utterly forsaken to ruin by God. If sin is not cast off by repentance, it must be borne to eternal confusion.

Key Word: Jerusalem's harlotry. vv. 16, 35.

Strong Verses: 59.

CHAPTER SEVENTEEN

Contents: Parable of the great eagle. Rebellion of Zedekiah and its results.

Characters: God, Ezekiel, Zedekiah, Pharaoh.

Conclusion: He who breaks covenant with God, and tramples the directions of His Word under foot, cannot hope to be delivered from that vengeance which is the just punishment of such treachery. God can without any difficulty root up sinful men and whole kingdoms.

Key Word: Broken covenant, vv. 18, 19.

CHAPTER EIGHTEEN

Contents: Ethical instructions for Israel in captivity.

Characters: God, Ezekiel.

Conclusion: He who makes conscience of conforming in everything to the will of God, who makes it his business to serve God, and his aim to glorify God, shall without fail be happy here and hereafter, and wherein he comes short of his duty, it shall be forgiven him. Let the impenitent thank themselves if they fall under God's curse, for the soul that sinneth shall neither have peace in this life nor salvation in the next. The God of heaven has no delight in man's ruin.

Key Word: Righteousness and wickedness, v. 20.

Strong Verses: 4, 9, 20, 21, 22, 23, 32.

CHAPTER NINETEEN

Contents: Lamentation for princes of Israel.

Characters: God, Ezekiel.

Conclusion: God's ministers who have foretold His judgments upon sinners should bitterly lament the destruction of sinners when it comes, as those who have not desired the woeful day. Sinners may thank themselves for the fire that consumes them, for they have by their wickedness made themselves like tinder to the sparks of God's wrath.

Key Word: Lamentation, vv. 1, 14.

CHAPTER TWENTY

Contents: Jehovah vindicated in the chastising of Israel. Israel's future judgment. Parable of the forest of the south field.

Characters: God, Ezekiel.

Conclusion: God takes it as an affront when those come to inquire of Him who are resolved to go on in their trespasses. He is indeed long-suffering with sinners, and it is owing purely to His mercy, which guards His own glory, that they are not immediately made an end of. If men will not acknowledge God as their ruler, they will have to face Him as Judge when it is too late.

Key Word: Jehovah's long-suffering, vv. 9, 14, 17, 22.

Strong Verses: 19, 20.

Striking Facts: vv. 33-44. This prophecy has to do with the future judgment of Israel at Christ's Coming. The issue determines who of Israel in that day shall enter the land for kingdom blessing. (Ezekiel 20:38; Psalm 50:1-7; Malachi 3:2-5; 4:1, 2.)

CHAPTER TWENTY-ONE
Contents: Parable of the sighing prophet, and of the sword of God. No king for Israel until Messiah comes to reign.
Characters: God, Christ, Ezekiel, King of Babylon.
Conclusion: When the sword is unsheathed among nations, God's hand must be owned in it, for His wrath against sin often puts an edge upon the sword, and the instruments He uses in executing judgments, He fills with strength and fury according to the service they are employed in.
Key Word: Jehovah's sword, v. 3.
Strong Verses: 27.
Striking Fact: v. 27. Jesus Christ has incontestable title to the kingship, not only of Israel, but the whole world, and in due time He will have the pos-, session. Until that time, there will be a general and continual overturning of kingdoms.

CHAPTER TWENTY-TWO
Contents: Sins of Israel enumerated. Parable of the dross in the furnace. Sins of priests, prophets and people.
Characters: God, Ezekiel.
Conclusion: Whatever God's wrath inflicts upon a people, it is their own way that is recompensed upon their heads, and God deals with them much better than their iniquity deserves
Key Word: Abominations, v. 2.
Strong Verses: 14, 30, 31.

CHAPTER TWENTY-THREE
Contents: Parable of Aholah and Aholibah. Sentence passed upon Judah.
Characters: Ezekiel, Aholah, Aholibah.
Conclusion: Whatever creature we dote upon we make an idol of, and what we make an idol of, we defile ourselves with. Forgetfulness of God is at the bottom of all such adulterous departures from Him.
If men will not part with their spiritual whoredoms, they must bear the consequences of them.
Key Word: Whoredoms, v. 8.
Strong Verses: 49.

CHAPTER TWENTY-FOUR
Contents: Parable of the boiling pot. Ezekiel again made a sign to Israel.
Characters: God, Ezekiel, King of Babylon.
Conclusion: There is a day coming when it will be said, "He that is filthy, let him be filthy still." The declarations of God's wrath against sinners are as inviolable as the assurances He has given His people of His favor.
Key Word: Vengeance v. 8.

CHAPTER TWENTY-FIVE
Contents: Prophecy against the Ammonites, Moabites, Edomites and Philistines.
Characters: God, Ezekiel.
Conclusion: Those who glory in any other defence than divine power and promises will sooner or later see cause to be ashamed of their glory. Those who rejoice in the calamities befalling God's people will shortly be reckoned with.
Key Word: Judgments, v. 11.

CHAPTER TWENTY-SIX
Contents: Coming judgment upon Tyre.
Characters: God, Ezekiel, Nebuchadnezzar.
Conclusion: It is just with God to blast the designs and projects of those who contrive to raise themselves upon the ruin of others, and let them not expect to prosper long, for the Lord of Hosts is against them to bring them down to the dust.
Key Word: Tyrus' destruction, v. 17.

CHAPTER TWENTY-SEVEN
Contents: Lamentation for Tyre.
Characters: God, Ezekiel.

Conclusion: `God takes notice of the vain conceits !men have of themselves in their prosperity. When they pride themselves on pomp and pleasure, and think themselves perfect, because of their worldliness, He will find a way to bring down their estate to the dust.
Key Word: Lamentation, vv. 2, 32.

CHAPTER TWENTY-EIGHT
Contents: Rebuke of the King of Tyre, and the fate of Satan who inspired him. Zidon's judgment and Israel's re-gathering.
Characters: God, Ezekiel, Daniel, King of Tyre, Satan.
Conclusion: Those who pretend to be rivals with God will certainly be shown that they are but men—weak, timorous, trembling and perishing men.
Key Word: Brought down, vv. 8, 17.
Strong Verses: 17 (See Rev. 20:10).
Striking Facts: vv. 12-18 go beyond the King of Tyre to Satan, the real but unseen ruler of Tyre. His unfallen state is here described. For his fall see Isa. 14:12-14.

CHAPTER TWENTY-NINE
Contents: Prophecy against Egypt.
Characters: God, Ezekiel, Pharaoh, Nebuchadnezzar.
Conclusion: Those who abuse their power will justly be stripped of it. Those who pride themselves in prosperity, forgetting that God is proprietor of the earth, will be forced out of it. God may even use bad men as tools to bring about His purposes.
Key Word: Desolations, v. 9.

CHAPTER THIRTY
Contents: Egypt in the day of Jehovah. God against Pharaoh in the war with Babylon.
Characters: God, Ezekiel, Nebuchadnezzar, Pharaoh.
Conclusion: Nothing can protect a provoking people when God comes forth to contend with them. God often makes one wicked man a scourge to another for the executing of His judgments upon sin.
Key Word: Judgments, v. 19.

CHAPTER THIRTY-ONE
Contents: Prophecy against Pharaoh.
Characters: God, Ezekiel, Pharaoh.
Conclusion: It is rare to find a humble spirit in the midst of great advancement. God can easily expel those who think themselves, and seem to others, to have taken deepest root. Pride goeth before a fall.
Key Word: Pride punished, vv. 10, 11.

CHAPTER THIRTY-TWO
Contents: Lamentation for Pharaoh and Egypt.
Characters: God, Ezekiel, Pharaoh, Nebuchadrezzar.
Conclusion: Great potentates, if they be tyrannical and oppressive, are in God's account no better than beasts of prey, and will be shortly devoured. The nation that has terrorized others will eventually be made a terror to itself. (God's messengers should sympathize with the miseries which sinners bring upon themselves. It becomes them to weep for sinners who will not weep for themselves.)
Key Word: Lamentation, vv. 2, 16. Terrors, v. 32.

CHAPTER THIRTY-THREE
Contents: Ethical instructions for the captivity. Rebuke to those who are not sincere in their professions.
Characters: God, Ezekiel, Abraham.
Conclusion: God warns sinners of the wrath to come that they may flee from it. Those who go promiscuously into the mouth of judgment, though they hear the warnings of God's servants against the dangers of sin, have destroyed themselves.
Key Word: Warning, v. 3.
Strong Verses: 8, 9, 11, 12, 13, 31, 32.

Striking Facts: vv. 12-13. Many have been ruined by trusting to the merit of their own righteousness, and thinking that God is so much their debtor that they may therefore venture to commit a little sin. "The righteousness of the righteous shall not deliver him." (Rom. 4:5-8; 10:1). Happy is the man who is clothed with the righteousness of Jesus Christ and in whom Christ lives. (Gal. 2:20.)

CHAPTER THIRTY-FOUR

Contents: Message to the faithless shepherds of Israel. Promise of restoration of Israel, and setting up of the kingdom.
Characters: God, Ezekiel.
Conclusion: Those will have a great deal to answer for in the day of judgment who took upon them the care of souls as under-shepherds, yet never took any care of them. Happy are they who know Christ, the Good Shepherd, being fed in His pastures and blessed with all spiritual blessings in Him.
Key Word: Shepherds, v. 2.
Strong Verses: 12, 15, 31.
Striking Facts: vv. 23, 29. Jesus is coming as the Great Shepherd (Heb. 13:20) to gather His people and make a final covenant of peace with Israel. He is the "plant of renown," far above all principalities and might and power and dominion, and every name that is named, not only in this world, but that which is to come.

CHAPTER THIRTY-FIVE

Contents: Prophecy against Mount Seir.
Characters: God, Ezekiel.
Conclusion: Those who have a perpetual enmity to God and His people must expect eventually to be made a perpetual desolation. Those who have lived to shed blood will be given blood to drink.
Key Word: Desolations, vv. 3, 9, 14.
Strong Verses: 6.

CHAPTER THIRTY-SIX

Contents: Message to the mountains of Israel. Restoration of Israel predicted. Israel's past sins.
Characters: God, Ezekiel.
Conclusion: Those who put shame and reproach upon God's people, though God may have made it serve a purpose to His end, will sooner or later have it turned upon themselves. God takes occasion from the insolence of enemies to show Himself concerned for His people, ready to do them good.
Key Word: Mountains of Israel, v. 1. Restoration, v. 24.
Strong Verses: 23 (b), 26, 27.
Striking Facts: The restoration of Israel is yet future. The remnant which returned after the seventy years and their posterity were continually under Gentile yoke. In A. D. 70 they were driven into dispersion, which still continues.

CHAPTER THIRTY-SEVEN

Contents: Vision of the valley of dry bones. Sign of the two sticks.
Characters: God, Holy Spirit, Ezekiel, Joseph, Ephraim, Judah.
Conclusion: He who made man so fearfully and wonderfully can in like manner make him new. Scattered atoms can be marshalled in their proper place and every bone can be made to come to its place by the same wisdom and power by which bones were first formed in the womb.
Key Word: Dry bones, v. 4.
Strong Verses: 5, 6, 28.
Striking Facts: v. 22. As bone came to bone, so the Israelites scattered over the earth will come to their respective families and tribes in the last day. Then Christ will come to be recognized as King, in allegiance to whom all will cheerfully unite. (Many believe David will sit upon the literal throne of Jerusalem as representative of Christ, the great Ruler in the air above.)

CHAPTER THIRTY-EIGHT

Contents: Prophecy against Gog.

Characters: God, Ezekiel.

Conclusion: God does not only see those who are now the enemies of His people, but foresees those who will be so in the last days, and lets them know by His Word that He is against them, and will make their movements to serve His own purposes.

Key Word: Gog, v. 3. (Latter days, v. 16.)

Striking Facts: This prophecy should be read in connection with Zech. 12:1-4; 14:1-9; Matt. 24:14-30; Rev. 14:14-20; 19:17-21. Many see a reference to the northern European powers headed by Russia in the last days to wage a great war. The reference to Mesheck (Moscow) and Tubal (Zobolsk) is thought to be clear identification. The prophecy belongs to the future battle of Armageddon.

CHAPTER THIRTY-NINE

Contents: Prophecy against Gog, continued. Vision of restored and converted Israel.

Characters: God, Holy Spirit, Ezekiel, Gog.

Conclusion: The powers in the last days that rise up to oppress Israel and work havoc in the earth will be made to know by dear-bought experience that Jehovah is the God of power and the Saviour of Israel, even though they seem long to have been neglected by Him. In that day the slaughter will be so great that there will not be a sufficient number of the enemies left alive to bury their dead. God will then let all nations know the meaning of all Israel's troubles, and will get glory to Himself, and their cleansing and restoration.

Key Word: Gog, v. 1.

Strong Verses: 21, 23, 24.

CHAPTER FORTY

Contents: Vision of the man with the measuring reed. The future temple and its service.

Characters: God, Ezekiel, sons of Zadok.

Conclusion: A great and beautiful temple, framed in detail in the counsel of God, is to be set up in Jerusalem in the millennial age, for the setting forth of the truths of God's Word.

Key Word: Temple

CHAPTER FORTY-ONE

Contents: Further description of the temple.

Characters: God, Ezekiel.

Conclusion: Same as Chap. 40.

Key Word: Temple.

CHAPTER FORTY-TWO

Contents: Further description of the temple.

Characters: God, Ezekiel.

Conclusion: Same as Chap. 40.

Key Word: Temple.

CHAPTER FORTY-THREE

Contents: Vision of God's glory filling the temple. Place of the throne of the future kingdom. The altar and offerings.

Characters: God, Holy Spirit, Ezekiel.

Conclusion: The glory of God shall return to earth in the kingdom age, filling the new temple, and Israel will once more offer their appointed and acceptable sacrifices in praise to God.

Key Word: Temple, glory (v. 2), throne (v. 7), offerings (vv. 18-27).

CHAPTER FORTY-FOUR

Contents: Gate for the prince. God's glory filling the temple. The priests.

Characters: God, Ezekiel, sons of Zadok, prince.

Conclusion: In the great temple of Jehovah in the kingdom age, Israel shall worship with a new heart, and every detail of the temple services will be carried out according to God's appointment.

Key Word: Temple services.

CHAPTER FORTY-FIVE

Contents: Jehovah's portion of the land and the prince's portion.
Characters: God, Ezekiel, prince.
Conclusion: In the kingdom age Israel will honor Jehovah with portions of land set apart for divine service. Sin offerings will be offered according to God's appointment, for while sin will be suppressed, the tendency to sin is not removed until the new heaven and new earth are established.
Key Word: Portion of land, v. 1.

CHAPTER FORTY-SIX

Contents: Worship of the prince and people, and the offerings.
Characters: God, Ezekiel, prince.
Conclusion: Israel will acknowledge their dependence upon Jehovah in the kingdom age with many offerings according to a divine plan for that period, by which perfect fellowship may be maintained.
Key Word: Offerings, v. 4.

CHAPTER FORTY-SEVEN

Contents: River of the new sanctuary. Borders of the land.
Characters: God, Ezekiel.
Conclusion: Rev. 22:1-2; Zech. 14:8-9.
Key Word: River of sanctuary, v. 1; borders, v. 13.

CHAPTER FORTY-EIGHT

Contents: Division of the land. The city and its gates.
Characters: God, Ezekiel, prince.
Conclusion: The tribes of Israel will in the kingdom age be distributed according to the divine counsels by a plan different from that previously known. The chief glory of the land will be the manifestations of Jehovah's presence in the city of His choice.
Key Word: Borders, v. 1.
Strong Verses: 35 (b).

DANIEL

Key Thought·	Number of Chapters:	Key Verse·	Christ seen as:
Kingdom	12	2:22	King

Writer of the Book:	Date:	Conclusion of the Book:
Daniel	*About 534 B. C.	

Conclusion of the Book: God is universal sovereign of all—and is yet to be acknowledged as such by all men.

SUMMARY.

CHAPTER ONE

Contents: Personal history of Daniel. Reason for appearance of Daniel and his friends before Nebuchadnezzar.

Characters: Nebuchadnezzar, Daniel, Hananiah, Judah, Mishael, Azariah, Ashpenaz, Cyrus, Jehoiakim, Melzar.

Conclusion: Plain living and high thinking go together. When God's people are in Babylon, they should take special care that they partake not of her sins (Psa. 141:4). It is to the praise of God's people not to relish the delights of sense, but to look upon them with indifference.

Key Word: Heart purpose, v. 8.

Strong Verses: 8.

Striking Facts: This book is written by a man "greatly beloved" (9:23), and deals with much the same prophecies as those of Revelation written by "the beloved disciple," (John). Note similarity between the two· 1. In captivity. Dan. 1:6; 8:2; Rev. 1:9. 2. Beloved. 10:11; John 13:23. 3. Heard the Lord's voice. 8:16; 10:9; Rev. 1:10. 4. Saw the Lord's face. Dan. 10:6; Rev. 1:14. 5. Prostrated. 10:8-9; Rev. 1:17. 6. Quickened. 10:10, 18; Rev. 1:17. 7 Angel taught. 10:11, 12; Rev. 1:1.

CHAPTER TWO

Contents: Visions of Nebuchadnezzar and their results. The forgotten dream and the failure of the astrologers. Daniel's interpretation after prayer for wisdom.

Characters: Nebuchadnezzar, Daniel, Shadrach, Meshach, Abedego, Arioch, Astrologers.

Conclusion: The wisest of men are clouded with a veil of flesh which confounds their understanding of divine things. The sacred things belong to the Lord our God, but believers by prayer are let into His mysteries concerning the last days. The kings of earth have no power but what is given them from above, and in due time all earth kingdoms will be done away with and replaced by the eternal kingdom of Christ on earth.

Key Word: Dreams, v. 1.

Strong Verses: 20, 21, 22, 44.

Striking Facts: The vision has to do with the course of the times of the Gentiles, during which four great world kingdoms would succeed each other. The last of the four (Rome) would divide into legs and then into ten toes (7:27). (Gentile world powers of the last days.) The smiting stone (7:34-35) is to destroy this system of kingdoms in its final form by a sudden blow from heaven (not by gradual process). (See Dan. 7:1-28; Rev. 13-19.) When this destruction comes it will be immediately followed by the kingdom of Christ, which will fill the whole earth at once. Christ is the stone cut out without hands, who will smite the nations, and then become a great mountain, filling the earth with His glory.

CHAPTER THREE

Contents: Pride of Nebuchadnezzar and his punishment. The image of gold. The three Jews refuse to worship the image. Fiery furnace proven harmless. The king convinced.

Characters: God, Nebuchadnezzar, Shadrach, Meshach, Abednego.
Conclusion: We should obey the powers that be until they tell us to disobey and dishonor God (Rom. 13:1), then we should obey God rather than man (Acts 5:29). If we are called to pass through the fire, Christ walked there before us, and will walk there with us (John 15:20), and nothing will be lost by being true to Him.
Key Word: Deliver, vv. 17, 28.
Strong Verses: 17, 28.
Striking Facts: v. 25. Many think this was the eternal Son of God, not a created angel. Hereby Christ shows that what is done against His people He takes as done against Himself. Whoever throws them into the furnace do in effect throw Him in (Isa. 63:9). Those who suffer for Him are therefore assured of His precious presence with them.

CHAPTER FOUR

Contents: Nebuchadnezzar's proclamation. The true vision and its interpretation. Vision fulfilled; the restoration of Nebuchadnezzar.
Characters: God, Daniel, Nebuchadnezzar, Astrologers.
Conclusion: God has power to humble the haughtiest of men who would in their pride act in competition with Him. Those so confident of their own sufficiency will be brought sooner or later to own God's dominion over them and their own utter weakness. Many have been brought to themselves by being made beside themselves.
Key Word: Pride abased, v. 37.
Strong Verses: 35, 37.

CHAPTER FIVE

Contents: Daniel's personal history under Belshazzar and Darius. The pride of Belshazzar and his downfall. The writing on the wall. Its interpretation and fulfillment.
Characters: God, Belshazzar, Queen, Daniel, Darius, Nebuchadnezzar, Astrologers.
Conclusion: God expects from the greatest of men that their hearts will be humbled before Him by acknowledgment that, great as they are, to Him they are accountable. If they persist in their pride and impenitence, they will be made to know that the Most High God rules.
Key Word: Found wanting, v. 27.
Strong Verses: 21.

CHAPTER SIX

Contents: Daniel's history to the accession of Cyrus. Decree of Darius. Daniel's steadfastness. Daniel in the lion's den and his deliverance. Darius' new decree.
Characters: God, Daniel, Darius, Princes.
Conclusion: "God first" means "safety first." That which believers do faithfully in conscience toward God may often be represented as done with obstinate motives by men, but God knows the heart, and whatever the test, will give peace and deliverance, and will clear the integrity of His trusting child.
Key Word: Delivered, vv. 16, 20, 23.
Strong Verses: 5, 10, 16 (b), 23 (b), 26.

CHAPTER SEVEN

Contents: The beast vision of Daniel, forecasting the four world empires and the final heading up under anti-Christ. Vision of Christ coming in glory. Interpretation of the beast vision.
Characters: God, Christ, Daniel, Belshazzar, anti-Christ.
Conclusion: The thrones of the kingdoms of this world in their final heading up will be thrown down. The people of God in every age should be encouraged under their troubles with the prospect of Christ's coming in glory, for God has sworn that he will in due time put His King upon the throne of earth and make an end of all unrighteous rule.
Key Word: Kingdom visions, v. 1.
Strong Verses: 9, 14, 27.
Striking Facts: vv. 13, 14; identical with Rev. 5:6-10. The order of events will be:

1. Investure of Christ's earthly kingdom (13, 14; Rev. 5:6-10).
2. The vexing of Psa. 2:5. See also Matt. 24:21, 22; Rev. 6:18. 3.
Return of Christ in glory to deliver the smiting blow of 2:45; 7:9-11;
Rev. 19:11-21. 4. Judgment of nations and setting up of kingdom
(7:10, 26, 27; Matt. 25:31-46; Rev. 20:1-6).

CHAPTER EIGHT

Contents: The ram and rough goat vision, and its interpretation.
Characters: God, Christ, Gabriel, Daniel, Belshazzar, anti-Christ.
Conclusion: Out from the kingdoms of the last days a king of fierce countenance, the anti-Christ, will arise, and acting by the power of Satan,
will bring transgression to the full. Though he will for a time prosper
in his hellish schemes, the sudden brightness of Christ's coming will utterly
destroy him.
Key Word: End-time Indignation, v. 19.
Strong Verses: 23, 24, 25.
Striking Facts: Two ends are in view in this chapter—historically the end
of the Grecian empire of Alexander; prophetically, the end of the times
of the Gentiles (Luke 21:24; Rev. 16:14), when the "little horn" of
7:8, 24-26, the beast, will arise, followed by the return of Christ.

CHAPTER NINE

Contents: Vision of the seventy weeks. Daniel's prayer and confession.
Characters: God, Christ, Daniel, Jeremiah, Darius, Gabriel.
Conclusion: God's Word is intended to encourage our prayers, and when we
see the day of the performance of His prophecies approaching, we should
the more earnestly confess our sins and pray, not only being forward to
speak to God, but as forward to hear what He has to say to us.
Key Word: Prayer, v. 3. Vision, v. 21.
Striking Facts: vv. 24-27. Reduced to calendar years, this 69 weeks of years
(v. 25) is 476 years. The edict to restore Jerusalem was issued 446
B. C. Applying 476 to this point brings us to Christ's birth and 30 years
over, the very time of the cutting off of Messiah by His crucifixion (v. 26).
Luke 3:23 says that Jesus began His ministry at 30 years and an error
is imagined by some, but Scripture is accurate, for when in the sixth cen-
tury, the time A. D. and B. C. was divided, an error of four years was made
in the calendar so that really 30 A. D. is 34. Christ's ministry extended
nearly four years; thus 30 A. D. in our chronology was the time of Christ's
death. At the close of the age, the other week of years will be fulfilled in
awful tribulation, after which Christ will appear suddenly in the clouds
to set up His eternal kingdom.

CHAPTER TEN

Contents: Visions of the glory of God. The heavenly messenger detained,
but comes at last to show Daniel things to come, in answer to prayer.
Characters: God, Christ, Daniel, Michael, Cyrus, Princes of Persia and Greece.
Conclusion: From the day that we begin to look toward God in the way of
duty, He is ready to meet us in the way of mercy. When we rightly understand the methods of God's providence and grace concerning us, we
will be better reconciled to them. Failure to complete transactions with
God is responsible for many unanswered prayers.
Key Word: Great vision, v. 8.
Strong Verses: 12, 19, 21.
Striking Facts: vv. 6, 16, 17. Christ here appears in the same resemblance
wherein He appeared to John in Rev. 1:13-15, viz., in His priestly dress,
girded ready to His work on behalf of His people.

CHAPTER ELEVEN

Contents: Prophecy covering the period from Darius to anti-Christ, showing
the conflicts of nations, and final heading up for destruction.
Characters: God, Daniel, Kings of Persia and Greece, anti-Christ.
Conclusion: That which God has declared in His Word concerning the end of
kingdoms shall surely come to pass, and then the sins of men and the
wickedness of anti-Christ and Satan shall be made to serve His purposes and

contribute to the bringing of his counsels to birth in their season. Though sin comes to an awful heading up under anti-Christ, it will surely come to eternal destruction when Christ comes to set up His glorious kingdom.

Key Word: Time of the end, v. 40.

Strong Verses: 32, 33

Striking Facts: v. 45. This was not fulfilled in Antiochus, for he died in Tabal, Persia. This man, the anti-Christ, will come to his end in Judea between Jerusalem and the Mediterranean, and it is the brightness of Christ's coming only that will bring him to his doom (2 Thess. 2:8; Rev. 19:20).

CHAPTER TWELVE

Contents: The great tribulation of the last days, and the resurrection foretold. The last message to Daniel.

Characters: God, Daniel, Michael.

Conclusion: The present age is to close in a time of tribulation such as the world has never known. Christ will come to save His people and to raise the bodies of many from the dust. Glorious rewards will be conferred upon those who have themselves been wise and have instructed others in the way of salvation.

Key Word: Time of the end, vv. 4, 9.

Strong Verses: 2, 3.

Striking Facts: The time of the end or day of Jacob's trouble (Jeremiah 30:7), will be a time of tribulation such as was not from the beginning of the world, nor ever shall be (Matt. 24:21). The New Testament adds many details concerning it. But for the appearing of Christ in glory no flesh would be spared through it. Those who know Christ as their Saviour will not be called upon to pass through it (Rev. 3:10), but will be caught up before it begins (1 Thess. 4:16-18).

HOSEA

Key Thought:	Number of Chapters:	Key Verse:	Christ seen as:
Return	14	14:9	Risen Son of God

Writer of the Book:	Date:	Conclusion of the Book:
Hosea	790-725 B. C.	God longs for the return of backsliders, pleads with them and makes every inducement for their repentance.

SUMMARY

CHAPTER ONE

Contents: Israel, Jehovah's dishonored wife, repudiated, but to be restored.

Characters: God, Hosea, Uzziah, Hezekiah, Jeroboam, Gomer, Jezreel, Jehu, Lo-ruhamah, Lo-ammi.

Conclusion: Giving glory to any creature which is due to God alone is as much an injury and affront to God as for a wife to embrace the bosom of a stranger, is to her husband. Thus many who have been in covenant relation with God have broken their marriage bond, turning away the mercy of God from their houses.

Key Word: Israel—whoredom, v. 2.

Strong Verses: 10.

Striking Facts: v. 11. The day will come (Rom. 11:25) when Israel will come forth out of the lands, acknowledging Jesus Christ whom they crucified, as their head (Zech. 12:10).

CHAPTER TWO

Contents: The chastisement of adulterous Israel. Yet to be restored.

Characters: God, Hosea, Ammi, Ruhamah, Baalim.

Conclusion: Those who exchange the service of God for the service of the world and the flesh will sooner or later be made to own that they have changed for the worse, finding themselves cast off of God and hedged about with thorns. Woe unto us, if God will not own Himself in relation to us.

Key Word: Israel's harlotry, restoration, vv. 5, 18.

Strong Verses: 18, 19, 20.

Striking Facts: vv. 14-23. In the final day of Israel's despair, God has promised to revive her with comforts—the sight of their coming Messiah. In that day they will be betrothed to Him anew forever, and the earth shall be filled with His eternal peace and righteousness.

CHAPTER THREE

Contents: Jehovah's undying love to Israel. The future kingdom on earth.

Characters: God, Hosea.

Conclusion: God's people (Israel) who have gone awhoring from Him must take upon themselves the shame of their apostasy and submit to the punishment of their iniquity. If God dealt with them according to the strict rigor of the law, He would have no more to do with them, but He will deal with them according to the multitude of His mercies, and not according to their iniquities. The remnant of Israel will yet seek the Lord and receive their King.

Key Word: Israel's harlotry, restoration, vv. 3, 4.

Strong Verses: 4, 5.

Striking Facts: vv. 4-5. The reference may be to the Lord Jesus Christ, the Son of David, to whom God gave the throne of His father David—Luke 1:32. The Chaldee translates it, "they shall seek the service of the Lord their God, and shall obey Messiah, the Son of David, their King."

CHAPTER FOUR

Contents: Charges against Israel for their sinfulness, idolatry and ignorance.
Characters: God, Hosea.
Conclusion: It is a sad and sore judgment for men when God has to say, "let them alone"—giving them up to their own heart's lust to walk in their own counsels until the measure of their iniquity is filled. Man's doings will surely return upon him, and his sins against God will be called over to him, either to his humiliation or to his condemnation.
Key Word: Jehovah's controversy, v. 1.
Strong Verses: 9, 17.

CHAPTER FIVE

Contents: Jehovah's face withdrawn from Israel.
Characters: God.
Conclusion: There is a time when Jehovah will not be found—when it is time for His judgments to fall on a rebellious, sinful people. He will take no notice of their troubles or prayers, until they become sensible of their guilt, and are brought to humble themselves before Him for it.
Key Word: Jehovah's withdrawal, vv. 6, 15.
Strong Verses: 15.

CHAPTER SIX

Contents: The voice of the remnant of Israel in the last days. Jehovah's response.
Characters: God.
Conclusion: The consideration of God's judgments upon us because of sin should awaken us to return to God by repentance, prayer and reformation. He who has smitten us will bind us up if we humbly return to Him.
Key Word: Return, v. 1.
Strong Verses: 1, 3, 6.
Striking Facts: vv. 1-3. This will be Israel's resolve in the last days, as the result of the "time of Jacob's trouble." The Lord Jesus will be to them as a refreshing rain after a long drought, and Israel shall be revived.

CHAPTER SEVEN

Contents: Jehovah's response to Israel's cry, continued. Israel's sad state.
Characters: God.
Conclusion: If sinful souls are not healed and helped, but perish in their sin and misery, they cannot blame God, for He could and would have healed them. They are not healed because they will not be, refusing to look to God even when they are reaping the sore results of sin. Let all such remember that all their works are remembered and will have to be faced.
Key Word: Wickedness, v. 2.
Strong Verses: 2.

CHAPTER EIGHT

Contents: Jehovah's response, continued. Sins denounced and captivity foretold.
Characters: God.
Conclusion: Those who sow to the flesh must reap corruption. All the hopes of sinners are cheats, and their gains are snares. Those who break friendship with God make themselves an easy prey to all about them.
Key Word: Sowing, reaping, v. 7.
Strong Verses: 7 (a), 11.

CHAPTER NINE

Contents: Jehovah's response, continued. Israel's coming distress because of sin.
Characters: God.
Conclusion: Joy is a forbidden fruit to those who have broken covenant with God, until they return and make their peace with God. If men make things of the world and flesh their portion, it is just with God to deny

them the comfort of them—to bring man to a sense of his folly. The day of recompense hastens on apace toward all who go a whoring from God.
Key Word: Days of recompense, v. 7.
Strong Verses: 5, 17.

CHAPTER TEN

Contents: Jehovah's response, continued. Further reproof for Israel's impiety.
Characters: God. Jareb, King of Israel.
Conclusion: If the grace of God prevail not to destroy the love of sin in us, it is just that the providence of God should destroy the fuel of sin about us, and that what men have made idols of should be spoiled. Because God does not desire the ruin of sinners, He does desire their chastisement.
Key Word: Chastisement, vv. 10, 15.
Strong Verses: 12, 13.

CHAPTER ELEVEN

Contents: Jehovah's response, continued. His tender love for Israel.
Characters: God.
Conclusion: Though men who have had relationship with God are ripe for ruin because of following their own counsels, instead of God's, God is slow to anger, loth to abandon them, longing to draw them with the cords of His love.
Key Word: Jehovah's love, vv. 1, 4, 8.
Strong Verses: 3, 4, 8, 9.
Striking Facts: v. 1. These words have a double aspect, being applied to Christ (Matt. 2:15). They speak historically of the calling of Israel out of Egypt, and prophetically of the bringing of Christ from Egypt, the former being a type of the latter. Christ's calling out of Egypt is likewise a figure of the calling of all who are His out of spiritual slavery.

CHAPTER TWELVE

Contents: Jehovah's response, continued. Further reproof of Israel's sins.
Characters: God.
Conclusion: Those who make creatures and things their confidence, put a cheat upon their own souls, and prepare vexation for themselves. God has His eye even upon the merchant weighing his goods, and knows his methods and the idols of his heart. If men put contempt upon God, God will let their neighbors look with contempt upon them.
Key Word: Recompense, vv. 2, 14.
Strong Verses: 6.
Striking Facts: vv. 9-10. As great an offense as Israel has been to God throughout the centuries, God's Word assures us that the prophecies regarding their restoration to glory in the earth will be certainly fulfilled in His own time. That time is connected with the time of Christ's Second Coming.

CHAPTER THIRTEEN

Contents: Jehovah's response, continued. Israel's ruin. Ultimate blessing in the kingdom age.
Characters: God.
Conclusion: Worldly prosperity, which feeds men's pride, makes them forgetful of God, and sends them on a downhill course in which they cannot easily stop themselves. Those whom God has in vain endured with long-suffering, and appealed to with much affection, will finally be made the vessels of His wrath.
Key Word: Ruined (vv. 8, 16), ransomed (14).
Strong Verses: 4, 6, 14.
Striking Facts: vv. 9-11. God will yet give Israel a King, whom they will receive as God-appointed, a Saviour to their nation. Israel, becoming weary of the theocracy, or divine government, rejected Samuel, crying, "Give us a king." God gave them a king and plenty of trouble with him. Christ is the true heavenly King, and He will at His Second Coming take the throne of His father David.

CHAPTER FOURTEEN

Contents: Entreaty and promise to Israel. Restoration foretold.

Characters: God.

Conclusion: Though backslidings from God are dangerous diseases of the soul, yet they are not incurable, for God graciously promises that if backsliders will return to be reconciled to Him and to His whole will, He will heal their backslidings and make them conscious of His love. ·

Key Word: Backsliding healed, v. 4.

Strong Verses: 4, 9.

Striking Facts: vv. 5-7. God will yet be as the dew unto Israel, refreshing them with His comforts, but not until they see it descending upon them in the person of Jesus Christ, their rejected King, when He comes in the clouds of heaven with great glory. Then their branches indeed shall spread, and they shall grow as the vine.

JOEL

Key Thought:	Number of Chapters:	Key Verse:	Christ seen as:
Judgment	3	2:13	Outpourer of the Spirit.

Writer of the Book:	Date:	Conclusion of the Book:
Joel	Either 860-850 B. C. or 400-380 B. C.	Repentance, a heart broken for sin and from sin, is necessary, if the judgments of God are to be averted.

SUMMARY

CHAPTER ONE

Contents: Joel's warnings of desolation upon Israel, and call to repentance. The plague of insects

Characters: God, Joel.

Conclusion: Those who will not be aroused out of their security by the Word of God will finally be aroused by His rod, for He has the meanest of His creatures at His command, and if He pleases can humble and mortify a rebellious people by the most contemptible creatures. Even locusts become as lions when armed with a divine commission.

Key Word: Destruction, v. 15.

Strong Verses: 15.

Striking Facts: This prophecy looks for its complete fulfillment to the end-time of the present age (Rev. 14, 16, 19). Joel gives the fullest view of the consummation of all written prophecy concerning Israel's woes and final glory under Christ.

CHAPTER TWO

Contents: Day of vengeance upon Israel. Invading hosts and awful scourges. Repentance of the Jewish remnant and Jehovah's response and deliverance.

Characters: God, Holy Spirit, Joel.

Conclusion: There is a great and terrible day of the Lord coming upon the world, to be ushered in with wonders in heaven and earth, blood and fire and pillars of smoke. Woe to those who are not prepared for that day when it comes unawares upon them. Those who are able to pass through it will be given a change of heart through the universal outpouring of the Holy Spirit, and God will reign gloriously in all the universe, restoring to great favor in the earth the remnant of Israel.

Key Word: Day of the Lord, vv. 1, 31.

Strong Verses: 10, 28, 29.

Striking Facts. v. 28. This has a partial and continuous fulfillment during "the last days" (Heb. 1:2), which began with the first advent of Christ (Acts 2:17), but the greater fulfillment awaits the "last days" as applied to Israel, when Christ shall come to be recognized as Lord of Lords and King of Kings.

CHAPTER THREE

Contents: Restoration of Israel, and judgment of all nations in regard to Israel. Full kingdom blessings under Christ.

Characters: God, Joel.

Conclusion: Though God has suffered the enemies of His people (Israel) to prevail very far and for a long time, they will, in the day of decision, be called to account for it. To those who have repented and looked toward God as their salvation, that day will be a joyful day, for the Lord will be the strength of Israel, and all the earth shall be filled with the knowledge of Him thereafter.

Key Word: Day of the Lord, v. 14.

Strong Verses: 14, 16.

Striking Facts: v. 2. All nations that wrong the Jews lay themselves open to God's vengeance, especially those in the last days who persecute the Jews. The coming of Christ will be the day of decision for them. The remnant of Israel will then be cleansed and restored, Jerusalem once more being made a praise in the earth.

AMOS

Key Thought: Punishment	Number of Chapters: 9	Key Verse: 4:12	Christ seen as: Thy God, O Israel.

Writer of the Book: Amos	Date: 870-783 B. C.	Conclusion of the Book: National sin inevitably spells national judg- ment.

SUMMARY

CHAPTER ONE

Contents: Judgments pronounced upon surrounding peoples—Syria, Tyre, Edom, Ammon.

Characters: God, Amos, Uzziah, Jeroboam, Hazael, Benhadad.

Conclusion: The God of Israel is the God of all the earth, and the nations that refuse to worship Him, and who persecute His people will be made to know that they are accountable to Him as Judge.

Key Word: Punishment, vv. 6, 9, 11, 13.

CHAPTER TWO

Contents: Judgments pronounced upon Judah, Moab and Israel.

Characters: God, Amos.

Conclusion: To keep not the commandments of God's Word, making no conscience of them, is to despise the wisdom, justice and goodness of the Author. Those who will not submit to the convictions of the Word will have to sink under the weight of God's punishments.

Key Word: Punishment, vv. 1, 4, 6.

Strong Verses: 16.

CHAPTER THREE

Contents: Jehovah's controversy with Israel.

Characters: God, Amos.

Conclusion: Judgment begins at the house of God. The nearer men are to God in profession, and the kinder notice God has taken of them, the more quickly and severely will He reckon with them if they by wilful sin disgrace their relation to Him. We cannot expect God to act for us unless we are reconciled to Him.

Key Word: Punishment, v. 2.

Strong Verses: 2, 3, 6.

CHAPTER FOUR

Contents: Threatening against the oppressors in Israel. Israel reminded of God's chastening in the past.

Characters: God.

Conclusion: God designs all His providential rebukes to influence men to turn to Him. The reason God sends worse troubles is because former and lesser troubles have not done their work. If men continue obstinate, they force God to do what He does not willingly do, but what is necessary to bring men to their senses.

Key Word: Israel's stubbornness, vv. 6, 8, 9, 10, 11, 12.

Strong Verses: 12 (b), 13.

CHAPTER FIVE

Contents: God's lamentation over Israel and captivity foretold. The day of the Lord.

Characters: God.

Conclusion: If men will not take a right course to obtain the favor of God, God will take an effectual course to make them feel the weight of His displeasure. Our transgressions do not pass Him unobserved, and He knows all hypocrisy in worship, and the punishment will be in proportion to the profession made.

Key Word: Lamentation, vv. 1, 16.

Strong Verses: 8, 9, 14, 15.
Striking Facts: vv. 22-23. Religious ceremonies are of no account with God, except as they express from the heart that for which they stand. "No man cometh to the Father but by Christ." Those ceremonies designed to set forth Christ are an abomination to God if the offerer does not from the heart recognize Christ in them and yield himself to Him. Though ritual sacrifices may be dispensed with, spiritual sacrifices in Christ cannot.

CHAPTER SIX

Contents: Woe pronounced upon those at ease in sin—abandoned by God.
Characters: God, David
Conclusion: Many are puffed up and rocked to sleep in carnal security by the position they occupy in the world—set upon their own pleasure and careless of the afflictions of others. Those who thus give themselves to mirth when God calls them to mourning will find it a sin that will be punished with terrible woes.
Key Word: Woe, v. 1.
Strong Verses: 1 (a).

CHAPTER SEVEN

Contents: Threatening judgments. The prophet's intercession no longer to prevail. Amos charged before the king and his answer.
Characters: God, Amos, Amaziah, Jeroboam.
Conclusion: God's patience, which has long been sinned against, will at length be sinned away—for to be often reprieved yet never reclaimed; often reduced to straits, yet never brought to God—is a great insult to God and merits His rejection. Those who have faithfully declared the counsel of God may expect to be misrepresented as enemies, and often by men in high religious standing.
Key Word: God-abandoned, v. 8.

CHAPTER EIGHT

Contents: The basket of summer fruit foretelling Israel's near ruin. Summary of the case against Israel.
Characters: God, Amos.
Conclusion: The time of God's patience draws surely to a conclusion, and if men do not make an end of sin, God will make an end of them, even though they be His professing people. To continually trample under foot the Word of God will end in a famine of the Word of God, which in a time of trouble will be the sorest judgment.
Key Word: The end, v. 2.
Strong Verses: 7 (b), 11.

CHAPTER NINE

Contents: Final prophecy of dispersion of Israel and their ultimate restoration and blessing in the kingdom age.
Characters: God, Amos.
Conclusion: The sword of war is the sword of divine vengeance, for God will thoroughly sift His people who ignore His constant pleadings. Evil is often nearest those who put it at the greatest distance from them (v. 10).
Key Word: Israel's sifting, v. 9.
Strong Verses: 6, 10, 11.
Striking Facts: vv. 11-15. The bringing again of dispersed Israel to their own land is the sure promise of God's Word. In the coming Kingdom of Christ, the Messiah, Israel shall take deep root in the world, never to be rooted out of it. They shall find in Him the happiness and rest they have so long sought, and God's favor shall again be with them to give abundance of all good things.

OBADIAH

Key Thought: Edom.	Number of Chapters: 1	Key Verse: 21	Christ seen as: "The Lord in His Kingdom."
Writer of the Book: Obadiah	**Date:** 900-880 B. C.		**Conclusion of the Book:** We should take solemn warning against the perils of pride and anti-Semetism.

SUMMARY

CHAPTER ONE

Contents: Edom's humiliation because of sin against God's people.

Characters: God, Obadiah.

Conclusion: If men in their pride and carnal security dare to challenge omnipotence, their challenge will be taken up, and God will promptly lay them low. God will not suffer men to be puffed up by the humiliation of His people, nor to gloat over them in their afflictions.

Key Word: Edom, v. 1.

Strong Verses: 4, 15.

Striking Facts: v. 17. Following the day of recompense, for which Christ is coming to the earth, the promise of deliverance and holiness for the people shall be fulfilled. The kingdoms of the world shall then become the kingdoms of the Lord and His Christ, who will take to Himself great power, and reign.

JONAH

Key Thought:	Number of Chapters:	Key Verse:	Christ seen as:
Repentance	4	3:2	Risen Prophet

Writer of the Book:	Date:	Conclusion of the Book:
Jonah	825-790 B. C.	God is the God of the Gentiles as well as of the Jew.

SUMMARY

CHAPTER ONE

Contents: Jonah's commission and effort to avoid God's will. Swallowed by a great fish.

Characters: God, Jonah, seamen.

Conclusion: Men may be distinctly called of God to proclaim His message, yet refuse to obey, but indisposition to preach will not rid one of the obligation to preach. God will send His storms to teach the wisdom of obedience.

Key Word: Fleeing prophet—v. 3.

Strong Verses: 9.

Striking Facts: Typically Jonah foreshadows Israel out of their own land, a trouble to the Gentiles, cast out but miraculously preserved. In the future, in their hour of deep distress, they will cry out to God, will be delivered and will go forth to the Gentiles as originally commanded, announcing the kingdom of Christ at hand and His Second Coming.

CHAPTER TWO

Contents: Jonah's prayer out of the depths and its answer.

Characters: God, Jonah.

Conclusion: Though we bring affliction upon ourselves by our sins, yet if we pray in humility and godly sincerity, we shall be heard at the throne of grace and God will speak the word of deliverance.

Key Word: Prayer—v. 1.

Strong Verses: 1, 7, 8, 9(b).

Striking Facts: v. 10. Israel swallowed up by the Gentiles in the sea of the nations must go down to the "bottom" before they will cry out to God and look to the one they pierced as their Saviour. When that hour comes, the nations will vomit them out upon their own land, where they will come face to face with Christ.

CHAPTER THREE

Contents: Jonah's second commission. Ninevah's repentance because of his obedience.

Characters: God, Jonah, King of Nineveh.

Conclusion: Those who would not destroy their souls must afflict their souls. God threatens so He will not have to punish, and makes His judgments conditional upon true repentance. There is mercy for those who will, before it is too late, confess and forsake their sin.

Key Word: Repentance, vv. 8, 10.

Strong Verses: 2(b), 10.

Striking Facts: v. 10. God is unchangeable in character, but He may change His conduct toward men as they change their attitude toward Him. Repentance in man is a change of will. Repentance in God is God willing a change.

CHAPTER FOUR

Contents: Jonah's displeasure over God's action toward Nineveh. The sheltering gourd.

Characters: God, Jonah.

Conclusion: Though there be those who find it in their hearts to quarrel with the goodness of God and His sparing, pardoning mercy to others (to which we all owe it that we are out of hell), yet God will justify Himself in the methods of His grace toward repenting sinners. As God values a human soul, so should we look upon it as worth more than all the world.

Key Word: Displeased, v. 1.

Strong Verses: 4, 2(b).

Striking Facts: Jonah (Matt. 12:40) is used as an illustrious type of Christ who was buried and arose (1 Cor. 15:4) after three days. As God prepared Jonah's grave, so He prepared Christ's. Both were buried in order to their rising again for the bringing of the doctrine of repentance to the Gentile world.

MICAH

Key Thought:	Number of Chapters:	Key Verse:	Christ seen as:
Controversy	7	1:8-9	The Bethlehemite

Writer of the Book:	Date:	Conclusion of the Book:
Micah	758-710 B. C.	God abhors injustice and ritualism. He takes delight in pardoning penitent sinners.

SUMMARY

CHAPTER ONE

Contents: Jehovah's case against Israel. Impending judgment.

Characters: God, Micah, Jotham, Ahaz, Hezekiah.

Conclusion: There comes a time when men who have persisted in sin must face ruin without remedy. God cannot help them because they will not by repentance and reformation help themselves.

Key Word: Incurable, v. 9.

Strong Verses: 3, 4.

Striking Facts: vv. 6-16. describes the Syrian invasion. This gives rise to the prophecy of the greater invasion in the last days (4:9-13), and of Christ's deliverance at Armageddon (Rev. 16:14; 19:17).

CHAPTER TWO

Contents: Jehovah's case against Israel, continued. Future deliverance of a remnant.

Characters: God, Holy Spirit.

Conclusion: Sinners cannot expect to rest in a land which they have polluted by their sins against God, for He will certainly cause it to spew them out with terrible judgments. With every threatening of judgment, however, there is a promise of mercy for a remnant who will acknowledge their King and walk in His ways.

Key Word: Sore destruction, v. 10.

Strong Verses: 1, 7.

Striking Facts: v. 13. Christ is the King who will, after the great Armageddon, pass before Israel to bring them into the land of their rest. While there is in this age an election out of Israel, the promises of restoration to the land here given will only have their accomplishment at Christ's Second Coming.

CHAPTER THREE

Contents: Coming judgments of the captivities. The priests and prophets rebuked.

Characters: God, Holy Spirit, princes, prophets.

Conclusion: Men cannot expect to do ill and fare well simply because they are recognized as religious. The time will come when those who have shown no mercy shall have judgment without mercy, for God will hide His face when they are sorely in need of His favor.

Key Word: Israel's sin, v. 8.

Strong Verses: 4.

CHAPTER FOUR

Contents: The future kingdom of Christ on earth and Israel's happy regathering. Battle of Armageddon.

Characters: God, Christ.

Conclusion: In the last days of the age, the Kingdom of Christ shall be mani fested in the earth with a lustre no earth kingdom has ever had. It will be a kingdom universal, peaceful, prosperous, and of the increase of Christ's government, and peace there shall be no end. Israel, long dispersed and cast off, will have a place of glory in the earth, recognizing Christ as King and Lord.

Key Word: Mountain of the Lord, v. 1.
Strong Verses: 1, 2, 3, 4, 5.
Striking Facts: vv. 1, 2. A mountain in Scripture is a symbol of great earth power (Dan. 2:35). The ultimate establishment of Christ's earthly kingdom is here foretold. Christ will be the King (v. 7) to protect and govern it and to order its affairs for the best to the end of time. —

CHAPTER FIVE

Contents: The birth and rejection of Christ foretold. His ultimate eternal kingdom after His rejection.
Characters: God, Christ.
Conclusion: Christ, who existed from eternity as Son of God, was to be born into the world as the child of woman, to be the Saviour of the world. Rejected, except by a remnant, He would await the consummation of the age, when He will be given a kingdom glorious to Himself; happy for His subjects; disastrous to sinners.
Key Word: Israel's ruler (Christ), v. 2.
Strong Verses: 2, 4.
Striking Facts: v. 2. See Isa. 7:13, 14; 9:6, 7. Note that the "child" was born in Bethlehem, but the "Son" was "from everlasting." Christ was pre-existent, else He could not have by His atonement made propitiation for the sin of the world.

CHAPTER SIX

Contents: Jehovah's controversy with Israel's past and present.
Characters: God, Omri, Ahab, Balak, Balaam.
Conclusion: God issues a challenge to all who have ever professed belief in Him, but have wandered from Him, to testify against Him, if they have found His demands unreasonable, or if He has not fully paid His accounts. If our ceremonies be accepted of Him, they must be backed by lives conformed to His will and in communion with Him, for He cannot be deceived by external ceremonies. If professors of religion ruin themselves by sin, it will be the most terrible of any ruin.
Key Word: Controversy, v. 2.
Strong Verses: 3, 7, 8.
Striking Facts: v. 7. Sacrifices and ceremonies have their value from the reference they have to Christ, the great propitiation, but if the believer disregards their meaning, they are an abomination. Thousands of rams and rivers of oil cannot take the place of one little stream of the blood of Christ, the power of which is truly appropriated to the heart.

CHAPTER SEVEN

Contents: Israel's sad present condition. The voice of the remnant in the last days.
Characters: God, Micah.
Conclusion: When a child of God has much occasion to cry "Woe is me"— when it seems that all flesh has corrupted their way—it is a great comfort that he has a God to look to, in whom there is rejoicing and satisfaction always. He cannot but marvel at God's pardoning mercy to men and rejoice at the promise that He shall yet reign supreme in the earth.
Key Word: God, my salvation, v. 7.
Strong Verses: 7, 9, 18, 19.
Striking Facts: v. 19. The gracious God is ready, because of the sacrifice of His Son, to pardon and pass over the iniquity of His people upon their repentance and turning to Him. Let the pardoned sinner remember that if he has not been dealt with according to his deserts, it is because Jesus Christ bore his sins on the cross, and made it possible for God to put His sins in the depths of the sea.

NAHUM

Key Thought:	Number of Chapters:	Key Verse:	Christ seen as:
Nineveh	3	1:8-9	Bringer of Good Tidings.

Writer of the Book:	Date:	Conclusion of the Book:
Nahum	About 660 B. C.	An awful doom awaits the apostate.

SUMMARY

CHAPTER ONE

Contents: Jehovah's holiness and power. Nineveh's destruction forecasted.

Characters: God, Nahum.

Conclusion: The wrath of God is revealed from heaven against His enemies, and His favor and mercy are assured to His faithful, loyal subjects. His mighty power makes His wrath very terrible and His favor very desirable.

Key Word: Vengeance, v. 2.

Strong Verses: 3, 7.

Striking Facts: v. 15. These words are quoted by the apostle both from Isaiah and Nahum, and applied to the great redemption wrought by the Lord Jesus and the publishing of His gospel to the world (Romans 10:15).

CHAPTER TWO

Contents: The battle in the streets of Nineveh.

Characters: God.

Conclusion: God has a quarrel with those who have done violence to His people, and when the measure of their iniquity is filled up, He will fill them with terror, while the fire of His indignation shall utterly consume all in which they have placed their confidence.

Key Word: Nineveh emptied, vv. 10, 2.

CHAPTER THREE

Contents: Nineveh reaps what it has sown—destruction and violence.

Characters: God, King of Assyria.

Conclusion: The people that have with their cruelties been a terror and destruction to others, will eventually have terror and destruction brought home to them. They are but preparing to themselves terrible enemies against the day of their own fall.

Key Word: Woe, v. 1.

Striking Facts: The great lesson of Nahum is that the character of God makes Him not only a stronghold to all who trust Him, but One who "will not at all acquit the wicked." He can be "just and yet the justifier of him which believeth in Jesus" (Romans 3:26), but only because His law has been fully vindicated in the cross.

HABAKKUK

Key Thought: Faith	Number of Chapters: 3	Key Verse: 2:4	Christ seen as: The Lord in His Holy temple.

Writer of the Book: Habakkuk	Date: 608-590 B. C.	Conclusion of the Book: God is perfectly consistent with Himself, even though evil is long permitted.

SUMMARY

CHAPTER ONE

Contents: Habakkuk's prayer concerning evil in dispersed Israel. God's voice to Israel and Habakkuk's testimony to God.

Characters: God, Habakkuk.

Conclusion: We must not think it strange if God sometimes suffers wickedness to prevail far and to prosper long, for He has good reasons for His attitude, and He cannot be the author or patron of sin. He takes full account of all sin committed, and will surely make men answer for it in His own time.

Key Word: Israel's iniquity, v. 3.

Strong Verses: 12, 13.

Striking Facts: v. 5. Acts 13:37-41 interprets this prediction of the redemptive work of Christ with Israel in dispersion. God did "work a work" which Israel did not believe. Paul quoted this to the Jews of the dispersion in the synagogue at Antioch.

CHAPTER TWO

Contents: Jehovah's response to Habakkuk's testimony. Vision of coming woes.

Characters: God, Habakkuk.

Conclusion: The lusts of the flesh, the lusts of the eye and the pride of life are the entangling snare of men, which, if yielded to, bring woes upon them. Those who will not be taught the knowledge of God's glory by the judgments of His mouth will be made to bear the judgments of His hand.

Key Word: Woe, vv. 9, 12, 15, 19.

Strong Verses: 4, 12, 14, 15, 20.

Striking Facts: v. 14. Isa. 11:9 fixes the time when the earth will be filled with the knowledge of the glory of the Lord—when the Righteous Branch of David, Christ, has come and set up His kingdom. The knowledge of the "glory" of the Lord cannot be until He is manifested in glory (Matt. 24:30; 25:31; Luke 9:26; 2 Thess. 1:7; 2:8; Jude 14).

CHAPTER THREE

Contents: Habakkuk's answer of faith to Jehovah. The terror of God's wrath against sinners.

Characters: God, Habakkuk.

Conclusion: The God of nature can alter and control all the powers of nature to make earth, sea and heavenly bodies carry out the purposes of His judgment against sinners, or for the salvation of His people. His true children can, in the midst of earth's distresses, rejoice in Him who is the God of their eternal salvation, since by them, their salvation cannot be hindered but only furthered.

Key Word: Jehovah's wrath, vv. 2, 8.

Strong Verses: 2(b), 18, 19.

ZEPHANIAH

Key Thought: Remnant) ͻ ι	Number of Chapters: 3	Key Verse: 1:4; 3:13	Christ seen as: The Lord in I. Israel's midst.

Writer of the Book:) · .Zephaniah͵ ͵ι·,) .· ·· ·.Ι·:· ·.· ͵ .	Date: 639-609 B. C. , ·· ·.	Conclusion of the Book: . Our God is a jealous God.

SUMMARY

CHAPTER ONE

Contents: Coming judgment on Judah prefiguring the coming day of the Lord.

Characters: God, Zephaniah, Josiah.

Conclusion: Those who will not improve the presence of God with them as a Father, may expect His presence with them as a Judge, to call them to account for all their contempt of His grace. The day of His wrath will strip sinners of all that they have and will leave them nothing but distress and pain with no way of helping themselves.

Key Word: Day of wrath, v. 15.

Strong Verses: 18.

Striking Facts: vv. 7, 14. The day of the Lord here is a small specimen of the great "day" that is to come, in which all earth judgments will culminate, to be followed by Israel's restoration and blessing under Christ.

CHAPTER TWO

Contents: Call to remnant of Israel in the day of the Lord. Judgment threatened upon Assyria, Philistia and other nations.

Characters: God.

Conclusion: The nations that rebel against the precepts of God's Word have the threatenings of His Word against them, and the effect will be no less than their total destruction in the day of His fierce anger. It concerns each one to make it sure to themselves that they shall be hid in the day of God's wrath, in a hiding place of God's providing.

Key Word: Jehovah's anger, v. 2.

Strong Verses: 3.

Striking Facts: v. 3. The only safe hiding place from the wrath of God against sin is the righteousness of Christ (1 Cor. 1:30; Rom. 10:1-3). To be "hid with Christ in God" (Col. 3:2) is to be in the chambers of safety.

CHAPTER THREE

Contents: Jerusalem's moral state in time of Zephaniah. The coming judgment of nations and kingdom blessing for restored Israel. ,

Characters: God.

Conclusion: The end of nations that have continued to be of the earth and of the devil, when Christ comes to set up His kingdom, shall be destruction. The reproach of Israel shall then be removed, and all who are permitted to enter that Kingdom will have occasion, with all their hearts, to eternally rejoice in Him, for God will have forever removed calamities from them, the noise of war will be silenced, sinful nature put under control and God and His Christ made all in all.

Key Word: Judgment of nations, v. 8. (Kingdom blessing, 14-20

Strong Verses: 8, 9, 17.

Striking Facts: v. 15. It is the Lord Jesus, the rejected and glorified King, who will be in the midst forever, to receive the homage of His subjects and to give out His favors.

HAGGAI Σ

Key Thought:	Number of Chapters:	Key Verse: -	Christ seen as:
Build	2	1:8	The Desire of all Nations.

Writer of the Book:	Date:	Conclusion of the Book:
Haggai	About 520 B. C.	God demands first place in life and in service.

SUMMARY

CHAPTER ONE

Contents: Jehovah's chastening because of the interrupted work on His house. The work on the temple recommenced.

Characters: God, Darius, Haggai, Zerubbabel, Joshua.

Conclusion: Those are strangers to their own interests who prefer the conveniences and ornaments of the temporal life before the carrying on of God's work in the community. If we would have the real comfort and continuance of temporal enjoyments, we should make God our friend by putting His interests first, otherwise that which we gain is put into a bag with holes.

Key Word: Temple, vv. 2, 14.

Strong Verses: 6, 7.

CHAPTER TWO

Contents: The various temples. Chastening because of priest's impurity and the peoples' delay. Future destruction of Gentile power.

Characters: God, Haggai, Zerubbabel, Joshua.

Conclusion: If we take no care of the interests of God's work, we cannot expect that He should take care of all our interests. If we are employed in His work, we should be jealous over ourselves, lest we spoil it by going about it with unsanctified hearts and hands.

Key Word: Jehovah's house, v. 3.

Strong Verses: 6, 7, 8, 9.

Striking Facts: v. 7. Christ is the desire of all nations, for in Him shall all the families of the earth be blessed with the best of blessings. The shaking of nations will take place in the great Tribulation, which will be followed by Christ's coming in glory.

ZECHARIAH

Key Thought: God's Ways	Number of Chapters: 14	Key Verse: 8:2	Christ seen as: Prophet, Priest and King.

Writer of the Book: Zechariah	Date: 520 B. C.	Conclusion of the Book: The infinite care and love of God is over His people through the cen- turies.

SUMMARY

CHAPTER ONE

Contents: Zechariah's symbolic visions, warning of Jehovah's displeasure with the nations.

Characters: God, Darius, Zechariah.

Conclusion: The judgments of God which those who went before us were under should be taken as warnings not to tread in their steps. A speedy reformation, while the mercy of God is extended, is the only way to prevent an approaching ruin.

Key Word: Jehovah's displeasure, vv. 2, 12, 15.

Strong Verses: 3.

Striking Facts: v. 17. The visions reveal Judah in dispersion, Jerusalem under adverse possession, and the Gentile nations at rest about it, the conditions that have prevailed throughout the present age. God's answer to the angel's intercession sweeps on to the end time, when the Lord shall yet comfort by the return of Christ in glory

CHAPTER TWO

Contents: Visions of Zechariah. Jerusalem in the kingdom age.

Characters: God, Zechariah.

Conclusion: Jerusalem is the apple of Jehovah's eye, jealously guarded by His angels and marked out for a glorious place in the earth in the day when Christ returns to dwell among men upon the earth.

Key Word: Jerusalem, v. 2.

Strong Verses: 8, 10, 11.

Striking Facts: v. 11. He whom the Lord of Hosts will send in the latter days to dwell among men can be no other than the Lord Jesus. All nations will at that time own Him as the one sent of Jehovah, which was not fulfilled in His first coming.

CHAPTER THREE

Contents: Visions of Zechariah. Joshua and Satan before the angel of the Lord. Jehovah's servant, The Branch.

Characters: God, Christ, Joshua, Satan, Zechariah.

Conclusion: By the guilt of our sins we are obnoxious to God's justice, and by the power of our sins we are odious to His holiness. Those who would belong to Christ will be enabled to cast off the filthy rags of corrupt affections and lusts, and will be clothed with the spotless robe of His righteousness. Only such can He place in positions of honor and trust in His service.

Key Word: Garments, v. 3.

Strong Verses: 4, 7.

Striking Facts: v. 8. Christ is the "Servant, the Branch," who was long hid, but in the fulness of time was brought forth into the world. His beginning was as a tender branch, but He will yet become a great tree filling the earth.

CHAPTER FOUR

Contents: Vision of the golden candlestick and two olive trees. Zerubbabel designated to finish the temple.

Characters: God, Holy Spirit, Zechariah, Zerubbabel, Joshua, the angel.
Conclusion: God will carry on and complete His work, not by human might or power, but by the power of His Spirit, working in those designated and called by Him. For those thus called, all difficulties shall be gotten over.
Key Word: Temple's completion, v. 9.
Strong Verses: 6 (b).
Striking Facts: v. 14. Some think Christ and the Holy Spirit are here meant. From Christ, the olive tree, by the Spirit, the olive branch, all the golden oil of grace is communicated to believers.

CHAPTER FIVE

Contents: Vision of the flying roll and the ephah.
Characters: God, Zechariah, angel.
Conclusion: God's holy law reveals the righteous wrath of God against those who by swearing, affront God's majesty and who by stealing, set aside their neighbor's rights.
Key Word: Curse, v. 3.

CHAPTER SIX

Contents: Vision of the four chariots. The symbolic crowning of Joshua.
Characters: God, Jesus, Zechariah, angel, Joshua, Heldai, Tobijah, Jedaiah, Josiah.
Conclusion: Following the day when God's judgments go forth to all the earth, Christ shall be manifested in His kingdom glory as the Priest-King on His own throne.
Key Word: The Branch, v. 12.
Strong Verses: 12, 13.
Striking Facts: v. 13. Christ is now a Priest, but still in the holiest within the veil (Lev. 16:15; Heb. 9:11-14, 24), seated on the Father's throne (Rev. 3:21). He will yet sit upon His own throne (Heb. 9:28), a Priest—upon His throne.

CHAPTER SEVEN

Contents: The mission from Babylon, and Jehovah's answer to the question of fasts. Why prayer was not answered.
Characters: God, Holy Spirit, Darius, Zechariah, Sherezer, Regemmelich.
Conclusion: When we offer up our requests to God, it must be with readiness to receive instructions from Him. God is not made men's debtor by fasts which are not observed with self-examination and a purpose to put away their sins.
Key Word: Fasts, v. 5.
Strong Verses: 9, 10, 13.

CHAPTER EIGHT

Contents: Jehovah's unchanging purpose to restore Jerusalem and bless Israel in the Kingdom.
Characters: God, Zechariah.
Conclusion: Jerusalem, the city of God, and Israel, the people of God, have God to plead their cause until the day when the dispersion shall be ended, Israel again is made fruitful, and Jerusalem a praise in the earth. In that day all men shall honor a Jew as one of the chosen people of God.
Key Word: Zion's restoration, vv. 2, 12.
Strong Verses: 16, 17, 22, 23.
Striking Facts: In the days after the coming of Christ in glory, Jerusalem will be made the center of earth's worship, and the Jew will be the missionary to all nations, bearing the messages of Christ.

CHAPTER NINE

Contents: Burden upon the cities surrounding Palestine. Christ presented as King-Savior in His first advent.
Characters: God, Christ.
Conclusion: Christ, Israel's King, who came as the meek and lowly One, riding upon an ass, will yet be recognized by Israel, and will bring them deliverance, slay all enmities and extend His kingdom to all the earth.
Key Word: Zion's King, v. 9.
Strong Verses: 9, 10.

Striking Facts: v. 9. Having introduced the King, which was Christ in vv. 9-10, the verses which follow look to the end time and the kingdom when He will come in glory. Except in v. 9, the present age is not seen in Zechariah.

CHAPTER TEN

Contents: The future strengthening of Judah and Ephraim. Israel's dispersion and regathering in one view.
Characters: God.
Conclusion: God has a hand in all the events concerning Israel, and they shall finally have His favor and presence, being owned and accepted of Him. The people long dispersed shall be brought together, purified and strengthened in the Lord.
Key Word: Israel's strengthening, vv. 6, 10, 12.
Strong Verses: 12.
Striking Facts: v. 12. It is Christ whom Israel will recognize as the crucified King, who will strengthen them, and cause them to bestir themselves to go up and down the land in His name.

CHAPTER ELEVEN

Contents: First advent of Christ foretold and His rejection. God's wrath against Israel as the result. The rise of anti-Christ and his judgment.
Characters: God, Zechariah.
Conclusion: Those who will not open the door to let the King in, but sell Him for a paltry price, will sooner or later have to open the door to let ruin in. (This is the desperate case of Israel in the present age.)
Key Word: Jehovah's wrath, v. 6.
Strong Verses: 12, 13.
Striking Facts: v. 7. Beauty and Bands—literally "graciousness and union" —signifying God's attitude toward Israel in sending His Son (Matt. 21:37), and His purpose to reunite Israel (Ezek. 37:15-22). Christ in His first advent came with grace (John 1:17) to offer union (Matt. 4:17), but was sold for 30 pieces of silver (vv. 12, 13). Beauty (graciousness) was thereby "cut in sunder." Bands (union) was broken, God's purpose to reunite Israel being for this age abandoned.

CHAPTER TWELVE

Contents: Jerusalem's coming siege by the Beast and his armies. Deliverance of Judah by the Lord Himself. The Spirit poured out and the pierced One recognized.
Characters: God, Christ, Holy Spirit, Zechariah.
Conclusion: Jerusalem, following the awful days of the end-time, shall be repeopled and replenished, but it will not be until Christ returning in glory is recognized by Israel as He whom they have pierced. He will put down all enemies and work a gracious work in His people.
Key Word: Jerusalem's deliverer, v. 10.
Strong Verses: 10.
Striking Facts: v. 10. The pouring out of the Spirit upon all who receive the Crucified One as Lord and Saviour in the present age is an earnest of what Israel shall receive when Christ's Kingdom comes.

CHAPTER THIRTEEN

Contents: Repentant remnant of Israel in the last days. Refined by great tribulation. Israel again restored to God's favor.
Characters: God, Christ, Zechariah.
Conclusion: Israel, at the end of the age, will pass through a period of fiery trial for purification, after which they will find Christ to be the Lamb slain for the putting away of sin. Their sin and uncleanness finally put away, they shall be restored to Jehovah's favor.
Key Word: Israel's refining, vv. 1, 9.
Strong Verses: 1, 6.
Striking Facts: v. 1. The fountain opened is the pierced side of Jesus Christ,

for thence came there out blood and water—precious blood, the price of our redemption. Those who now look to Christ pierced are saved—but this Israel does not see and will not until His Second Coming (v. 6).

CHAPTER FOURTEEN

Contents: The return of Christ. Armageddon. The changes in Palestine. The kingdom established on earth.

Characters: God, Zechariah, Christ.

Conclusion: In the last days, Christ shall return in glory, His feet touching in that day upon the Mount of Olives. All opposing powers shall be put down, Israel shall be gloriously established, Christ shall be owned by all as King and Lord forever, and all men will serve and worship in the beauty of holiness.

Key Word: Kingdom, v. 9.

Strong Verses: 4, 9, 20.

Striking Facts: v. 9. The prayer (Matt. 6:10) "Thy kingdom come, Thy will be done on earth as it is in heaven," will have its final answer in the coming of the King in the power of His might. It will not be a spiritual and gradual coming, the effects of preaching, but a personal, literal coming in the clouds of heaven (v. 4).

MALACHI

Key Thought:	Number of Chapters:	Key Verse:	Christ seen as:
Robbery	4	3:8	Sun of Righteousness

Writer of the Book:	Date:	Conclusion of the Book:
Malachi	440-410 B. C.	Remember Jehovah, repent toward Him, return to Him and render to Him that which is His due.

SUMMARY

CHAPTER ONE

Contents: Jehovah's love for Israel. The sins of the priests and hypocrisy of the people.

Characters: God, Malachi, Jacob, Esau.

Conclusion: God would have His people know that He loves them, therefore justly takes it very ill to have His favors slighted and His ordinances partaken of in hypocrisy. Those who come to holy ordinances irreverently, going away from them never the better, and under no concern, in effect say, "The table of the Lord is contemptible."

Key Word: Jehovah's displeasure, vv. 10, 13.

Strong Verses: 13.

CHAPTER TWO

Contents: The message to the priests concerning their sins. The evils among the people.

Characters: God, Holy Spirit, Malachi.

Conclusion: Woe to those appointed to be God's mouth to the people, but who instead are a stone of stumbling. All who rest in external performances of religion will not only come short of acceptance with God in them, but will be filled with shame and confusion.

Key Word: Israel's abominations, v. 11.

Strong Verses: 7, 10, 17.

Striking Facts: v. 10. Cp. Acts 17:24-29. The reference in both instances is to God as "Father of our spirits"—or creation. It has no reference to salvation. "We are children of God by faith in Christ Jesus."

CHAPTER THREE

Contents: Mission of John the Baptist, and Christ's first advent foretold. Israel exhorted to return to God.

Characters:—God, Christ, Malachi, John the Baptist.

Conclusion: Those who deny God His part of their estates may justly expect a curse upon their own part of them. Those who rob God rob themselves of His benefits and protection. In view of the immanence of Christ's coming, we should see to it that our accounts with God are balanced.

Key Word: Return, vv. 7, 18.

Strong Verses: 1, 10, 11, 17.

Striking Facts: v. 1. The first "messenger" is a prophecy of the appearing of the forerunner, John the Baptist (Matt. 11:10; Mark 1:2), which Isaiah had foretold (40:3). "The messenger of the covenant" is Christ Himself, but for its final fulfillment looks to the second coming of Christ, the messenger having been rejected at His first advent. His sudden coming to the temple, connected with judgment, awaits fulfillment (Heb. 2:20). Malachi, like other O. T. prophets, saw both advents of Messiah blended in one horizon, but not the separating interval.

CHAPTER FOUR

Contents: The day of the Lord and coming of Christ as "sun of righteousness." Elijah to be forerunner of the day of the Lord.

Characters: God, Moses, Elijah, Christ, Malachi.

Conclusion: The great day of the Lord is impending, a time of terror and destruction upon all whose hearts have been stout against God, but followed by the coming of Christ as the sun of righteousness with healing in His wings for all who have looked to Him. "Come quickly, Lord Jesus."

Key Word: Day of the Lord, v. 5.

Strong Verses: 1, 2.

Striking Facts: v. 2. The Old Testament closes with the promise of the rising of the "sun" of righteousness. The New Testament closes with the promise of the rising of the "morning star" (Rev. 22:16). The morning star precedes the coming of the sun, which finally ushers in the day. Christ is coming to the Church as the "morning star" in the last dark hours of the age (1 Thess. 4:13-16—prior to the great tribulation). At the close of the tribulation He is coming as the "sun" ushering in the Millennial day, and Israel's history will then be resumed.

22466910R00123

Printed in Great Britain
by Amazon